84-1796

LB2332   Regulating the intellectuals
.R43

REGULATING THE INTELLECTUALS

REGULATING
THE
INTELLECTUALS

Perspectives on
Academic Freedom
in the 1980s

edited by
Craig Kaplan
and
Ellen Schrecker

PRAEGER SPECIAL STUDIES • PRAEGER SCIENTIFIC

New York • Philadelphia • Eastbourne, UK
Toronto • Hong Kong • Tokyo • Sydney

Library of Congress Cataloging in Publication Data

Main entry under title:

Regulating the intellectuals.

  Includes index.
  1. Academic freedom—Social aspects—United States—
Congresses. 2. Academic freedom—Economic aspects—United
States—Congresses. 3. Learning and scholarship—United
States—Congresses. I. Kaplan, Craig. II. Schrecker,
Ellen.

LB2332.R43 1983	378'.121	83-17836

ISBN 0-03-063943-3 (alk. paper)

Published in 1983 by Praeger Publishers
CBS Educational and Professional Publishing
a Division of CBS Inc.
521 Fifth Avenue, New York, NY 10175 USA

©1983 by National Emergency Civil Liberties Committee (NECLC)

4567890 052 987654321

Printed in the United States of America
on acid-free paper

To Our Parents:
Bea Kaplan
and the memory of
Clinton Kaplan,
who gave me more than he ever realized,
and
Edwin Wolf II
and the memory of
Margaret D. Wolf

Acknowledgments

This volume grew out of a conference entitled "Academic Freedom in the 1980s," which was held at New York University in May 1982. Some of the contributors to this book spoke informally or presented scholarly papers at that conference; others wrote essays specifically for this volume. In addition to our contributors, the editors wish to thank the National Emergency Civil Liberties Foundation, Inc., and its president, Harry Rand, under whose auspices this conference was held; and the National Emergency Civil Liberties Committee, its staff, its executive committee, its associate general counsel, Michael Krinsky, its director, Edith Tiger, and its chair, Corliss Lamont, under whose aegis this volume was prepared.

We acknowledge our debt to Donald Hazen and Newsweek, Inc., to Colin Greer and The New World Foundation, and to The Boehm Foundation for their interest in and support of our project.

We thank also all those who participated in the planning and production of the conference and in the development of this book. Especially, we thank Stanley Aronowitz, whose creativity appears to know few limits, and Nancy Anderson, who could be counted on for needed doses of constructive criticism.

Craig Kaplan thanks Adamantia Pollis, once his teacher and since then his best friend, for her encouragement and for her example—an academic of unwavering intellectual honesty.

Ellen Schrecker thanks Marvin Gettleman, her colleague and husband, for all his domestic, intellectual, and political support.

Finally, we thank Lynda Sharp, our Praeger editor for her good humor and her patience.

Contents

REGULATING THE INTELLECTUALS

•1•
Introduction
Craig Kaplan

The threat to academic freedom in our times must be seen in the fact that, because of the alleged external danger to our country, freedom of teaching, mutual exchange of opinions, and freedom of press and other media of communication are encroached or obstructed. This is done by creating a situation in which people feel their economic positions endangered. Consequently, more and more people avoid expressing their opinions. . . . This is a state of affairs which a democratic government cannot survive in the long run.

—Albert Einstein[1]

Regulatory policy is increasingly made with the participation of experts, especially academics. A regulated firm should be prepared to co-opt these experts . . . [by] hiring them as consultants or advisors or giving them research grants and the like. . . . [T]he experts themselves must not recognize that they have lost their objectivity and freedom of action.

—Bruce Owen and Ronald Braeutigam *The Regulation Game*[2]

The rhetoric in higher education circles now is the rhetoric of the corporation, with questions about productivity. . . . [S]hould my books be 10% longer? The use of the word enforces the concept of the university as an independent corporate model with managers and increased output.

—Joseph S. Murphy[3]

American capitalism has always required the creation and perpetuation of democratic illusions to sustain and maintain itself.

Often it was the illusion of endless and equal opportunity couched, for example, in Greeley's "Go West" exhortation or the log cabin to White House (now ghetto to corporate boardroom) parable or the volumes of Horatio Alger triumphs. Sometimes, however, mixed with the effects of smoke and mirrors came real, concrete changes—although generally less significant and less, in fact, than at first perceived. The incipient welfare statism of the New Deal, for example, actually and concretely expanded the parameters of what people in America could legitimately expect from government programs and activities in the way of objective economic and social support. Certainly, it can be argued that the New Deal co-opted deeper yearnings for a thoroughgoing structural shift in the economic and social life of America. But, if it did this, it did so by creating real jobs for real people with real needs.

During the business boom of the late 1950s, the 1960s, and the early 1970s, there was relatively less need for government and business to resort to obfuscation. Until the long-term impact of the military spending necessitated by the Vietnam debacle and aggravated by the energy crisis of the early 1970s pushed the economy into its seemingly (until very recently) endless inflationary spiral, business, fueled by increasing productivity and government contracts, was amassing healthy profits. At the same time, the civil rights movement was making palpable gains (though leaving structural racism untouched), disposable income was growing, and liberal rhetoric was spawning the war on poverty. Happily, crime and political and social unrest were quarantined to campus and ghetto.

In such periods of economic expansion, the capitalism of the developed West has exhibited the remarkable capability to pay two pipers. There is, in fact, enough to go around. An equilibrium that pays off on its promise to the rich also provides just enough to the not-so-rich and to the poor to keep the capitalist house of cards in place. The fact that the redistributive tendency within this framework is relatively weak is a generally acceptable reality. When business and/or government respond to the demands of the poor and middle classes, especially when the demands are framed in terms of social need, we rarely witness an exhibition of corporate or governmental understanding, nor do we see guilt or weakness. Rather, we observe the cold application of hard cost-benefit analysis. While this approach, in the short run, successfully defuses some portion of the underlying discontent with the discriminatory nature of the economic structure and creates an opportunity for a buy-in to the economic system for some, thereby performing a significant legitimating function for the system as a whole, it frequently fails to consider adequately the relationship between long- and near-term objectives.

What creates structural stability at any given moment may cause havoc later on. Short-term cost-benefit predicated determinations generate, in addition to temporal system persistence, a contervailing group of tendencies that sound in the conflict between rights and privilege, between entitlement and charity, between empowerment and noblesse oblige. It is this set of tensions that undermines and erodes the delicate systemic balance by creating a situation earmarked by a just rising of expectations among the population.

In the lexicon of the tradition of Parsonian systems analysis, the major intrinsic quality of a social or political system is its desire to maintain its equilibrium, to perpetuate itself, to persist. To do this, it struggles to balance the demands placed upon it with its capability to satisfy them; while at the same time vigilantly policing its boundaries in order to ward off extrinsic destabilizing pressures. All political systems, according to the adherents of this model, can be analyzed and understood by examining the nature and number of demand inputs and the character and quality of its outputs. As long as the system is reasonably responsive to the demand structure, it shall remain in a self-regulated equilibrium. Obviously, however, when there is a change in demand or an overload, disequilibrium results.[4]

Among the numerous input/output functions in almost all political systems is education. It is probably among the most important and among the most problematic. The formal education process is a recognized socializer. In *Who Governs?*, Robert Dahl, a doyen of Yale's political science department and leading "democratic" theorist, endeavored to develop an empirical base upon which to rest a "systems analysis" of local politics. At one point in his exposition of how political decisions were made in New Haven in the late 1950s, Dahl commented upon the role of education.

> Widespread adherence to the democratic creed is produced and maintained by a variety of social processes. Of these, probably formal schooling is the most important. The more formal education an American has, the more democratic formulas he knows, expresses and presumably believes.[5]

Dahl's insight is clearly not original. After all, one can expect that all Yale political theorists have read Plato and Aristotle. Nonetheless, Dahl's positioning of education as central to political stability is a judgement worth repeating. However, the narrowness of the paradigm in which Dahl labored precluded him from recognizing the context in which he was correct and limited him to a context in which he was wrong. I shall develop this point below. Suffice it to note here the strength of a contrary perception regarding the value of mass education.

In commenting upon the "increasing and accelerating democratization of the polity," Carl Kaysen observed that

> It is known that political activism rises with the level of education. Thus, the nation is producing a population that will be more interested in political activity, more ready to listen to the kinds of political entrepreneurs who create issue politics, whether they are called the Friends of the Earth, or Defenders of the Consumer.[6]

In systems analysis terms, Kaysen is concerned about the difficulties a democracy has in dealing with the problem of "stress" or demand overload. How can the balance be struck between the desire for democracy so dependent upon an alive, alert, sophisticated, and educated populace and the need for a limited, controlled, and regulated demand?

Mass education in the humanities and social sciences is a prerequisite for relevant, active participation in our political process. This is especially so within a political system premised upon the rhetoric of democracy. Since the rhetoric cannot be totally jettisoned in order to reduce the stress upon our governmental structures, legitimacy can only be maintained through a combination of attempts to reduce expectations, and increase in direct repression, the creation of economic insecurity throughout the society, and, in the specific context of academia, a restructuring of our institutions of higher learning. It is this central conundrum of democratic theory that places the education apparat with its staff of academics and intellectuals in such a pivotal position.

The discussions of this issue take many concrete forms, often revolving around questions of finance, governance, and curricula. Of course, more broadly at issue is the role and control of education in an avowedly democratic polity. In the immediate post-sputnik world of the late 1950s there was a general consensus in America that the question of Why Johnny can't read be addressed. In the context of the perceived threat from the Soviet Union, happily little thought was given to the possible ramifications of teaching all the Johnnys not only how to read but to write and to count and to think critically.

In the realm of higher education, the goal was to galvanize a flaccid and timid educational system—a structure that had ossified during the years of post–World War II reaction—to produce, especially in the sciences, the work force required to meet the perceived Soviet challenge to U.S. intellectual hegemony.

Even before this, however, mass university education had become part of the North American mainstream. The U.S. federal government spent $5.5 billion between 1944 and 1956 educating GIs under the Serviceman's Readjustment Act.[7] This trend continued into the 1970's with Congress, in 1972, transforming the financial benefits of the 1965 Higher Education Act into "direct entitlements to needy students." Additionally, government research programs, military and nonmilitary, became a major source of university funding. Through the development of programs to meet these two broad objectives—"expanding student access and generating new knowledge"—the nexus between government and the university system evolved to a new level.[8] Rather than functioning pursuant to a generally shared perception regarding the optimal nature of the polity, as had been traditionally the case, government, through the power of the purse, exerted significant control, albeit indirect, on the structure and function of higher education.

This development broadened and deepened in the context of seemingly unlimited overall economic growth. The importance of this factor cannot be understated. At once it both created room for risk taking by students and faculty because it eliminated the need for narrow goal-oriented inquiry and by so doing opened up whole new areas for intellectual examination, especially in the so-called "soft" social sciences and the humanities; and at the same time it limited the need for external constraint upon free and open inquiry. This is not to suggest that intellectual nirvana existed on American campuses during the halcyon days of the 1960s. Even during this relatively liberal period—a decade or so of debate and confrontation over free speech on campus, censorship of student newspapers, university research commitments, and civil rights and the war in Vietnam—the government cum corporate establishment continued to exercise influence over university structure and governance. As many of the articles in this volume suggest, the issue was not whether the campus and its intellectual activity were being regulated. Rather what was so singular about the 1960s was the extended length of the leash.

Relative freedom existed for students and for faculty because of the relatively "good fit" between what the university produced and society's capability to absorb it. The short-term view of the educational process is nearly always an instrumental one: What does the labor market need, and how may it be provided? Unfortunately, invariably there are time lags in this process, so that real complementarity between the educational apparatus and the economic system rarely lasts for extended periods. There is a frequent need then to reformulate and to rearticulate the role of education to meet new economic realities. Clark Kerr[9] did this for the period of university expansion and growth. Ronald Reagan's National Commission on Excellence in Education is attempting to do it for the new period of contraction. In any case, most new agendas create conflict. This volume examines, although not systematically, how the notion of academic freedom fares in this conflict.

As the contributors to this collection make clear, there is little consensus regarding the meaning of academic freedom although there is agreement that it is something worth protecting. The concept has been invoked in support of many contrary causes and positions. It, for example, was used to justify student activism and to repress it, to defend radical faculty and to defend their suppression, to support inquiry into admissions or promotions or tenure decisions and to deny such inquiry.

It is, at best, a slippery notion, but clearly a notion worthy of analysis. At one level, academic freedom provides security, albeit mostly psychological, in the form of procedural and due process safeguards to iconoclasts and dissenters in academia who chose to feel relatively secure in the belief that the ivy-covered walls of the university truly provide protection from shifts in the political winds. Ellen Schrecker exposes in her essay just how limited and self-delusional this perspective is. She describes in some detail how universities, often by the institutional manipulation of all too willing administrators and faculty, sacrifice individual scholars—and do so in the name of academic freedom. In one sense this recalls only too vividly the Vietnam era soldier who claimed he had to burn a village in order to save it.

At another level, the concept of academic freedom offers itself to the university as a ready-made, principled rationale for institutional resistance to state intrusion into academic decision making. Elizabeth Schneider's article on law school clinical programs develops one aspect of this argument as well as its internal contradiction. In his exposition of Princeton's utilization of academic freedom principles in defense of a university's right to exclude certain ideas from its campus, Sanford Levinson illustrates just how malleable the concept is. Similar difficulties arise when academic freedom–based arguments are proffered by universities resisting governmental inquiry prompted by allegations of discrimination in hiring, firing, tenure, promotion, and admissions.

Part of the problem lies in the multifaceted nature of the concept. The early idea of academic freedom was primarily procedural and individual. It was ostensibly advanced as a unitary value that established due process requirements for dealing with individual cases of classroom deviation from the prescribed norms of the prevailing intellectual perspective. It did not, however, encourage or even protect those who aggressively challenged the collective wisdom of the age. Indeed, there was precious little general debate on the issues of course offerings and curricula, much less on the role of the university itself within the larger society. In fact, academic freedom, while being advertised as a value-free safeguard for unfettered study, research, and publication, and even appearing to be so because of its procedural rubric, served to help mask the ongoing participation of the academy in the maintenance of the status quo.

This is not to suggest that the academic freedom notion did no more than legitimate the controls and constraints which existed and foster a tendency toward oppressive self-regulation. Even in its earliest formulations, the principle of academic freedom created valuable space for the courageous scholar. It was not until the 1960s, however, that there was a more general impact. During the middle of that decade, the idea of academic freedom underwent a dual transformation. New-left activism coupled with the postbehavioral revolution within the social sciences forced, in a public way, community-oriented values upon the academic freedom construct. Initial analytic puncturing of the facade of value-free neutrality was followed by frontal assaults on the substantive, conservative content that inhered in the prevailing notion.

The academic freedom debates raged over campus recruitment, Defense Department research, and ROTC, as well as over affirmative action, distribution versus core curricula, and grading policy. The "new" academic freedom became a weapon for those who advocated an engagé academy—a university responsive to the value-laden demands of communities, minorities, and outsiders. Its due process and procedural aspects were often invoked, but almost exclusively in support of broader political and social claims.[10]

Even during this arguable aberrant period, academic freedom continued to sound in the traditional liberal rhetoric of the "free marketplace of ideas." Of course, it was also during this period that radicals had the political clout to demand stalls in the market. In this sense the liberal ideology was temporarily co-opted by the left.

The current period has brought with it a revival of the pre-1960s academic freedom construct. The university is being, in some sense, reclaimed by those who espouse the conventional wisdom. The battle for the dissenter and iconoclast, and the activist, becomes then to preserve a portion of the space won 15 years ago. Procedural struggles take on new, short-range importance as the political and social movements are manifestly weaker. The increasing amount of litigation emanating from the campus on issues of tenure and promotion attests to this.

With the greater reliance on procedural protections comes a reassertion of the notion of a value-free process devoid of political/social content. Thus the university will invoke financial exigency or curriculum requirements to cover its political/racial/sexual motivations. Various aspects of this theme are developed in the articles by Evelyn Hu-DeHart, Joseph S. Murphy and Emily K. Abel.

Possibly even more destructive to the long-term health of a freely inquiring academy is the increased involvement of corporations in university affairs. Certainly, this is not a new problem, as there has always been corporate influence in university decision making by boards of trustees, alumni organizations, and contributors.[11] Recently, the mode of intrusion has become the research contract. The extent of this intrusion is markedly on the rise. College and university susceptibility to corporate seduction, although always notable, has never been at a higher level. As Joseph Murphy develops in his article, much of the academy's vulnerability is directly attributable to the Reagan cutbacks in federal aid to education and the reduction in state aid because of budgetary difficulties. This is true in both the public and private sectors. Additional responsiveness to corporate blandishments stems from the demographic shifts that have resulted in reduced enrollments, especially in the private liberal arts institutions, which, as Stanley Aronowitz analyzes, are finding their function made more and more irrelevant by virtue of the overall economic conditions.

The academic freedom card is available to all participants in the corporate-university game. It is invoked by universities and faculty wary of "allowing corporate sponsors to influence their research or limit the publication of their findings."[12] It is also interposed by individual faculty members who assert, for example, that inquiry into their financial interests in companies that finance their research violates their right to privacy and infringes on academic freedom.[13] As articulated by Harvard Dean Henry Rosovsky in referring to the role of the academic: "If our role is to be social critic, does it affect us when we accept money from corporations or the government? I haven't noticed that the system inhibits professors from being social critics.[14]

Of course, it may not be inaccurate, although possibly disingenuous, to assert there is really no objective difference between government interference with academic decision making and private corporate intrusion. Both provide research money and thereby dictate research directions and set research priorities. Does it really matter from an academic freedom perspective whether the directions come to Harvard from Hoechst A.G. or Du Pont or to Washington University from Monsanto[15] rather than from the Departments of Defense or Agriculture or Health and Human Services? Typically, consistent with most discussions about academic freedom, almost any answer will be ambiguous.

In expressing concern about corporate influence in academia, the Carnegie Foundation report entitled *The Control of the Campus* stated:

> The connection between higher education and major corporations—in both research and curriculum decisions—imperils colleges and universities in much the same way as the church and the state have threatened university integrity in the past. And preoccupation on the part of the academy with the priorities of business and industry may mean that the larger social mandates . . .—equality of access to education, fiscal accountability, social justice—will be compromised.[16]

This view suggests a distinction, and one with an important difference, between corporate and governmental overtures. Although the government has and continues to direct research, now primarily through the Pentagon,[17] and to set research priorities and even determine curricula, it must do so in the context of an articulated and arguably positive social agenda that at least may be the subject of public debate and discourse. Not so with private investments and contracts, which are subject only to the test of profit production. As Henry Manne, the director of the University of Miami's corporation-sponsored and -funded Center for Law and Economics, maintained: "Every time businessmen acknowledge a public interest in what they do, they invite political control of their activities."[18] This prospect is anathema to Manne and to his corporate clients. His observation, in any case, should cause any university to proceed with extreme caution and skepticism regarding the acceptance of corporate dollars regardless of the seeming symbiotic nature of the arrangement. Corporate interest in the university is explored in some detail by Michael Useem.

The resolution of the academic freedom problematic is central to the primary issue of the role of education in the 1980s in North America. Those who dwell only on the purported diminution of academic standards, who bemoan the loss of excellence, and who wring their hands over lowered SAT scores and therefore call for renewed emphasis on the basics, more skill training, and a longer school year are rightly demanding that the educational system, at all levels, "get its act together." But they miss what may be the essential point by not also calling for renewed emphasis on the social sciences and the humanities, on philosophy and sociology, on critical thinking in conjunction with physics and chemistry.

Stanley Aronowitz writes that

> As the United States' economic power diminishes, America needs
> different skills and understandings to deal with an increasingly
> interdependent world. . . . The American academic system is the only
> place where a new generation of serious scholars about the world
> economy, diverse political systems and different cultures can be
> educated.[19]

But to the extent that higher education is dominated by a narrow
instrumentalist perspective, the type of scholarly endeavors necessary
to the creation of new insights will not be undertaken.

Aronowitz's general argument has been embodied, at least in some
form, although most definitely not intentionally, in what Andrew
Kopkind describes as an ". . . ambitious scheme of government
funding, direction and control of virtually all important research in
international studies in America."[20] He refers to a proposed program of
funded research to be developed under the auspices of the National
Security Council which would distribute $15 to 20 million for the
support of international studies research projects around the country.[21]

This initiative is the brainchild of Robert E. Ward, director of the
Center for Research in International Studies at Stanford. It appeared in
the *Washington Quarterly,* a publication of Georgetown's prestigious
Center for Strategic and International Studies and had been earlier
presented at a meeting of the International Research Council. Not
surprisingly, given its parentage and circumstance of birth, the
proposal is receiving serious consideration in Washington, if not on
many campuses. For no other reason, it commands our attention since
it is likely typical of the form of future government overtures to
university centers.

As important, while Ward's explanation for why the proposal is
needed illustrates a number of key shared perspectives regarding the
importance of critical education among those holding very different
political and social perspectives and positions, it also exemplifies just
how deep are the contradictions for those who espouse academic
freedom principles without really being willing to take the risks
entailed in taking these principles seriously.

The motivation behind this proposal is truly significant. The mere
floating of the project and the attention it has received is indicative of
the current academic establishment's recognition of the poverty of the
noncritical, functionally oriented, positivistic educational world view
that they have created and its concomitant inability to produce
intellectuals capable of creative policy development. As characterized
by Kopkind: "The need for new policies to stem the receding tide of

American power is matched by the need for new cadre to formulate them." He suggests that the scholar now providing policy advice and the younger academic in the pipeline is "... the conformist, unimaginative, unquestioning kind who does not produce interesting research or useful analysis."[22]

> "There is a paradox" an untenured professor ... told me. "They want new people so they set up a program to get people but they won't get the people they want. It's a contradiction between the defense 'liberals' on the academic side and the military 'conservatives' on the government side. The right-wing wants to set the agenda and pick sympathetic scholars, but the liberals want a theory that will help them run the world. The two are not compatible."[23]

This particular formulation of the conflict may not provide a sense of relief to those of us who neither want to run the world or to blow it up. Still, it does put an important aspect of the academic freedom problem into focus because it shows just how right Robert Dahl really was in *Who Governs?* Education, albeit somewhat different than Dahl's "education for democracy," is in fact necessary for the preservation of democratic freedoms. It may also be necessary, as those who are developing the NSC program have come to realize, for the preservation of U.S. international hegemony. Although this confluence of interests may be upsetting to some, it does provide the basis for an explicit alliance in defense of academic freedom and provides at the same time the basis for socially relevant and creative scholarship.

It does not, admittedly, protect the committed academic from being the subject of discrimination and manipulation by his or her institution, department, or, alas, colleagues. Nor does it insulate the serious scholar from being directed and regulated by a combination of government, corporate, professional, and institutional interests. Only vigilance and courage can do this.

As the title to this volume suggests, intellectuals on the campus—and, to a lesser extent, those off the campus as well—are as subject to regulation as the poor that Frances Piven, a contributor to this book, and Richard Cloward wrote about in their works on the functions of welfare and the welfare rights movement.[24] If there is any lesson in this analogy and in the theme of this volume, it may be that intellectuals, nearly as much as other people, must become more conscious, and self-conscious, of the roles they and their institutions play in democratic society.

NOTES

1. Letter to Clark Foreman, Director, Emergency Civil Liberties Committee, March 3, 1954.

2. Bruce Owen and Ronald Braeutigam, *The Regulation Game* (Cambridge, Mass.: Ballinger Press, 1978), p. 7.

3. Joseph S. Murphy, address to plenary session, Conference on Academic Freedom in the 1980s, National Emergency Civil Liberties Foundation, May 22, 1982.

4. The classic formulation of this analysis is David Easton, *The Political System*, 2nd ed. (New York: Knopf, 1971), further developed in *A Framework for Political Analysis* (Englewood Cliffs, N.J. Prentice-Hall; 1965). Also see Samuel P. Huntington, *Political Order in Changing Societies* (New Haven, Conn.: Yale University Press, 1968), in which he applies this argument to developing societies, and *The Crisis of Democracy* (New York: New York University Press, 1975), in which he extends his analysis to the United States.

5. Robert Dahl, *Who Governs?* (New Haven, Conn.: Yale University Press, 1967), p. 317. Also see Robert Dahl, *A Preface to Democratic Theory* (Chicago: University of Chicago Press, 1956), for an elaboration of his approach.

6. Carl Kaysen, as quoted in David Dickson and David Noble, "By Force of Reason: The Politics of Science and Technology Policy," in *The Hidden Election*, ed. Joel Rogers and Thomas Ferguson (New York: Pantheon, 1981), p. 278.

7. *The Control of the Campus*, Carnegie Foundation for the Advancement of Teaching (Princeton, N.J.: Princeton University Press, 1982), p. 45.

8. Ibid.

9. Clark Kerr, *The Uses of the University* (Cambridge, Mass.: Harvard University Press, 1963).

10. It is illustrative that during the late 1960s, the notion of academic freedom was frequently argued by campus radicals and community activists and rarely, if ever successfully, invoked by besieged university administrators.

11. Thorstein Veblen, *The Higher Learning in America* (New York: Hill and Wang, 1957).

12. "Coast Teachers Warned on Ties to Corporation," *New York Times*, February 2, 1983, p. A16.

13. Ibid.

14. Fox Butterfield, "The Professor as Paid Expert," *New York Times*, June 12, 1982, p. 44.

15. David E. Sanger, "Corporate Links Want Scholars," *New York Times*, October 17, 1982, p. 4 (business section).

16. *The Control of the Campus*, p. 86.

17. See, for example, William Rosenau, "The Warriors of Academe," *Inquiry Magazine*, February 15, 1982, p. 13.

18. Henry Manne, as quoted in David Dickson and David Noble, "By Force of Reason: The Politics of Science and Technology Policy," in *The Hidden Election*, ed. Joel Rogers and Thomas Ferguson (New York: Pantheon, 1981), p, 270. Also see, generally, Leonard Silk and David Vogel, *Ethics and Profits* (New York: Simon & Schuster, 1976).

19. Stanley Aronowitz, infra at p. 96, this volume.

20. Andrew Kopkind, "A Diller, a Dollar, an NSC Scholar," *The Nation*, June 25, 1983, p. 783.

21. Robert E. Ward, "From the Research Council: Studying International Relations, *Washington Quarterly* Spring 1983, p. 160.

22. Kopkind, "A Dillar, a Dollar, an NSC Scholar," p. 800.

23. Ibid., p. 801.

24. Frances Piven and Richard Cloward, *Regulating the Poor: The Functions of Public Welfare* (New York: Pantheon Books, 1971), and *Poor People's Movements* (New York: Pantheon Books, 1977), Chap. 5.

I
Institutional Perspectives: Editors' Note

Academic freedom is not an abstraction. We must place it within its institutional setting, within a system of higher education that serves very definite social, as well as cultural and political, functions. What these functions are and should be determine the actual meaning of academic freedom and its value to the university and to our society as a whole. Clearly, the university has become increasingly central to North American society—as a training and socializing mechanism, as a source for new and creative ideas and critical thought, and, as Bertell Ollman asserts, as the institutional basis for our country's legitimating social myth, equality of opportunity. The fact that the university occasionally transforms this and other myths into reality merely increases the importance of the institution. This is especially true because, as several of the essays in this volume develop, a major ramification of the social changes of the 1960s and early 1970s was the entrance of different groups of people—members of the working class, women, minorities, and new faculty—onto the campus.

Because of the academy's complexity, functionally and structurally as well as demographically, academic freedom has not one but several roles to fulfill. Not only must it protect the university itself and the jobs and civil liberties of dissenting professors and staff, but it must also preserve the social and intellectual gains of the last 20 years. This is a difficult task. The traditional guarantees of academic freedom, such as tenure and peer review, have, as Ellen Schrecker points out, been unsuccessful in preserving individual political freedom and, as Ollman argues, may actually constitute a subtle form of repression and discrimination against radicals. (In a later section, Evelyn Hu-DeHart addresses some of the particular problems of women and minorities in this regard.) Additionally, the financial cutbacks and political conservatism of the past few years pose a new kind of threat to academic freedom. The danger is no longer merely to individuals but to disciplines, to student bodies, to departments, and even to entire institutions.

•2•

Academic Freedom
and
Political Dissent

Frances Fox Piven

The tradition of academic freedom is both mythical and practical. In the mythical dimension, we set forth the values or aspirations connoted by academic freedom. The practical dimension is the actual set of organized activities by which those values are presumably realized in the everyday life of the university. In fact, there is a good deal of tension between the myths and the practices of academic freedom. To explain why, I have to begin with the myths.

The mythical aspects of academic freedom grow out of a mythical model of what a university is. The university is depicted as a very special place, an enclosed place surrounded by high walls that set it apart from the larger society and protect it from the influences of the larger society. Sometimes, in a mocking spirit, academics call their institution an ivory tower. The mockery, however, is usually of the oddity of an institution that is thus set apart and protected. It is not a mockery of the notion that there could be such a place. The myth that an institution of higher learning is sheltered from the stormy motions of the society and from the corrupting passions and influences of the larger society holds sway in American academic life.

The university is thus depicted as a monastery. And within the sheltered enclave of the monastery, scholar-monks pursue their sacred mission, preserving the accumulated wisdom and technique of our culture, transmitting it to new generations, and pushing ever outward the boundaries of ignorance and darkness in our understanding of the nature of the universe and human existence. Academic freedom is an important part of this mythic model, for it is by nurturing and celebrating the capacity for reason and free inquiry that learning is preserved, transmitted, and expanded. And reason and inquiry can rule only because the university is a protected place, sheltered by high walls that prevent the intrusion of those worldly concerns for wealth, or for power, or for privilege that have always been at war with the search for truth.

This is the image of the structure and mission of an institution of higher learning in which the ideal of academic freedom is lodged. Even ideals, however, can be complicated. The image of the ideal university is not only of an institution that is protected from outside influences but of an institution that selects and cultivates academic excellence. To protect scholarly activity from extraneous influences is not to grant the scholar license under the guise of pursuing truth. High standards for the exercise of reason and the scholarly inquiry must also be developed and observed. The apparent dilemma is one of warring ideals, of freedom against excellence. How can the standards of excellence demanded of an institution of higher learning be ensured if scholars are simply granted license? But how can scholars be judged for their competence without the risk of curbing free inquiry?

The real-world practices of academic freedom are framed and justified by this dilemma. The core practice is known as peer review. Academics should be judged only by their fellow academics, for then the criteria employed will be scholarly criteria and thus excellence and academic freedom will be preserved. When scientists judge scientists or humanists judge humanists, the often harsh discipline demanded by excellence can be exercised without curbing free discourse. And to ensure that these scholarly judgments are indeed untainted by external pressures, they are typically conducted in secrecy; strict confidentiality is taken to be a further guarantee that extraneous influences will not intrude into the councils of scholars.

Of course, the university is not a monastery, and no high walls shield it from outside influences. Rather, the university is an actual and real organization, with an actual and real material existence. A university has actual buildings, and actual employees, and actual equipment. And a real organization with all of these real and material manifestations requires a material base. In other words, universities cost money—as it happens, a great deal of money. And money is not produced within the monastery. It must come from beyond the walls.

Contemporary American universities depend on three main sources for money: private gifts, research grants and contracts, and tuition payments. Private gifts ordinarily come from the very rich. Most research is funded by government, although of late corporations have been showing a renewed interest in sponsored university research. And tuition payments, partly underwritten by government, also depend on the market value of higher education—on the increased earning power (and status) yielded by a college degree.

In other words, actual universities depend on the rich, on the state, and on the market. Dependence means vulnerability to influence, and the sources of influence are surely not monastic. Ideals notwithstanding, those on whom the universities depend for funds have something to do with how the university pursues its mission, with which parts of our intellectual heritage are preserved and transmitted, and which bodies of knowledge and technique are expanded. Naturally enough, universities try to do what they do in ways that will ensure continued contributions from the wealthy, the government, and the markets on which they depend.

These real influences that shape real universities arise from a stratified society, and so therefore are universities stratified in reflection of their differentiated dependencies. The most prestigious universities receive gifts from the wealthiest and most powerful businesspeople, who in turn sit on the boards of trustees of these great universities. Lesser businesspeople settle for ties to lesser universities. Relations between government and the universities follow a broadly similar pattern. If Harvard scholars advise the president, scholars from Rutgers or the City University of New York are more likely to advise a mayor or a city council. And finally, the most prestigious schools are oriented to the top of the labor market, training the young to occupy leading positions in our institutions. By contrast, community colleges train people for work as health-care aides or computer technicians.

But stratification aside, my main point is this: What universities teach, how they teach it, and what passes for scholarship in the universities are all necessarily influenced by the exigencies of institutional preservation and expansion—in other words, by money. What, then, of academic freedom? What of the ideal of an institution in which the pursuit of learning is protected from corrupting external influences? And what about the actual procedures for peer review developed within the universities in the name of this ideal?

The answer, briefly, is that these procedures are a weak reed in the face of influences on which jobs and salaries and buildings and equipment and research facilities depend. Typically, we academics like to think it is mainly administrators who are the conduit for these ugly considerations, and they often are. After all, it is the job of administrators to be concerned about the material base of the university and to make the connections with corporate and government elites that will maintain and expand the material base of the university. Accordingly, administrators are in fact responsible for a good number of the most blatant and notorious affronts to academic freedom, and particularly for affronts to the procedures of peer review that we think ensure academic freedom.

But administrators are not the whole of the problem. Procedures for peer review have always been the vehicle for bending the functions of the university to the interests or prejudices of those on whom the university depends. The procedure that is defined as a process for evaluating competence and judging scholarship can also be used to bar the scholar whose ideas or methods are deviant, or critical, or radical, from the point of view of the university. The language with which this is done within the conventions of peer review is not a language that reveals that interests and prejudices are being protected, that it is politics which is at work. Instead, academic politics employs its own very academic language, a language that preserves the myth of academic freedom by announcing with each expulsion that it is excellence and not freedom that is at issue. That all of this is done in secrecy can have the perverse effect, not of protecting peer deliberations from extraneous considerations, but rather of concealing the role of these considerations in the decisions that are reached.

To appreciate the sometimes devastating effect on freedom of inquiry, you must remember the vulnerability of those who are subject to peer review. A scholarly career begins with graduate studies. Whether it will go any further depends not only on whether the student will pass rounds of written and oral exams but on whether she or he can interest a professor in supervising work on the dissertation, and that in turn is likely to depend very much not only on the quality of the dissertation proposal but on its orientation as well. A completed dissertation must then meet the approval of a faculty committee. Then there is the job search the outcome of which depends on the goodwill and effort of faculty who provide leads and references. It all goes well and a position is found, the young scholar is then subject to six or seven years during which she or he is repeatedly evaluated by senior faculty. The outcome of these evaluations is either the promised land of tenure or a broken career. Even tenured status may not bring the ideals of academic freedom much closer, for then there are the concerns for recognition, for salary increases, for further promotions—all conditional on the outcome of peer review.

The problem, however, is not with peer review. Rather it is with a conception of academic freedom that denies the reality of real-world influences on the university. In fact, in the context of these influences, peer review is of some value, for it does provide some protection from the pressures exerted by the wealthy, by government, and by market considerations. Even at its worst, peer review is only indirectly the vehicle of such pressures, and that can be an advantage. Moreover, peer review is a formal procedure that at least partly defines the rights and obligations of different parties. Similarly, the standards for academic excellence are at least partly articulated. Together, procedural rights and articulated standards can sometimes be used to protect the critical or the deviant, and perhaps more successfully because peers are only indirectly susceptible to external influences. This means that peer review can sometimes be made to protect the deviant and the critical, because it is accountable to formal procedures and to standards that are at least partly objective. We can at least ask the grounds when a candidate is rejected and can at least demand to know, for example, whether the candidate has published more or less, in more or less prestigious places, than other candidates. In other words, peer review is not what it is often taken to be; it does not protect scholars from the interferences of power and wealth, and it does not ensure freedom of inquiry. It is a very imperfect mechanism for achieving these ends. But it is not worthless either.

Still, it is not mainly a procedure that shields scholars from external influences that yields us what space there is in our universities for diverse and critical perspectives. To the contrary, it is the intrusion of worldly influences, albeit of a very different kind than I have so far mentioned, that have broadened our universities and given the ideal of academic freedom some reality. I can illustrate this in my own academic experience. I studied at the University of Chicago in the 1950s where we were instructed to read Plato and Aristotle, Thucydides and Herodotus, Saint Augustine and Spinoza, Locke and Hobbes, Freud and Durkheim. My university is renowned for the boldness of its curriculum and the freedom of its atmosphere. However, we did not read Marx or Luxemberg or Lenin. This point is often made about American universities. But I make it again to show you a difference.

Students today do read Marx, not because peer review has done its work, but because a new kind of worldly influence intruded upon the university. In the 1960s, the universities were forced to notice the radical movements around them, particularly because these movements enlisted large numbers of young people who were, so to speak, within the walls, and some of whom eventually joined the ranks of young scholars. It was this diversification, even democratization, of the worldly influences to which the university had to defer that enlarged academic freedom. In consequence, our universities became better than they were: the diversification of worldly influences came to be reflected in a greater diversity of scholarly interpretations. The university thus moved a little bit closer to the mythic ideals of academic freedom. It did this, not by shielding itself from the world around it, but because that intrusive world had become a little bit better, a little bit more politically equal, a little bit freer.

The expansion of academic freedom that occurred in response to the political movements in the 1960s and 1970s is under assault today. We should not overstate what is happening. There has been no full-scale purge. A good part of the narrowing of outlook, of the contracting of the intellectual space achieved over the last decade, is the result of economies made necessary by declining enrollments and government cutbacks, just as the liberalization of the 1960s and 1970s was facilitated by the extraordinary institutional expansion that was then occurring. Still, the cuts made necessary by contraction are not likely to be neutral or evenhanded. Inevitably, those who are more controversial, more difficult, more deviant (and perhaps for such reasons better and not worse scholars) are inevitably more likely to be the ones who are terminated.

Fiscal pressures will also make the universities more vulnerable to the preferences of those who provide money: the wealthy, government, and employers. And because government funds are being reduced, the influence of private-sector donors will increase. There are signs that corporate leaders have developed a position and a program to make use of their increased influence, a program for reforming the university, for reversing the drift to the political left with which the university has come to be associated. Institutions like the American Enterprise Institute and the Heritage Foundation are exemplars of the corporate program for academic renewal. And that all of this is happening in the context of a politics at least momentarily dominated by the intolerance of the Republican right is further cause for worry.

These assaults on academic freedom are occurring at a very important moment in American history. With the election of 1980, the national government became the vehicle for a corporate effort to transform American institutional life in the name of higher profits. The effort is both material and ideological. In material terms, wages are being reduced, the economic insecurity of working people is being increased, business regulation is being dismantled, and business taxes have been slashed. In ideological terms, there has been a concerted effort to convince Americans that the economic, environmental, and political gains made by ordinary people over the course of the last 50 years are simply no longer possible, not because of the opposition of powerful groups, but because these gains interfere with the "natural" workings of the economy. In a similar way, there is a concerted effort to persuade Americans of the enormity of the Soviet-Cuban-Nicaraguan threat to our security and the consequent need for vastly increased armaments.

In other words, we are in the midst of a large and expensive propaganda effort that is intended to persuade Americans of the truth of the Republican right's interpretation of our current social reality. It is a campaign of ideas, of explanations of how it is that we have gotten into the mess we are in, and how we can get out of it. Ideas have to be fought with alternative ideas. There are not many places in our society in which the space to develop alternative interpretations is protected. That is why the space created within the university over the last two decades is important. It has made our universities better in a scholarly sense. More to my point, the ideas developed and transmitted in the university are part of American political life. In the end, that is why academic freedom is important. And it is especially important now, because ideas are likely to figure largely in the emerging political conflict.

•3•

Academic Freedom: The Historical View

Ellen Schrecker

Academic freedom is a fuzzy concept. As we try to expand the definition of that concept to include substantive protections for the social changes of the past 15 years, we must be aware of the context within which that definition has developed. Although the traditional description of academic freedom, invariably presented in abstract language, seems often designed to glorify existing institutions, there is more to the concept than public relations. Even in its most idealized and institutionally gratifying aspects, the notion of academic freedom is not without value. The ideal sets a standard that, while not always adhered to, nonetheless does provide some protection for most academics. But it is a limited protection, and anyone who ventures beyond the mainstream risks losing whatever benefits academic freedom can confer. As we shall see, this has always been the case, especially with regard to political dissent. Moreover, during times of stress, when the acceptable limits of political discourse narrow, the academic community has responded by redefining academic freedom so as to ensure that it remains within these new limits. The process is instructive; for it is only by understanding how academic freedom actually, rather than theoretically, functions will we be able to consolidate and expand its protection to those groups, ideas, and individuals that need it today.

In preparing and revising this article, the author would like to acknowledge the assistance of Sheldon S. Wolin and Fred Zimring.

If we look at the academic freedom cases of the past 80 or 90 years, it becomes clear that we are dealing with not one but three separate concepts. The first is what most of us would immediately recognize as the classical form of academic freedom, that type of civil liberty which relates to the specific work of the professor: the freedom to teach, do research, and publish without interference. Obviously, the recent epidemic of creationism threatens this freedom, as do the legislative attempts to restrict the caseloads of law school clinics that Elizabeth Schneider describes elsewhere in this volume. The second type of academic freedom protects individual college teachers and allows them to exercise the same civil and political rights as other citizens without endangering their academic status. This type of freedom is far from absolute and, as we shall see, can only guarantee the teaching jobs of people who do not challenge the status quo. Students have a similar claim to academic freedom, particularly with regard to their civil and political rights, but the stake of faculty members is greater. The third type of academic freedom is corporate. It is a collective right that, roughly defined, is the set of practices guaranteeing the autonomy of the academic profession as a whole. These practices ensure that academics control the conditions of their own employment, that they determine who shall teach and what shall be taught, and that they make these decisions according to the criteria that they themselves have established without any interference from the outside.[1]

Although these types of academic freedom are related, they are not identical. The first two are individual freedoms, the third a corporate one. This distinction helps us understand how academic freedom functions; for when we look at the history of academic freedom in the United States, it becomes clear that the academic profession has defended its collective freedom by making concessions with regard to that of its individual members. In other words, in order to make sure that outsiders do not meddle with matters like hiring, promotion, and curriculum development, the academic profession took upon itself the task of policing itself and making sure that none of its members would do anything that would bring about such intervention. This means that the profession essentially acts as a transmission belt for political pressures from the outside. Ironically, the more coherently organized the academy is, the more sensitive it becomes to those pressures and the more quickly it responds to or even anticipates them. Thus, the more effectively the academic profession defends itself, the more likely it is to sacrifice those of its members who cause it trouble.

This self-policing mechanism does not always work. There are times when outside pressures cannot be internalized because they attack the independent status of the professoriate. Then the academic community rouses itself, as it did in opposition to the California Loyalty Oath in 1949, and declares that academic freedom is, indeed, in danger.[2] But such crises are rare, and the academic profession usually has little trouble maintaining its autonomy. It does this in an indirect manner, by claiming that the fulfillment of its professional responsibilities requires such autonomy. And it defines those responsibilities in appropriately scholarly terms. As a result, in order to protect itself, the academy has come to exclude from the realm of scholarship those individuals, activities, and ideas it feels may endanger the profession's autonomy.

First, the academic profession sanitized its own teaching and research. This process essentially eliminated the advocacy of controversial issues from acceptable academic discourse. This had not always been the case. In the late nineteenth century, among the first generation of professionally trained academic economists were a handful of men who were essentially social reformers and who hoped to contribute their expertise to the solution of the nation's social ills. At the same time, however, they were ambitious men who had chosen to make their careers within the academic world, and when their advocacy of social reform got them in trouble with trustees and administrators, they chose to save their careers rather than their principles. Because some of these men were among the leaders in their field, the compromises that they made set a pattern that was to dominate the academic profession from then on.

Perhaps the most important of these late nineteenth-century academic freedom cases was that of Richard T. Ely. The most well-known and prolific economist of his time, Ely wrote for a popular as well as a scholarly audience, advocating measures that, because he was so outspoken, seemed far more radical than they actually were. As a result, in 1894, one of the regents of the University of Wisconsin, where Ely taught, charged him with supporting strikes, hobnobbing with union organizers, and writing "utopian, impractical, or pernicious" books. The other regents were upset, and a trial followed. Instead of fighting the regents' attempt to pass on his scholarly output, Ely chose to prove that the specific charges against him were false. Were they true, he admitted, they would "unquestionably unfit me to occupy a responsible position as an instructor of youth in a great university." Ely's stature in his field, as well as his willingness to accept a restricted notion of what constituted appropriate academic behavior, probably saved his career.

Ely's student, Edward Bemis, was neither so flexible nor so eminent. He was fired from the University of Chicago in 1895 because he refused to give up his advocacy of such measures as the public ownership of railroads and utilities. Significantly, the Chicago administrators and senior professors who dismissed Bemis insisted that they did so because of his scholarship and teaching, not his politics. As a result, Bemis never taught again. The rest of the academic world took note and redefined the scholarly vocation as an objective one, one that viewed the open advocacy of social change as none of the scholar's business.[3]

This notion was universally accepted; its adoption essentially protected the professoriate from lay interference with its professional activities. By defining the educational mission as one that would not threaten the status quo either in print or in the classroom, the academic establishment was able to assert the inviolacy of a professor's academic work. It was a bargain that even radicals did not question until the 1960s. It was also the official doctrine of the American Association of University Professors, the supposed guardian of academic freedom. Established in 1915 by such luminaries as philosopher John Dewey, the AAUP was the academic counterpart of the many organizations that were then being set up to enhance the status and consolidate the power of the various professions. Its founding document, the 1915 Report of Committee A on Academic Freedom and Tenure, established a code of scholarly behavior and developed the procedures for ensuring that the enforcement of that code would be in scholarly hands. The report stressed the notion of objectivity and insisted that, in order to qualify for the protection of academic freedom, a professor must be an unbiased scholar whose conclusions "must be the fruits of competent and patient and sincere inquiry and . . . should be set forth with dignity, courtesy, and temperateness of language."[4] Significantly, although the report did not indicate that these criteria had any political content, the only academic responsibility that is spelled out in detail was the treatment of controversial material. Here, professors must give all sides of the issue and must not indoctrinate their students. It is obvious that, whatever educational advantages such neutrality conveyed, teachers who concealed their own opinions by presenting every side of an issue will not indulge in the kind of advocacy that got Ely and Bemis in trouble.

The core of the report was procedural. It stressed the necessity for faculty participation in all personnel decisions and laid out detailed rules for the granting of tenure and the dismissal of tenured professors. Only faculty members could decide such matters because only they possessed the special knowledge that such decisions required. At no point did the fledgling AAUP admit the criteria according to which academics judged each other's performance were anything but scholarly or that they had been established to ensure that individual professors did not endanger the autonomy of the rest of the profession by engaging in activities that would have invited intervention by such outsiders as trustees or state legislators. For any such admission—that the academic profession applied political standards to its criteria for membership—would destroy the credibility of its claim that only academics could judge other academics. After all, no one needs a Ph.D. to identify a radical.

From the start, political radicalism posed the greatest danger to the autonomy of the academic profession. The political radical was a provocation, not simply for what he did inside his classroom, but for what he did outside as well. A left-wing professor was an open invitation for outsiders to intervene. Few radicals went into academic life. American universities were, for the first half of the twentieth century at least, such conservative places that there was no need to erect formal barriers against left-wingers.[5] Accordingly, there were few significant violations of this type of academic freedom. One of the first involved the well-known apostle of subsistence living, Scott Nearing, who in the early twentieth century agitated against child labor and taught economics at the University of Pennsylvania. Although his department unanimously recommended his retention, the trustees of the university abruptly fired him in the summer of 1915 because, as they later claimed, his activities were "constantly misunderstood by the public and by many parents of students." Even the AAUP couldn't swallow that one, and it condemned Penn for violating academic freedom.[6]

More significantly, however, the AAUP did nothing, perhaps because it could have done nothing, to get Nearing reinstated. A few years later, it admitted that "our experience has shown pretty clearly that we can rarely expect to obtain the actual redress of an individual grievance. . . . We do not believe that we should intervene merely to secure the professional rehabilitation of one unjustly accused."[7] Henceforth, its policy was to focus its activities on defending the principle of academic freedom. Of course, by defending principles instead of people, the AAUP as much as announced that professors who indulged in radical politics did so at their own risk and could expect little or no corporate support from their peers.

The cases of teachers like Granville Hicks and Jerome Davis in the 1930s or Bruce Franklin and Michael Parenti in the 1960s and 1970s indicate that even during these presumably tolerant decades, America's colleges and universities often fired their most politically conspicuous faculty members.[8] We must recognize this fact; for, however much we may, and should, disapprove, it is clear that the academic profession never has protected and is unlikely ever to protect the jobs of its most outspoken radicals. The professional criteria that must be fulfilled in order to qualify for the protection afforded by the corporate guarantee of academic freedom indicate that it was probably never intended to protect the political radical.

A far more serious problem has been the tendency of the academic community, in times of national crises like wars, to redraw the boundaries of acceptable professional behavior so as to come to terms with the prevailing political consensus. At such times, outside pressures for purging the academy of its supposedly disloyal members increase; and the academy, many of whose members themselves believe in the need for loyalty, finds itself confronted with a choice between defying national opinion in the name of academic freedom or redefining academic freedom so as to accommodate the national mood.

The first such crisis was World War I. Because public opinion was seriously divided about the war, the repression of dissent became an ideological crusade, one in which the academy enlisted. Scott Nearing, who was teaching at the University of Toledo when the United States entered the war, was only one of dozens of insufficiently patriotic professors to lose his job. Columbia's president, Nicholas Murray Butler, spoke for the overwhelming majority of his academic colleagues, professors and administrators both, when he announced to the graduating class of 1917 that

> What had been tolerated before becomes intolerable now. What had been wrongheadedness was now sedition. What had been folly was now treason. ... There is and will be no place in Columbia University ... for ... any among us who are not with whole heart and mind and strength committed to fight with us to make the world safe for democracy.

Butler was to back these words with deeds by dismissing two faculty members. One had no tenure; but the other, James McKeen Cattell, was a distinguished, though prickly, psychologist whose apparent offense was to petition Congress for the passage of a law exempting unwilling draftees from having to fight in Europe. Although a few of Cattell's colleagues protested, and one, the historian Charles Beard, even resigned, most of the Columbia faculty did nothing.[9]

Nor, it turned out, did the AAUP. Instead of responding to Cattell and the other academic casualties of the First World War in its ordinary manner, by investigating their dismissals and issuing reports on them, the organization set up a special committee. Its report, the work of the distinguished philosopher, Arthur O. Lovejoy, did not deal with specific cases. Instead, it redefined academic freedom in such a way as not only to condone most of the wartime violations of that freedom but also to support the worst of the nation's phobias. The AAUP actually advised professors of German or Austrian descent not to talk about the war in public or to criticize it in private.[10]

The cold war brought yet another redefinition of academic freedom. This time it was to stress not loyalty, but candor. Once again entire categories of academics were to be declared suspect and denied the protection of academic freedom. The first were members of the Communist party, who, as early as 1940, had begun to come under pressure. The academic world had reluctantly tolerated Communists during the 1930s, but when public opinion was aroused against the party in the aftermath of the Nazi-Soviet pact, the academy caved in under the pressure and prepared to expel Communists from within its ranks. The most intensive of these early purges took place in New York City, where a special legislative committee, the so-called Rapp-Coudert Committee, questioned dozens of New York City college teachers about their alleged Communist affiliations and forced the city to dismiss more than 40 of them. It was an abortive purge; for Hitler's invasion of the Soviet Union soon transformed Communists back into loyal Americans. But, truncated though it was, the action set precedents and established patterns that were to influence academic policy for the next 15 years.[11]

Redefining academic freedom was crucial here, for the traditional definition would not sanction firing teachers whose only sin was to belong to an unpopular, but nonetheless legal, political organization. Significantly, neither during the Rapp-Coudert investigations nor later during the cold war itself did anybody seriously charge Communist teachers with propagandizing in class or indoctrinating their students. Such charges might actually have been difficult to prove, for the suspect teachers made a point—in some cases almost a fetish—of segregating their political from their professional activities. Security was an important consideration. Expounding the party line or recruiting students for party causes would reveal a teacher's political affiliation and thus endanger his or her job.

Moreover, the Communist professors were highly trained academics who, despite their radicalism, shared their colleagues' commitment to the standards of their profession, in particular its concern with objectivity and fairness. They believed that it was unprofessional to use the classroom for other than educational purposes. As a former Harvard Communist explained, "We had a lurking feeling that it wasn't quite good sportsmanship to try to influence young people—at least to make use of our position in the classroom to do this." Even at the City College of New York, which boasted the largest and most militant group of academic party members, Communist teachers prided themselves on their fairness. "I have never," one of them declared, "made any effort whatsoever to impose my point of view on my students. There has always been full freedom of discussion in my classes." Student testimony corroborated these assertions. And the only even remotely classroom-related charge that was ever brought against any of these teachers was that the leaders of the student left-wing organizations took his courses.[12]

This is not to say that academic Communists necessarily concealed their political views from their students. Some were quite open. Herbert Phillips, a philosopher at the University of Washington, told his classes that he was a Marxist and warned them to take that fact into account when assessing his lectures. Others, however, did keep their politics out of the classroom. Since probably close to half of the academic Communists were scientists, this was not very difficult. When they later got into trouble, many of their students and colleagues were surprised to find out that they had been in the party. Even the most active student Communist at CCNY had no idea which members of the faculty were in the party until the Rapp-Coudert Committee exposed them.[13]

Because none of these teachers had violated the traditional norms of academic conduct, forcing them out of the academy without admitting that their exclusion was a political matter required revising the criteria for membership in the academic profession so that membership in the Communist Party would automatically disqualify someone. This was done by describing the party as an organization so totally antithetic to everything the American professoriate held dear that simply belonging to it extinguished someone's right to a teaching career. The people who shaped this new definition of academic freedom—the former New York University philosopher Sidney Hook was only the most prolific of them—focused on two specific aspects of party life: its intellectual rigidity and its clandestine nature. According to this interpretation, academic Communists were unappetizing creatures, part robot and part conspirator.

Almost everybody in the academic community believed, as one university president explained, that "a member of the Communist party is not a free man—that he is instead a slave to immutable dogma." This assumption that all Communists invariably followed every twist and turn on the party line was based more on what party literature said its members did than on what they really did. In fact, party discipline was never as strong as its leaders or its opponents claimed. And, in any event, the party handled its academic adherents with special care and kept them on a comparatively loose tether. "We made our own decisions," a former Harvard Communist admitted. "I cannot recall any directive coming down." If these academics followed the party line, it was usually because they believed in it. As Herbert Phillips put it, "I am a member of the Communist Party because I hold the ideas I do; I do not hold the ideas I do because I am a member of the Communist Party." Certainly, academic Communists had reservations about some aspects of the party line, but they supported most of it most of the time. And had the party demanded absolute conformity in intellectual matters, its academic members would have quit sooner than most of them eventually did. At one point in the 1950s, for example, the party's leaders tried to get some of their main academic supporters on the magazine *Science & Society* to endorse Lysenko's genetic theories. The magazine's editors refused and the matter was dropped. Such behavior, of course, did not accord with the public image of academic Communists as intellectual automatons.[14]

Secrecy was another matter. Most Communist professors did conceal their membership in the party. But they did this largely as a matter of self-protection; they were trying to keep their jobs, not deceive their students and colleagues. In fact, a lot of them were quite uncomfortable with having to hide their political affiliation. Even at the time they felt that the party's emphasis on secrecy, although understandable, was probably a mistake. Later events proved them right. Because this clandestine behavior was the only genuinely disreputable activity that Communist professors engaged in, the academic establishment seized upon it as proof of a Communist conspiracy. As a result, by the late 1940s, candor about one's political beliefs and affiliations became a new requirement for membership in the academic profession. That it was specifically directed against Communists and, a little later, against ex-Communists who refused to name names seems obvious in retrospect.[15]

The first postwar application of this new definition of academic freedom took place in Seattle, where, in 1949, after a highly publicized set of hearings by the state legislature's Fact-Finding Committee on Un-American Activities, otherwise known as the Canwell Committee, the University of Washington fired Herbert Phillips and two other tenured professors. Phillips and Joseph Butterworth, a Chaucer specialist, admitted that they were Communists and the administration urged that they be dismissed for that reason alone. The third professor, who had refused to tell either Canwell or the university whether or not he was a Communist, was charged with lack of candor.[16]

The faculty committee that heard the case refrained from recommending the dismissal of the two Communists, but only for technical reasons. The majority of its members agreed with the university's president, Raymond J. Allen, that members of the Communist party were, by definition, unqualified to teach. As Allen explained, because a Communist could not "be a sincere seeker after truth, which is the first obligation and duty of the teacher," the two professors were, " by virture of their admitted membership in the Communist Party . . . incompetent, intellectually dishonest, and derelict in their duty to find and teach the truth." Neither Allen nor the faculty committee ever seriously investigated the two men's academic performance; to have done so would have created problems, for there was no evidence whatsoever that either Butterworth or Phillips had misused his classroom or indoctrinated his students. But, as Allen himself admitted, politically there was no way the university could keep a Communist or suspected Communist on the faculty; and his rationalizations may well have served to legitimize the inevitable.[17]

By 1949, the notion that Communists were unfit to teach had become so commonplace within the academic community that even the firing of three tenured professors provoked little outcry. True, the AAUP had in 1947 adopted a resolution against the automatic exclusion of Communists from the teaching profession, and its annual conventions continued to reaffirm that resolution throughout the 1950s. But this statement had no impact at all, especially since the association never followed it up with any action. The rest of the profession, as indicated by faculty polls, resolutions at faculty meetings, and official statements, had clearly decided that, as the 1949 convention of the National Education Association resolved, by a 2,995–5 vote in support of a measure drawn up by Harvard president James Bryant Conant, among others, membership in the Communist party "and the accompanying surrender of intellectual integrity, render an individual unfit to discharge the duties of a teacher in this country." Many schools specifically revised their by-laws during this period to exclude Communists and other totalitarian types.[18]

That such a consensus was politically convenient does not necessarily mean that it was hypocritical. On the contrary, the cold war was at its most menacing, and most academics, like most American citizens, sincerely believed that Communist teachers not only belonged to a worldwide conspiracy but also, as Sidney Hook explained, "that the party line must be introduced wherever possible."[19] To reject such a view, because it did not accord with reality, would have required not only a certain amount of independent research but also what would have been for most academics an uncomfortable alliance with the left. Few made the effort.

But there were soon few Communists to protect. By 1950, when the Korean War broke out, what few Communists there were on American faculties had either left the party or the academy. The problem that the academic community now had to face was that of so-called "Fifth Amendment Communists," men and women who refused to tell congressional investigating committees whether they were or had ever been members of the Communist party. Because of the refusal of the Supreme Court to place any substantive constitutional limits on the right of a congressional committee to question witnesses about their political beliefs and activities, the only way someone could legally refuse to answer a committee's question—in particular, refuse to name names—was to take the Fifth and claim that answering such a question would tend to incriminate him or her. Unfortunately, because answering any question about their political activities would waive the privilege, witnesses had to take the Fifth in response to all sorts of embarrassing questions simply to avoid becoming an informer. To a public little versed in the niceties of constitutional law, such behavior seemed highly suspect. The congressional investigators made it more so. Joseph McCarthy claimed, for example, "that a witness's refusal to answer whether or not he is or is not a communist on the ground that his answer would tend to incriminate him is the most positive proof obtainable that the witness is a communist." In fact, although many of the people who took the Fifth were Communists, many more, certainly most of the academics, were ex-Communists who did not want to expose their friends.[20]

How was the academic world to handle such people? Uncooperative witnesses, as a Michigan faculty committee noted, brought "embarrassment to the University of a quite needless sort." These people, so most administrators and fellow professors believed, hurt their universities and should put loyalty to their institutions before loyalty to their former friends. The issue, of course, was public relations; and, significantly, at many institutions the most complete records of these cases were in the files of the schools' public information officers. Nobody questioned the necessity for some kind of official action; yet everybody recognized that to fire unfriendly witnesses out of hand, merely for exercising their constitutional rights —as private industry and the federal government did—would violate academic freedom. Somehow the academy would have to find a way to deal with Fifth Amendment witnesses without tearing itself apart over the issue. Academic freedom would have to be revised yet again so as to enable the academy to rid itself of this new category of undesirable professors.[21]

Here again, as during the earlier redefinition of academic freedom, the theorizing was coterminous with the firings it rationalized. Not every institution participated in the process, however. The New York

City municipal colleges probably dismissed the largest number of Fifth Amendment witnesses, more than a dozen men and women who had survived the Rapp-Coudert purges only to be called up by the Internal Security Subcommittee of the Senate Judiciary Committee in late 1952 and early 1953. Although AAUP regulations and academic tradition demanded that tenured professors receive a hearing before dismissal, the city's Board of Higher Education evaded this requirement by relying on a section of the New York City Charter that provided for the automatic dismissal of any city employee called before a legislative investigation who "shall refuse to testify or answer any question . . . on the ground that his answer would tend to incriminate." Because of this statute, the city authorities did not have to confront the issue of academic freedom. "The Board of Higher Education does not discharge the teacher," the president of Queens College explained to one of the uncooperative witnesses as he notified him of his dismissal, "rather the teacher by his own act in refusing to testify thereby brings about a termination of his employment."[22]

Other schools lacked such a handy bureaucratic device and, as a result, almost all of them granted the unfriendly witnesses on their faculties some kind of a hearing. Some of these hearings were quite elaborate. At Michigan, the proceedings involved three separate faculty panels and thousands of pages of testimony. Other schools were more prefunctory. Harvard did not even set up a faculty committee; its controversial teachers met instead with members of the university's ruling Corporation. The actual procedures did not matter much. Michigan fired two people, and Harvard, despite its seeming disregard for AAUP regulations, ostensibly fired no one.[23]

It is important to differentiate between the procedural and the substantive aspects of academic freedom in this context. Obviously, schools whose trustees and administrators either did not consult with or else overruled the recommendations of a faculty committee violated academic freedom. They had encroached upon the corporate rights of the academic profession, its autonomy and control over its own membership. On the other hand, those institutions whose authorities respected the decisions of faculty committees also violated academic freedom, but only that of the individual professors. This was because the committees, whatever their final verdict was, imposed political tests on their colleagues and forced them to discuss their political beliefs so as to prove that they were not in the Communist party. Because of the virtual consensus about the undesirability of Communist professors, few academics, or anyone else for that matter, recognized the extent to which faculty committees infringed upon the unfriendly witness's civil liberties.

Instead, the academic community—trustees, administrators, and professors—addressed itself to the task of trying to redefine academic freedom so that the dismissal of Fifth Amendment witnesses would not result in a violation of it. If the academy could draw up and enforce a code of behavior that would define taking the Fifth before a congressional committee as professionally unacceptable, then the academic profession might be able to avoid a confrontation with its employers and those outside forces that were trying to purge it of its undesirable members. It would do the job itself and in that way ensure, procedurally at least, that academic freedom would be preserved.

The necessity for such a reformulation became particularly acute at the end of 1952 after the Rutgers University Board of Trustees overruled the recommendations of a special faculty committee and dismissed two teachers—a tenured mathematician and the well-known classicist M. I. Finley—specifically for taking the Fifth. By the time the Rutgers' case broke, it was clear that the congressional investigating committees, which until then had largely ignored the academic world, were about to descend. It was equally clear that the nation's colleges and universities might have to deal with dozens of uncooperative witnesses. Rutgers' policy of automatically dismissing any professor who invoked the Fifth seemed somewhat crude for an institution of higher learning. Clearly, a more reasoned and scholarly guide would be helpful, not only to avoid open confrontations between faculties and trustees, but also to convince prospective witnesses that they had a professional obligation to cooperate with the committees. As a result, the first few months of 1953 saw a rash of official and semiofficial statements that purported to explain how a currently politically undesirable behavior—taking the Fifth Amendment—was professionally undesirable as well.[24]

One of the earliest and most important of these statements was a letter that two professors in the Harvard Law School wrote to the student newspaper discussing the legal implications of taking the Fifth. The two professors, Zechariah Chafee and Arthur Sutherland, argued that, unless a witness was "subjecting himself to some degree of danger of conviction of a criminal offense," he had no right to shirk his duty as a citizen "to cooperate in government." Whatever injustices the committees perpetrated, taking the Fifth was not a legitimate way to protest against them. In addition, the two men pointed out, "The Fifth Amendment grants no privilege to protect one's friends." This statement had enormous significance. Not only did it purport to be the most definitive interpretation of the Fifth yet to appear but it bore the name of Zechariah Chafee, probably the most distinguished civil libertarian in America. The president of Rutgers was to invoke it as an ex post facto justification for his university's actions. And academic administrators from Berkeley to Wesleyan distributed the Chafee-Sutherland letter to their faculties, presumably to warn the prospective witnesses on them against invoking the Fifth.[25]

An even more important statement came from an organization called the Association of American Universities, a group composed of the presidents of the nation's 37 leading universities. This statement, which was released in March 1953, was intended to be the basis of official policy for the entire academic community. A grant from the Rockefeller Foundation enabled the organization to distribute thousands of copies to teachers, journalists, and politicians. The formulation that the AAU adopted stressed the academy's new professional requirement of candor. "Above all," the statement insisted,

> the professor owes his colleagues in the university complete candor and perfect integrity, precluding any kind of clandestine or conspiratorial activities. He owes equal candor to the public. If he is called upon to answer for his convictions, it is his duty as a citizen to speak out. It is even more his duty as a professor. Refusal to to so, on whatever legal grounds, cannot fail to reflect on a profession that claims for itself the fullest freedom and the maximum protection available in our society.
>
> In this respect, invocation of the Fifth Amendment places upon a professor a heavy burden of proof of his fitness to hold a teaching position and lays upon his university an obligation to reexamine his qualifications for membership in its society.[26]

Few universities or colleges shirked these obligations. During 1953 and 1954, when the congressional probe into subversion on campus was at its peak, more than 100 college teachers appeared in public. Most of them refused to cooperate, and most of them lost their jobs. Of course, each school dealt with its own witnesses in its own way. Even so, patterns emerged. Every school conducted some kind of an inquiry in which at least some members of the faculty participated, although often only in a token way. State-supported schools were the most repressive. With only one or two exceptions, they fired every uncooperative witness on their faculties. Private schools had more flexibility. In most cases, the crucial determinant was the willingness of the Fifth Amendment witnesses to cooperate with their institution's investigation and talk about their previous political activities. They had to explain why they had invoked the Fifth and, if they had once been Communists, had to prove to the satisfaction of their colleagues and administrations that they were no longer. Without exception, every single professor who balked at taking this political test—whether at a liberal and progressive school like Reed College or a state university like Michigan—lost his job; for, in the language of the day, he had not been candid. Of course, every teacher who did not have tenure was, with only one exception, not reappointed.[27]

There was little opposition from within the academic community, certainly little organized opposition. Even academics who opposed every other aspect of McCarthyism agreed that professors had to discuss their political beliefs with their colleagues. The AAUP, which officially denounced some aspects of this new obligation of candor, did nothing else. Its general secretary was a cautious man who apparently did not want to create a schism over the issue. In addition, he was in poor health and was not functioning very well during these crucial years. Often he did not answer his mail or return phone calls. As a result, it was not until after his death that the AAUP took a public stand on any of these cases. Then, in 1956, seven years after Washington had fired its three tenured professors and three and a half years after Rutgers had, it issued a special report that censured a handful of schools, Rutgers among them. This pronouncement had little effect—and not only because it came too late but, more importantly, because it did nothing to rectify the injustices it denounced.[28]

Most of the men and women who were fired or not reappointed for political reasons during the McCarthy period found themselves unable to teach in the United States. M. I. Finley, whose scholarly credentials were to earn him a knighthood, had to take a job in Cambridge, England, because no American university would offer him one. And his case was no exception. The academic blacklist, although not as well known as that in the entertainment industry, functioned just as effectively. Not only did it exclude from college teaching just about every unfriendly witness whose institution had fired him or her but it also screened out people who might become unfriendly witnesses. Harvard's dean expected ex-Communists to clear themselves with the FBI before he would put their appointments through; California's public and private universities checked out their potential teachers with the state legislature's Un-American Activities Committee. Usually, however, a letter of recommendation sufficed to warn a department against hiring a potentially embarrassing colleague. As a result, although a few of these people did find academic jobs, primarily at small, denominational black colleges in the South, most either had to leave the academy or the country. When they did return, as most of them eventually did, they had lost about ten years from their careers.[29]

If nothing else, the existence of the academic blacklist during the 1950s and 1960s shows how little the academic community as a whole could or would do to help those of its members who were politically tainted. This is significant because most of these people were no longer politically active. By the time the committees got around to subpoenaing them, they had long since left the Communist party and were pursuing ordinary academic careers. Yet, because an outside authority, even as discredited an outside authority as HUAC was by 1954, intervened to identify them as politically undesirable, their careers were disrupted and in some cases destroyed.

Obviously, these were bad times for academic freedom, but only for that of individuals. The freedom of the profession as a whole, its control over the terms of its own employment, remained pretty much intact. Professors everywhere not only endorsed the exclusion of Communists and Fifth Amendment witnesses from the academy but also participated in the process of excluding them. In only a few, a very few, cases did a university's administrators and trustees impinge upon the prerogatives of the faculty and fire someone a faculty committee had wanted to retain. And even in those cases, those in which the AAUP censured the schools in question, the professors involved found themselves blacklisted just as thoroughly as if they had been fired with the advice and consent of all their peers.[30]

Clearly, then, the traditional structure of academic freedom with its emphasis on the procedures for faculty self-governance did not and does not protect the rights of politically unpopular professors. We need a new approach, one that recognizes several types of academic freedom and acknowledges that the type of academic freedom that protects individual dissenters has never existed, except on paper. This will not be easy. At the moment, university administrations are taking advantage of the present fiscal crisis to nibble away at the corporate privileges of the professoriate, thus putting the classic variety of academic freedom itself in question. The answer may well be some type of collective organization, unionization, perhaps—although the Supreme Court's decision in the Yeshiva case poses real obstacles for it, at least in its traditional form—at private colleges and universities. But unless the academic profession recognizes that it must organize collectively to protect the individual rights of all its members, not only will the jobs of political dissenters be in danger, as they always are, but the status and autonomy of the profession as a whole may be as well.[31]

NOTES

1. The general literature on academic freedom is rather unsatisfactory. Most theoretical formulations, like those of the American Association of University Professors, are self-serving, and the historical ones, although far superior, are limited. Typical of the genre are such books as Robert M. MacIver, *Academic Freedom in Our*

Time (New York: Columbia University Press, 1955), and Walter Metzger, *Academic Freedom in the Age of the University* (New York: Columbia University Press, 1955).

2. The best book on the California Loyalty Oath crisis is David P. Gardner, *The California Oath Controversy* (Berkeley: University of California Press, 1967).

3. The best study of the Ely and Bemis cases is in Mary O. Furner, *Advocacy and Objectivity* (Lexington, Ky.: University of Kentucky Press, 1975), pp. 143–205. See also Benjamin G. Rader, *The Academic Mind and Reform* (Lexington, Ky.: University of Kentucky Press, 1966), pp. 28–129, and Metzger, *Academic Freedom*, pp. 151–62.

4. Committee on Academic Freedom and Academic Tenure, "Report," *AAUP Bulletin* 1 (December 1915).

5. The best studies of the political culture of the professoriate are Claude Bowman, *The College Professor in America* (Philadelphia: University of Pennsylvania Press, 1938), and Laurence Veysey, *The Emergence of the American University* (Chicago: University of Chicago, Press, 1965), pp. 381–438.

6. Scott Nearing, *The Making of a Radical* (New York: Harper & Row, 1972), Chap. 5–6; "Report of the Committee of Inquiry on the Case of Professor Scott Nearing of the University of Pennsylvania," *AAUP Bulletin* 2 (May 1916).

7. Committee A, "Report," *AAUP Bulletin* 4 (March 1918): 19.

8. Granville Hicks was dismissed from Rensselaer Polytechnic Institute in 1935; Jerome David lost his job at Yale in 1936. See "Academic Freedom and Tenure: Rensselaer Polytechnic Institute," *AAUP Bulletin* 22 (January 1936), and "Academic Freedom and Tenure: Yale University," *AAUP Bulletin* 23 (May 1937). Both Bruce Franklin and Michael Parenti were casualties of the Vietnam War era unrest. Franklin was fired from Stanford and Parenti from the University of Vermont.

9. The best study of these wartime cases is Carol Gruber, *Mars and Minerva: World War I and the Uses of the Higher Learning in America* (Baton Rouge: Louisiana State University Press, 1975). The Nicholas Murray Butler speech is on p. 199.

10. "Report," Committee on Academic Freedom in Wartime," *AAUP Bulletin* 4 (February–March 1918): 40–41.

11. The best study of the Rapp-Coudert investigations is Lawrence H. Chamberlain, *Loyalty and Legislative Action* (Ithaca, N.Y.: Cornell University Press, 1951). See also Robert Iversen, *The Communists and the Schools* (New York: Harcourt, Brace, 1959), pp. 208–23.

12. Robert Gorham Davis, testimony, February 25, 1953, HUAC, 83rd Congress, 1st session, 47; Marvin E. Gettleman, "Communists in Higher Education: C.C.N.Y. and Brooklyn College on the Eve of the Rapp-Coudert Investigation, 1935–1939," unpublished paper, 1977; Howard Selsam, reply to a questionnaire, Paul Tillett files, in the personal possession of Virginia Wilson, Princeton, N.J.; "Academic Freedom & New York University: The Case of Professor Edwin Berry Burgum", pamphlet, New York, 1954: Alvin L. Schorr to Marvin E. Gettleman, May 11, 1979.

13. Jane Sanders, *Cold War on the Campus* (Seattle: University of Washington Press, 1979), pp. 51–2; Leon Wofsy, interview with the author, April 12, 1980.

14. Granville Hicks, *Where We Came Out* (New York: Viking Press, 1954), p. 46; George Mayberry, testimony, July 1, 1953, HUAC, 83rd Congress, 1st session, 1924; Herbert Phillips, quoted in *Harvard Crimson*, March 24, 1950; Joseph Starobin, *American Communism in Crisis, 1943–1957* (Cambridge, Mass.: Harvard University Press, 1972), p. 300.

15. Academic Communists took party names, for example; at schools like CCNY and Brooklyn College, where there were a lot of party members, the party units published "shop papers," which were written and edited anonymously. Among the academic Communists who regretted the clandestine nature of their political affiliation were

Richard Schlatter, "On Being a Communist at Harvard," *Partisan Review* 44 (December 1977): 611–12, and Mark Nickerson, testimony, University of Michigan, Special Investigating Committee, "Proceedings," V-1, box 21, Marvin L. Niehuss Papers, Michigan Historical Collections, Bentley Historical Library, University of Michigan, Ann Arbor.

16. There are two useful books about the University of Washington cases: Sanders, *Cold War on the Campus*, and Vern Countryman, *Un-American Activities in the State of Washington* (Ithaca, N.Y.: Cornell University Press, 1951).

17. Raymond J. Allen, "President's Analysis," *Communism and Academic Freedom* (Seattle: University of Washington Press, 1949), p. 90; Countryman, *Un-American Activities*, pp. 224–25.

18. "Report of Committee A," *AAUP Bulletin* 34 (Spring 1948); *Harvard Crimson*, June 9, 1949. Among the schools that revised their by-laws during this period were Cornell, New York University, and Michigan. See "Minutes, Faculty Meeting," May 30, 1951, Dean of the Faculty Records, Box 2, #11/2/926, Cornell University Archives, Ithaca, N.Y.; *Minutes of meeting of University Senate, March 13, 1947, April 8, 1948,* New York University Archives, Bobst Library, New York University; and *Report of the Joint Committee on Demotion and Dismissal Procedures,* box 21, Niehuss Papers, University of Michigan.

19. Sidney Hook, "What Shall We Do about Communist Teachers?" *Saturday Evening Post*, September 10, 1949. Just about every academic committee that dealt with the problem during this period subscribed to what I would call the Allen-Hook thesis. See Ellen Schrecker, "An Obligation of Candor," *New York University Education Quarterly* 14 (Summer 1983).

20. There is a large literature on the use of the Fifth Amendment before congressional investigating committees. A particularly helpful discussion is Telford Taylor, *Grand Inquest* (New York: Simon and Schuster 1955), pp. 195–208. See also Thomas I. Emerson, David Haber, and Norman Dorsen, *Political and Civil Rights in the United States* (Boston: Little, Brown, 1967), Vol 1, pp. 350–424; Daniel Pollitt, "Pleading the Fifth Amendment Before a Congressional Committee," *Notre Dame Lawyer* 32 (1956); and Erwin N. Griswold, *The 5th Amendment Today* (Cambridge, Mass.: Harvard University Press, 1955).

Joseph McCarthy is quoted in Dan Gillmor, *Fear, the Accuser* (New York: Abelard, 1954), p. 146.

21. Report of the Special Advisory Committee (Michigan), 34, in Niehuss Papers, box 21; "Academic Freedom and Tenure in the Quest for National Security," *AAUP Bulletin* 42 (Spring 1956): 60.

22. Robert Morris, *No Wonder We Are Losing* (Point Pleasant, N.J.: The Bookmailer, 1958), 135–45; Iversen, *The Communists and the Schools*, pp. 266–67; John J. Theobald to Oscar Shaftel, February 26, 1953, personal papers of Oscar Shaftel.

23. Michigan fired Chandler Davis and Mark Nickerson in August 1954, even though the faculty committees that dealt with the case recommended that Nickerson, who had tenure, be kept. Clement Markert, an assistant professor, was kept. Harvard kept Wendell Furry, a tenured associate professor. It also kept Leon Kamin, a teaching fellow, and Helen Deane Markham, an assistant professor in the Medical School, but both were later let go. "Statement by the Harvard Corporation in Regard to Associate Professor Wendell H. Furry, Teaching Fellow Leon J. Kamin, and Assistant Professor Helen Deane Markham," May 20, 1953, pamphlet.

24. Report of the Special Faculty Committee of Review (Rutgers), December 3, 1952, and Resolution of the Rutgers University Board of Trustees, December 12, 1952, are the primary documents in the case. They were widely distributed; and mimeographed copies of these documents appear in the archives of every university I have investigated.

25. Zechariah Chafee and Arthur Sutherland, letter to the editor, *Harvard Crimson*, January 8, 1953; Leopold Kohr to Zechariah Chafee, September 8, 1953, box 35, file 19, Zechariah Chafee Papers, Harvard Law School Library, Cambridge, Mass. Arthur Sutherland's papers, in the Harvard Law School Library, contain more than 50 requests for copies of the statement from a wide variety of schools, including Sarah Laurence, Ohio State, California Institute of Technology, Mount Holyoke, Smith, Brooklyn College, Syracuse, Michigan State, Oberlin, Oregon State, NYU, Cornell, Colorado, Vassar, and the University of Vermont.

26. Association of American Universities, "The Rights and Responsibilities of Universities and Their Faculties," Princeton, N.J., March 25, 1953; Association of American Universities, Minutes of Meeting, October 27–28, 1953, in Grayson Kirk Papers, Low Library, Columbia University.

27. The academics who were dismissed after refusing to cooperate with their institution's investigations were Chandler Davis (Michigan), Horace Bancroft Davis (University of Kansas City), Edwin Berry Burgum (NYU), Ralph Gundlach (University of Washington), Stanley Moore (Reed), and Morris Judd (University of Colorado). This may or may not be a complete list. Some cases I simply don't know about; others are unclear. Did the three professors at the Jefferson Medical School who were willing to tell their school's loyalty committee about their own politics but not about other people's cooperate or not? There were also half a dozen people at the University of California who, during the Loyalty Oath controversy, refused to discuss their political views with a faculty committee.

28. "Academic Freedom and Tenure in the Quest for National Security," *AAUP Bulletin* 42 (Spring 1956); Ralph Fuchs, interview with the author, October 6, 1978.

29. For the Harvard story, see Sigmund Diamond, "Veritas at Harvard," *New York Review of Books*, April 28, 1977. For the California one, see Richard E. Combs, testimony, Senate Internal Security Subcommittee of the Committee on the Judiciary, March 19, 1953, 83rd Congress, 1st session, pp. 605–22. M. I. Finley, reply to a questionnaire, Paul Tillett files, in personal possession of Virginia Wilson, Princeton, N.J.

30. The schools that the AAUP censured in 1956 were the University of California, Jefferson Medical College, Rutgers, Temple, and Ohio State. Later on the organization investigated other schools in greater depth and censured NYU, Vermont, the University of Michigan, the University of Oklahoma, Dickinson College, Lowell Technological Institute, and the University of Southern California. Reports on all these cases can be found in the *AAUP Bulletins* from 1956 to 1959.

•4•

Academic Freedom
in America Today:
A Marxist View

Bertell Ollman

Three brief case studies:

In 1915, Scott Nearing, a socialist professor of economics, was fired from the University of Pennsylvania for publicly opposing the use of child labor in coal mines. With an influential mine owner on the Board of Trustees, the president of the university decided he had to let Nearing go. As far as I can discover, he is the first professor fired from an American university for his radical beliefs and activities.[1]

Some have argued that this honor belongs to Edward Bemis, who was dismissed from the University of Chicago in 1894. A major charge in this case was that Bemis had the poor judgment to hold discussions with union leaders during the famous Pullman railroad strike of that year. In a letter to the president of the University of Chicago, Bemis admitted that he had talked to the union officials, but, he insisted, only with the purpose of urging them to give up the strike. It didn't help. The strike went on—and the dismissal stuck.[2] However, in light of Bemis's admission, I find it difficult to view him as the first radical to lose his job because of his political beliefs. That honor belongs to Nearing. This doesn't mean that the universities were tolerant earlier. Before Nearing, there simply were no radical professors.

Second, in 1940, the Rapp-Coudert Committee of the New York State legislature began its infamous investigation of subversives in the municipal college system of New York City (now City University of New York, CUNY). By 1942, more than 40 professors were fired or did not get their contracts renewed either because they were Communists or because they refused to divulge their political beliefs and connections.[3]

Third, in 1978, Joel Samoff was denied tenure by the political science department of the University of Michigan. Although he had published widely and was about to receive the university's Distinguished Service Award for outstanding contributions to the scholarly life of the university, he was faulted for not publishing enough in orthodox political science journals and for using an unscientific Marxist approach to his subject matter.

In each case, a professor's right to pursue truth in his own way was abrogated. In the Nearing case, the ax was wielded by the university's higher administration. For the CUNY 40, it was the government that was primarily responsible for the blow that befell them. And Samoff's academic demise resulted from a decision taken by a majority of his own colleagues.

Where does academic freedom lie in all this? Although there is general agreement that academic freedom involves the right of teachers and students to investigate any topic they wish and to discuss, teach, and publish their conclusions freely, there is an anguished debate over where to draw the line (nowhere is everything allowed) and, more particularly, over who should be allowed to do it. Where does the threat to academic freedom come from? The case against government interference in academic decision making is most easily made and probably most widely supported. Here, academic freedom is ensured when the government adopts a hands-off policy toward the university.

Many dissatisfied professors and students, however, maintain that a greater danger to academic freedom today comes from university presidents and boards of trustees who try to impose their values and judgments on the entire university community. Still others, including victims of peer evaluation like Joel Samoff, would argue that faculty bias does the most damage, that without a sincere toleration of unorthodox approaches on the part of the professoriate there can be no thoroughgoing academic freedom.

The situation is more complicated still, for even the people who advocate government interference in university affairs often do so—in their words—"to protect academic freedom," in this case against the deceivers and manipulators of youth. In short, everyone is in favor of academic freedom; only the emphasis and enemies are different. In 1978, when I was denied a job as chairman of the Government Department at the University of Maryland because of my Marxist political views, I called this denial an attack on my academic freedom. The faculty who had chosen me for the job also said their academic freedom had been infringed upon. Students who wanted to study with me made the same claim. President John Toll, who rejected me, insisted he was acting on behalf of academic freedom, his to do what he thought best in disregard of all outside pressures. And many state politicans, whose threats of financial retribution against the university constituted the most powerful of these outside pressures, likewise spoke of defending academic freedom against the likes of me.

The problem of sorting out the various uses of "academic freedom" is both very easy and terribly complex—easy, if it is simply a matter of taking a stand, of choosing the most compatible notion of "academic freedom" with one's own values and declaring other uses illegitimate, complex if we try to explore the relations between these different uses to discover what as a group they express about the conditions they are intended to describe. It is by taking this latter path that I hope to cast some light on the state of academic freedom in the United States today.

The time-honored way of breaking out of the confusion that surrounds the discussion of academic freedom is to label what has hitherto passed as a definition as the ideal and to add the words "unfortunately, it doesn't always apply." The implication, of course, is that this is what most people want, and that actual practice is close and closing in on the ideal. Focusing on the ideal in this way, practice can be shortchanged. What actually happens is viewed teleologically, in terms of what one thinks it is going to become eventually, in time, with patience and more propagandizing of the ideal. The possibility that the gap between the actual and the ideal is more or less fixed, and *that the ideal may even play a role in keeping it so,* is hardly entertained and can't be as long as what occurs is not examined on its own terms and within its real social and political context. In any case, the confusion over the different uses of academic freedom can never be sorted out as long as the discussion remains on the abstract level of ideas. For this, we must keep our feet on solid ground and find out who is doing what to whom and why.

The locus of our study, of course, will be the university. And not just any university, but the university in capitalist society. Can't we just examine the nature of universities in general? I think not. Why not should be evident if we look no farther than the big business–dominated boards of trustees of all our major universities. If we were studying institutions of higher learning in a foreign country and discovered that a majority of the members of all their boards of trustees were generals, we would not hesitate to make certain conclusions about the character and aim of education there. Yet even people who know that our boards of trustees are run by a business elite seldom question why this is so or try to think through what follows from this fact. Are businesspeople really more clever than the rest of us, or more public-spirited, or more concerned with the development of rational and critical thought? If not, we must try to understand what capitalists want from the university and what they do there and how all this relates to academic freedom.

Capitalism is a form of society where the means of production are privately owned, and all production decisions are made on the basis of what will earn the largest profits for owners. So much holds true for the entire history of our republic. But the American capitalist system has also undergone a number of major changes. The Marxist economist Sam Bowles points out that the capitalist economy and riding a bicycle have one important thing in common: In both, forward motion is necessary for stability.[4] (Perhaps, someone should point this out to Ronald Reagan.) As capitalism grows and changes so does the nature of its requirements from education—indeed, as well as from other sectors of capitalist life.

Among the major developments in American capitalism over the last 100 years are the following: With the growth of technology, the amount of capital investment going to workers in the form of wages has decreased as a percentage of total investment, leading to a general and long-term squeeze on profits (surplus value, of which profit is a portion, is produced by labor; hence, a relatively smaller percentage of investment going to labor means a constricted base for profits); the percentage of the work force that is self-employed (entrepreneurs and professionals) has gone down from 40 to 10 percent; the number of managers and professionals on salaries (chiefly employed by big business) has increased sevenfold; in big business, complex hierarchies have developed that determine power, status, and salary; more jobs require minimal skills; and intensification of the division of labor has led to an increased fragmentation of tasks for both white- and blue-collar workers, decreasing the degree of control that each individual has over his or her job; mainly in order to maintain profits, the government has come to play a more direct role in running the economy on behalf of the capitalist class; and ideology—that is, one-sided, partial, essentially mystifying interpretations of reality—has spread from the factory to the media, market, and schools, chiefly as a means of disguising the increasingly obvious pro-capitalist bias of the state.

The major changes that have occurred in American higher education during the last 100 years reflect these developments in the capitalist mode of production and have operated in general to facilitate the efficient functioning of the new capitalist order. For example, whereas in 1870 only 2 percent of the 18 to 21 age group went to college, today it is about 50 percent. The liberal arts and classics that formed the core of the traditional university curriculum have been replaced by science, math, public administration, business, and other vocational training. In both the natural and social sciences, universities have assumed more and more research and development tasks for private industry, increasing their profits by reducing their necessary costs.

Increasingly, university life has been organized on the basis of a complex system of tests, grades, and degrees, so that everyone knows exactly where he or she fits, what he or she deserves, what has to be done to rise another notch on the scale. Discounting, as most educators do, their negative effects on scholarship, critical thinking, and collegiality, these practices have succeeded in instilling a new discipline and respect for hierarchy, lowering student expectations, and generally creating a sense that you get what you work for and have talent for and, therefore, that failure is due to some personal fault (laziness, stupidity, or ill will). Overseeing this reorganization of the academy, codifying its ends and rationalizing its means, dispensing incentives, cost accounting, building bridges to the "community" (chiefly business leaders and politicians) is the work of a vastly expanded cast of professional managers. At Columbia University, for example, in the period 1948–68, the faculty grew by 50 percent, the student body by 100 percent, and the administration by 900 percent.[5]

Of all the ideas that help keep democratic capitalism in the United States functioning as smoothly as it does, none is more important than the idea of "equality of opportunity." Here, too, the university has a special role to play. It seems that people are willing to live with great social and economic inequalities if they believe they had, or have, or will have the chance to make it up, or even that their children will have such a chance. In the nineteenth century, the belief in equality of opportunity was fed chiefly by the existence of "free" land in the West. When the frontier closed, this dream was kept alive by the possibility of starting a small business, which, with a little luck and hard work, might one day make you rich. Now that nine out of every ten small businesses end in failure (U.S. Department of Commerce statistics), it is our relatively open system of higher education that serves as living evidence for the existence of equality of opportunity.

For universities to play their appointed role in this capitalist drama, it is not enough that everyone who wants to get an education be able to get into a university. In both its structure and content, higher education must appear to give everyone a more or less equal chance to prepare for the best jobs. Should the universities be perceived as vocational schools, providing low-level skills and indoctrinating students with the values and attitudes deemed important by their future capitalist employers, as a simple continuation of the tracking system already begun in high schools, the crucial ideological work of the university in promoting belief in the existence of a real equality of opportunity would suffer irreparable damage.

The university's role in helping to justify democratic capitalism carries over, as we might expect, to the content of its courses. Particularly today, with the government's more direct involvement in the economy on the side of the capitalists and so many young members of the working class in college with time to read and think about that involvement, there is a great need for ever more sophisticated rationalizations for the status quo. In this effort. the university must maintain the appearance of allowing all points of view, including some critical of capitalism, to contest freely. Otherwise, the ideas that emerge from universities would be tainted, viewed as propaganda rather than "knowledge" and "science," and have less hold on people. Not only students would be affected but also the general public, many of whose beliefs and prejudices receive their legitimation as value-free social science by academic decree.

Finally, to complete our list of main ways in which higher education serves capitalism in the modern period, we should mention that the universities provide local capitalists with a reserve army of low-paid, nonunionized, part-time workers, while at the same time offering a kind of custodial care for young people who cannot find jobs, becoming in Ira Shor's apt phrase, "warehouses for unneeded workers."[6] Here, too, students will only willingly accept these degrading roles and conditions if they believe they are receiving a real education and being prepared for something better.

Does all this mean that the university is not a place where knowledge and skills get passed on from one generation to the next and where some people teach and others actually learn how to think critically? Not at all. Like universities in all periods and in virtually all societies, American universities embody, to one degree or another, all the fine qualities that are extolled in commencement day speeches. Unfortunately, these speeches neglect to mention other functions that clearly stamp our universities as products of capitalist society, and any attempt to grasp the dynamics of the present situation must begin by focusing on these historically specific qualities—that is, those that mark them as universities existing and functioning in a capitalist society.

The time has come to reintroduce the idea of academic freedom and to see how it works. The first thing that strikes us from the above account is that American universities require a little critical thought, which means a few critical teachers, which means, too, a little academic freedom for them to work, in order for universities to function as they are meant to and have to in a capitalist society. The presence of some radical professors helps to legitimate the bourgeois ideology that comes out of universities as "social science" and the universities themselves as something more than training centers. So a few radical professors are necessary to make the point that real freedom of thought, discussion, and so on exist and that people in the university have the opportunity to hear all sides in the major debates of the day.

But a key question is, At what point do a few radical professors become too many? For the presence of radicals in universities at a time of burgeoning working-class enrollment and a declining economy constitutes a real and growing threat to the capitalist system. In the story of the "Emperor's New Clothes," it didn't take many voices to convince the crowd that the emperor was naked. At a time of deepening economic crisis, the promises of capitalism are no less vulnerable.

Given the need for some radical professors, and the dangers of too many, the debate over where to draw the line, who should do it, and on the basis of what criteria goes on continually. It goes on in government, in university administrations, and among faculty in almost every university department. Because the language in which these questions are posed is different on each level, even participants are not always aware that they are involved in the same debate. Without explicit coordination, using apparently different criteria and procedures, and while lost in their own internecine disputes over turf and power, the government, university administrations, and departmental faculties are taking part in the same balancing act.

Viewed from the perspective of their victims (of those who suffer because they fall on the other side of the line), however, the practice of academic freedom in our universities appears as a kind of policing mechanism that operates on three levels. On the level of government, its means (repressive laws, administrative harassment, threats to reduce funding, and so on) and ends are evident, although even here there is some attempt to disguise the ends in terms of preserving students' academic freedom from the predations of deceptive radical professors. For the administration, the disguise takes the form of preserving university autonomy from direct government interference, on one hand, and making universities run smoothly (radicals tend to make waves), on the other. At the faculty level, this "internal policing" (the label is Milton Fisk's[7]) takes the form of making so-called objective, value-neutral decisions on what constitutes political science or economics or philosophy, and which journals in each discipline warrant the academic "good housekeeping seal of approval" so that publishing elsewhere, which usually means in radical journals, doesn't count for promotion, tenure, and the like.

Only on the first level, that of government, is academic repression expressed in political terms, as an effort to keep radicals or Marxists out of the university because of their political beliefs. Hence, whenever governments are forced to act against radicals, the ideological work of the university, which relies so heavily on assumptions of tolerance, is seriously jeopardized. Better by far if university administrators, using institutional arguments, refuse to hire radical professors or turn them down for tenure. Best of all, of course, is when departmental faculties, using what appear to be purely professional criteria, take the initiative themselves. Consequently, and as a general rule, politicians only get involved in academic repression, or threaten to do so, when university administrators fail to act "responsibly," or give signs that they are about to; while administrators only overrule their faculty on this matter when it is the latter who have failed to act "responsibly."

In distinguishing among the forms of academic repression peculiar to the government, university administrators, and departmental faculties, I do not mean to suggest that these three levels are autonomous. Quite the contrary. The influence of the government on university administrations, for example—through appointing presidents and boards of trustees, determining budgets, setting research priorities, licensing programs, and so on—is so overwhelming that Michael Brown would have us view administrations in public universities as part of the state apparatus.[8] The situation in what are still called "private" universities differs only in degree. Nor do I wish to play down the ties of interests and values that bind government, university administrations, and most departmental faculties to the capitalist class, a connection that another Marxist scholar, Milton Fisk, tries to highlight by designating university professors a "class of functionaries" with a special servitor relationship to capitalists.[9] I have been chiefly concerned, however, to examine how the contradictory functions of the capitalist university (in particular, educating, socializing, and legitimating capitalist social relations) result in different kinds of academic repression that turn out, upon analysis, to be different aspects of the same thing—and this just because of the intimate ties (sketched by Brown, Fisk, and others) among the capitalist class, the government, university administrations, and most faculty members.

As regards academic freedom, what I have been arguing is that a kind of academic freedom already exists. It takes the form of a three-tiered mechanism of academic repression. It is how this repression functions, for whom and against what—*that* is academic freedom. The underside of who is allowed to teach is who cannot; just as what cannot be studied is organically related to what can be studied. Setting this ever changing boundary is the act of freedom of some that determines the kind (muted) and degree (very little) of freedom available to all. Unfortunately, academic freedom, interpreted as the actual practice of freedom in the academy, its expression as repression, is not quite what we always thought it was. What, then, can be said about what we always thought it was, or what is often referred to as the ideal of academic freedom?

First, it is clear that as long as the capitalist class controls the universities, which is to say as long as capitalism exists, the gap between the ideal of academic freedom and its practice (described above) is more or less fixed. But I have also suggested that this ideal itself may play a role in keeping this gap fixed, that rather than part of the solution, the ideal of academic freedom may be part of the problem. How can this be so? Partly, it is so because the ideal of academic freedom helps to disguise and distort an essentially repressive practice by presenting it as an imperfect version of what should be. Putting what everyone is said to favor at the start relegates what actually exists to the role of a passing qualification. Viewed in the way, and in this order, the dynamics of who is doing what to whom and why, together with the structural reforms needed to change things, can never be understood.

Futhermore, the ideal of academic freedom, beginning as the soft core of people's description of real events, gradually substitutes itself as an explanation of what is happening that is so feeble that, with minor qualifications, all the worst villains can embrace it. Although everyone may favor academic freedom, it is in the nature of ideals—it is said—that they can never be fully realized. Something similar occurs with the ideal of consumer sovereignty in which the assumed goal of the exercise replaces and then helps to explain what people actually do in supermarkets, where they generally choose products that they have been socialized to want. Likewise, the ideal of democracy plays a similar twofold role in respect to what happens in real elections, in which money and control of media play the decisive roles. In every instance asserting a valued goal becomes the means for misrepresenting and explaining away a reality that has little to do with it, except insofar as this reality requires for its continued functioning people's misuse of this goal. In other words, it is only because most people in the university misunderstand academic repression in terms of an imperfect academic freedom that academic freedom can continue to function so effectively as academic repression. If the practice of academic freedom in capitalism is academic repression, the ideal of academic freedom is the ideology that both permits and provides a cover for its occurrence.

So much follows from privileging the qualities of academic freedom as an ideal, but the contribution that the ideal of academic freedom makes to preserving the status quo also comes from its narrow focus on freedom. Talk of freedom, whether in the marketplace, in politics, or in the academy, assumes equality in the conditions that permit people to use their freedom or the irrelevance of such conditions. For freedom is not just about wanting something, but includes the ability to do or have what one wants. It is a want embodied in a practice, but, unlike the simple want, the practice requires the existence of certain conditions. Unfortunately, in a class-divided society, such conditions are never equal and always relevant. Simply put, some people have the money, jobs, or education to act freely, and others do not. In every case, the privileged few also benefit from a ready-made rationalization of their privileges: They are simply making use of their freedom. Let others, they say, try to do as much.

In the academy, the people with power use their freedom to repress radicals in the ways described. If the police mechanisms embodied in the practice of academic freedom give them the means to do this, it is the ideal of academic freedom that gives them an effective way of rationalizing it—hence the constant patter about exercising their academic freedom as they go about their work of repression. In the university, as throughout capitalist society, a commitment to freedom in the absence of an equally strong commitment to social justice carries with it the seeds of even greater injustice. For the ideal of academic justice to take its place alongside the ideal of academic freedom, however, we shall have to await the coming of a society that no longer needs its universities to help reproduce and rationalize existing inequalities, that is, a socialist society

So far I have examined the role that the ideal of academic freedom plays in keeping things as they are, but now I am only too pleased to admit that this ideal also plays a part in helping to change them. That is, at the same time that the ideal of academic freedom hides, distorts, and helps to rationalize academic repression by government, university administrations, and departmental faculties, it also opens up a little space and provides some justification for the presentation of critical opinion. Rhetorically and occasionally procedurally, it also serves as a modest defense for radical teachers who avail themselves of this space. Although wishing doesn't make it so and error exacts compound interest, what people believe to be true (even if false) and what they consider good (even if impossible) are not without influence. If only through constant repetition, liberal cant occasionally takes hold, particularly on younger members of the academy, producing a subspecies of academic freedom groupies, people too afraid to act on their ideas but willing to support those who do. With the help of the few real exceptions, liberals who try to incorporate their beliefs into their daily lives (a self-destructive impulse for all but the most established scholars), the ideal of academic freedom sometimes plays a progessive role in the struggle to extend the boundaries of what can be studied in our universities.

The ideal of academic freedom, vague, unclear, contradictory, but repeated often enough, also exercises—in my view—a very general restraining influence on what the perpetrators of academic repression are able and even willing to do. It is not always true that it is better to deal with honest villains than with hypocritical ones. In our understandable disgust with their hypocrisy, many radical critics have neglected to look for its positive side. The complex effects of hypocrisy on hypocrites, in the university as indeed throughout capitalist society, requires further serious examination.

Finally, and most important, the ideal of academic freedom also helps contribute to the development of critical thinking in the university insofar as it contains within itself elements of such thinking. At its best, this means recognizing, as part of the ideal, how the conditions of modern capitalist society have turned the practice of academic freedom into academic repression and used the ideal to cover its tracks. A critically constituted ideal understands the conditions of its own misuse as well as the structural changes necessary to reverse this process. Saved from displays of moral outrage, we are freed to work for academic freedom by helping to build the democratic socialist conditions that are necessary for it to exist. In developing this expanded understanding of the ideal of academic freedom, in sharing it in the university and with the public at large, we are beginning the work of putting it into practice. Academic freedom, by this interpretation, lives and grows in the conscious struggle for a socialist society.

Unfortunately, none of these progressive trends is dominant. At present, they are all subordinate to the role played by academic freedom in helping to police the university and only deserve our attention once this central role has been made clear. Otherwise, there is a danger of falling victim to all the distortions mentioned above and even contributing to them. But once the capitalist context in which academic freedom appears has been laid out, once its main function in this context is understood, its other role in helping to undermine capitalism requires equal attention.

In summary, academic freedom is about both freedom and repression, how they are linked to each other, not only as opposites, but also as preconditions, effects, and potentials, each on the other. Their proper order of treatment is first repression and then freedom. In this way, freedom is less distorted and the contribution that freedom (in its ideological form) makes to repression is minimized. The Marxist approach to academic freedom involves analyzing it as a practice, one inextricably tied to capitalist power relations, and an accompanying ideology. This analysis embodies and helps to develop a new critical practice and an alternative vision that can also be subsumed under the broader notion of academic freedom.

What, then, is the situation today? What is the state of these contradictory tendencies in academic freedom in the mid-1980s? One first remarks that there has been a considerable increase in the number of Marxist and other kinds of radical professors in the universities. Together with the growing crisis in capitalism and the inability of most bourgeois scholarship to explain it, this has led to the increased legitimacy of Marxist scholarship in practically every discipline. At the same time, there are also more radical professors not getting hired or tenured.[10]

Probably the most striking development is a gradual breakdown of the the three-tiered policing mechanism of academic repression. With a growth in the number of radical scholars and the increased legitimation of radical scholarship, the bottom tier, professors in the departments, is no longer excluding radicals with the regularity that it once was. I was jolted into recognizing this change by my experience at the University of Maryland, where a search committee made up of ten political scientists chose me, a Marxist, for their chairman. I don't think this could have happened ten years earlier. And if this happened in political science, traditionally the most conservative of the social sciences, it is happening (although sometimes very slowly) in all disciplines and in universities throughout the country (again, although many exceptions exist). In mine and other cases, this has simply forced university administrations and politicians (the second and third tiers) to take a more direct part in academic repression. But, as I have argued, there are limits to how much they can do without paying what is for them an unacceptable price in terms of legitimacy.

Consequently, on occasion, there have been important victories. Most recently, among the more prominent are Fred Block (Department of Sociology, University of Pennsylvania) and Dick Walker (Department of Geography, University of California, Berkeley), who received tenure, and Erwin Marquit (Department of Physics, University of Minnesota), who won promotion—all after protracted struggles. Although the cards are stacked against us, they are not all dealt out, and the way a particular struggle is conducted can count.

In the coming period, I would expect to see, for reasons already given, a still greater increase in the number of radical teachers, a rise in the amount of academic repression (primarily by university administrators and to a lesser degree by the government), and, as a result of both, a continued weakening of the university's role as a legitimator of capitalist ideology. How these conflicting tendencies will finally work themselves out, of course, will depend far more on the social and political struggles of the larger society than on the positions we take within the university. Yet what we do as professors will count for something in the balance, so we must become better scholars, better critics, better teachers. We will also need courage, and we will need to be steadfast—all of which brings me back to Scott Nearing.

Scott Nearing is still alive and well. At age 99, he continues his fight, our fight, against the system of injustice that deprived him of his job at the University of Pennsylvania back in 1915 (and again in 1917, at the University of Toledo, for opposing U.S. entry into World War I). Recently, he sent me a letter containing an important message, which he asked me to share with everyone to whom it applies:

To my comrades in the struggle for a kindlier and juster world, I send fraternal greetings. During the present period of worldwide change and unrest, study and teaching are particularly important. We as scholars have the right and duty to teach and impart what we believe in and what we have learned. The right to do this is the keystone of our profession. The need to do it arises whenever any authority challenges our responsibility to learn and communicate—to study and to teach. The present period offers scholars and students a challenge to meet and a part to play that may have vast consequences for the future of man. My salutations to the brave men and women who are opposing and resisting the forms of reaction, regression and despotism in North America.[11]

NOTES

1. R. M. Frumkin, "The Eternal Professor: Scott Nearing Is Still Teaching," *ZEDEK* (February 1981). *ZEDEK* is the newsletter of the Social Activist Professor Defense Foundation, 19329 Monte Vista, Detroit, Michigan 48221. It is the best source of information on the repression of radical academics. Subscriptions are $6 a year.

2. Walter P. Metzger, *Academic Freedom in the Age of the University* (New York: Columbia University Press, 1961), pp. 152ff.

3. Morris U. Schappes, "Forty Years Later—But Not Too Late," *Jewish Currents* (April 1982). On October 6, 1981, the Board of Trustees of the City University of New York voted an apology to Morris Schappes and other victims of the Rapp-Coudert Committee's investigation that took place some 40 years before. Similar apologies for "excesses" committed during the McCarthy period were offered recently by the boards of trustees of Reed College (in the case of Stanley Moore), Temple University (Barrows Dunham), and the University of Vermont (Alex B. Novikoff).

4. Samuel Bowles and Herbert Gintis, *Schooling in Capitalist America* (New York: Basic Books, 1976), p. 237.

5. Michael Brown, "The Ollman Case and Academic Freedom," *New Political Science* (Spring 1979), p. 46. For more extended discussions of the developments in higher education and their relationship to the changing requirements of capitalism, see Bowles and Gintis, *Schooling*; Ira Shor, *Critical Teaching and Everyday Life* (Boston: South End Press, 1980); Martin Carnoy, ed., *Schooling in Corporate Society: The Political Economy of Education in America* (New York: David McKay, 1972); and Henry A. Giroux, *Ideology, Culture and the Process of Schooling* (Philadephia: Temple University Press, 1981).

6. Shor, *Critical Teaching*, p. 6.

7. Milton Fisk, "Academic Freedom in Class Society," in *The Concept of Academic Freedom*, ed. Edmund Pincoffs (Austin: University of Texas Press, 1972), p. 16. Along with the Brown article cited above, this represents the best of what little work Marxists have done on the subject of academic freedom.

8. Brown, "Ollman Case," pp. 37–39.

9. Fisk, "Academic Freedom," p. 8.

10. For the increase of Marxist scholars and the spread of Marxist scholarship in the universities, see Bertell Ollman and Edward Vernoff, eds., *The Left Academy: Marxist Scholarship on American Campuses* (New York: McGraw-Hill, 1982). For the rise of academic repression, see the various issues of *ZEDEK*.

11. Scott Nearing, letter to author, November 29, 1981.

II
Economic Perspectives: Editors' Note

These are hard times almost everywhere, and academe is no exception. The contributors to this section document and attempt to explain some of these troubles and to show how the economic crisis of the 1970s and 1980s and the institutional responses to this crisis have deformed the university's mission and seriously constricted the type of intellectual activity that occurs on campus. Tightened budgets and changing student demands have, as Robert Lekachman reveals, prompted the academic community to shift its own intellectual and institutional resources away from the humanities and social sciences and into more allegedly utilitarian disciplines and areas of research. The political and social ramifications of this reallocation of attention, energy, and resources effectively further constrict the already overly rigid tracking system that has come to exemplify the pattern of educational opportunity within our society.

In this section Joseph Murphy reviews some specific manifestations of these changes and their implications for the City University of New York, in particular. Stanley Aronowitz places the shift into a structural framework in his analysis of the relationship between the economic and social spheres in terms of the role of education both in sustaining and undermining the position of the United States in the world economic and political systems.

Michael Useem augments Aronowitz's approach, focusing on the conscious campaign by what he calls the "inner circle" of the corporate elite to protect private profit by curbing the growth of the public sector. To the extent that this campaign has succeeded in reallocating the nation's resources, it has, albeit indirectly, reoriented the priorities of academe and severely weakened any notion of academic freedom. Useem joins Aronowitz in looking at the ideological component of this offensive—one that on the campus, in particular, intensifies its economic consequences. The corporate sector's attempts, strongly supported by the current national administration, to gain legitimacy for its drive to reduce public spending and regulation tempt the academic world to rationalize the institutional changes that these reductions have

61

forced upon them. At the same time, the very acceptance of and adaptation to these changes, as the articles in this section explain, have and will continue to result in the production of narrow and second-rate scholars, policy analysts, and decision makers whose inadequacies will create the opportunity for reviving critical education on a broad scale.

•5•

Academic Freedom
and
Social Change

Joseph S. Murphy

I am concerned about three things in education. Though none of them relates specifically to academic freedom, at least as we used to know it, they are all crucial to an enlarged version of academic freedom, one that stresses social justice as well as civil and political liberties.

My initial concern is that, for the first time in 50 years, an important tradition in American social and educational life is being threatened. I refer to the diminution of the importance of class or class origin as a basis for the structure of an educational system and the effort to reduce that factor in our national life. This tradition is being threatened by a national administration that increasingly wishes to privatize all its institutions. That is to say, it seeks to invest ever larger numbers of dollars in the private sphere at the expense of the public one, thus making a relatively small group of people wealthy and a much larger group of people impoverished. In short, it is a national policy that is apparently committed to the concept of public poverty and private opulence.

This policy is affecting our entire school system; it is certainly affecting our colleges and universities. It is affecting them adversely in a way that brings to mind an old debate in American life, although when it occurred it was in a narrower context—about Booker T. Washington's idea of education, on the one hand, and W. E. B. Du Bois's, on the other.

At the core of the debate was the notion that somehow there ought to be an educational system that trains one group of people—chosen by virtue of their economic status, their race or religion, or the recentness of their arrival in the United States—to do society's menial tasks, and another kind, an elitist education, that would train the children of the wealthy and the privileged to rule the rest of us. This debate was resolved, at least within the black intellectual community, by agreeing that what we really want for our children are opportunities for them to begin wherever they may find themselves, and then to go as far as each can go, with the support of a community that understands that talent, ability, vigor, energy, and determination are all independent of race, national origin, and religion.

These concerns about class and the reassertion of class are even more poignant in the light of the second point I want to stress: that we have established different tiers in our educational system. Probably the most striking current manifestation of that stratification is the rapidity with which educators give in to the insistence that there be more and more vocational courses, courses designed to prepare people for a certain kind of labor market. Not too long ago, I was at a meeting in the Bronx at which representatives of private industry made it quite clear that their appreciation of community colleges was contingent upon the degree to which a community college educated undergraduates to perform *exactly* those tasks that local industry required. This is a common viewpoint: No issue of the *New York Times,* or any other mass media publication, addresses itself to education without discussing the relationship between education and the scientific, vocational, and technical needs of our society and the economy. We can carry this a bit too far unless we recognize that education has got to be a good deal more than simply preparation for a job or a task or the performance of specific activities required by a labor market in a particular place at a given time.

There is, I think, an antidote to the problem, at least in some contexts, and that is the reassertion of the integrity and utility of a liberal arts education. It is commonplace for anyone representing education these days to say good things about the liberal arts. It has never been quite clear to me what they mean by "liberal arts." When I ask which liberal arts, they never name philosophy or sociology. They almost always say computer science and mathematics. What is it about a liberal arts education that both prompts us to say good things about it and, at the same time, be somewhat fearful and reserved about the liberal arts in our everyday life? I think I have a theory of what it might be.

Let us begin with the *Executioner's Song,* by Norman Mailer, either the book or the rather brilliant television production of that work. The story covers the casual and mindless murders committed in Utah by a man named Gary Gilmore, who became a national figure by virtue of his insistence that, he having taken a life, his life be taken. No one seemed to notice, incidentally, that this was Sir Matthew Hale's theory of punishment, that you ought to pay in like coin for a crime you have committed. So if you have murdered, the state has an obligation to take your life—to me, a most curious notion. Both the book and the television production made me wonder what precisely led someone like Norman Mailer to produce a thousand pages of essentially dull writing, dull because it was taken from tapes, dull because it was monosyllabic, dull because it was so devoid of words and language that adequately described people's feelings and sensibilities.

It occurred to me that this was a tour de force. I am probably one of the few people who read the whole thousand pages to find out whether Mailer could actually sustain such a tour de force, and he does. The book was about ignorance. Or, in my view, the book was essentially about being uneducated. The book was about people living lives without having the concepts or words to describe their feelings. They had no way of knowing anything about the forces that operate on their lives, about forces that were generated by virtue of their own character and internal life, that were imposed upon them from without, that were changeable, that were not, what was subject to free will, what was not.

In fact, being so deprived of language, they simply were incapable of grasping the notion that *they* controlled things. They spoke, throughout the entire book, of destiny, of luck, of stars, of a variety of mystical kinds of influences on their lives that, in fact, had nothing to do with the actual terms and conditions of their existence—influences that had nothing to do with their inability to understand the nature of their lives. They did not know that, since the beginning of intellectual life a thousand or more years before the birth of Christ, extraordinary efforts had been and are still being made by thinkers to define what laws determine how social and historical changes occur; what laws determine the interior psychological and unconscious life of individuals; what laws govern the way in which bodies in motion behave; what laws govern the biological life of individual human beings and of whole species.

There was no comprehension of these things because there was no liberal arts education. There was no liberal arts education that obliged people to read, not just Plato and Aristotle, Saint Thomas Aquinas and Shakespeare, but also Darwin and Marx, and Freud and Einstein, to understand that we in the twentieth century live in a penumbra of theories aimed at explaining the totality of our lives. These theories may not succeed in supplying complete answers, but they try, and the direction and meaning of that effort provide us with some picture of where we fit in the world. Not to have that frame of reference is to be "imprisoned." There are many people who, no matter how extensive their education might be, feel imprisoned for want of the background provided by a liberal arts education.

My third point is the relationship between the concept of education generally and the theory of social justice. Whatever that relationship is, or was, it is now in danger. What happened at my own university, the City University of New York, shows that all too clearly. This university is, I think, the only university in the world whose policies are often determined far away from its own locale. It is probably the only university in the nation for which, back in 1976, the president of the United States decided tuition policy. Until then, there was no tuition at the City University.

But the notion that somehow higher education should be free stuck like a bone in people's throats. The notion that people should have an opportunity to be educated, to better themselves, and to do so in a city that for 140 years understood that the education of its people was the best economic and social investment it could make. That lesson somehow did not reach all quarters, and when those unreached quarters gained the power to undo this city's commitment to free higher public education, free public higher education was undone. Its undoing sent a signal. The signal was not simply that nothing is free any longer but that, in fact, this university, which had always been doing what it was doing, except perhaps doing more of it than any other university, was overdoing things. And one of the things it was overdoing was producing too many people whom the labor market could not absorb. The result was a way of finding a formula for diminishing the number of people who sought and were getting higher educational opportunities. It reduced the size of the university from some 240,000 students to about 173,000 students. Not all of that attrition was due to an imposition of tuition, but it was a very substantial reason for the reduction in enrollments.

The City University has another mission, which these cutbacks impair. It is probably the only university in the world whose student body comes in large part as a consequence of events that occur in other corners of the world.

CUNY came into existence as the Free Academy in 1847 due to a determination by the board of education that there were too many poor and homeless kids in the streets who might very well profit from going on to college if only there were a place that would take them. In those days, of course, the City College of New York was a white Anglo-Saxon Protestant institution. By the 1870s and 1880s, however, the potato famines in Ireland had changed the constitution of the student population of the City College, and, in fact, through 1890, the vast majority of students in the Free Academy were the children of Irish immigrants evicted from the land by landlords. Between 1890 and the First World War, there was a vast infusion of peoples from southern Italy and Sicily due to famine and social unrest and also from Eastern Europe due largely to pogroms, as well as famine and unrest. The City University became the recipient of that flood of immigrants. And so it went.

After the Second World War, large numbers of dispossessed people from the South, black people coming to the city to seek opportunities from themselves and their children, found the City University of New York, and they find it now. By the same token, the Eastern Airlines flights leaving San Juan brought a million and a half Puerto Rican people to the city of New York, also driven to leave their country largely by economic opportunities here and their absence there. What all this leads up to is that the City University is unlike any other. It is committed to doing what no other institution ever has done, at least to the degree that this university has done it, which is the acculturation and the assimilation of hundreds of thousands who have come here, very often under adverse circumstances and under conditions of extreme pain.

The university will continue to serve in this way. There are other universities in the land that will do the same, but we do it under a cloud of increasingly ominous threats of retrenchments. Recently, we came very, very close to losing, by a very substantial margin, a billion dollars of the federal Pell grants. These grants run about $2.6 billion; 5 percent of that total goes to the City University and the State University of New York. In short, more than 3 percent of the entire national program designed for poor students goes to the City University of New York. Cutting our share would have meant tens of thousands of students being stricken from our rolls overnight. I think at the moment that threat has diminished somewhat. I am hopeful that we will successfully fight off any renewed efforts to suggest cuts in such areas.

Nevertheless, I suspect that anybody interested in education, whether public, private, parochial, or of any kind, had better face one fundamental fact: The present national administration is not a friend of education. I am sorry to have to say this in such blunt terms, but if there are any people who have not gotten that message, they ought to heed it now. There has been no indication that, without fight, without organization, and without effort, there will be any spontaneous perception in Washington that education is the best investment any national government makes, anywhere in the world—be it the third world or the richest country in the world. And to attack education or to reduce the present levels and hoped-for levels of expenditures for education at the national, state, or city levels is to eat our own seed; it is to devour our future. It is not only shortsighted, it is sure devastation.

•6•

Academic Freedom
in a
Failing Economy

Robert Lekachman

Just to demonstrate that it is possible, I shall begin with an item or two of comparatively good news on the academic freedom front. But before I do, let me indulge in a nostalgic recollection connected with the particularly outrageous case of Bertell Ollman whose appointment at the University of Maryland was vetoed, after Ollman had jumped through all the proper procedural hoops, by the incoming president, a certain John Toll. In the mid-1960s and early 1970s, the very same Toll was president at the Stony Brook Campus of the State University of New York. For advocates of dissenting opinion, Toll was bad news a decade and a half ago and manifestly still bad news today—an inspiring example of human consistency. The difference was in the political climate. Toll lost many of his attempts to deny tenure to campus radicals then. These are battles going in the opposite direction in Reaganland.

Yet—and here I tiptoe up to my good tidings—the threat to academic freedom as it is defined by the American Association of University Professors is less outrageous than in the dear bygone days of Joe McCarthy. It represents a tiny gain that in few places will a radical be openly fired on political grounds. The current threats to academic freedom are more subtle, connected substantially, although of course not entirely, with money. In some varying degree, all universities are feeling financial pressure. Hypocritical as it may be, the best way to handle untenured, inconvenient faculty is simply to deny reappointment on "appropriate" academic or even fiscal grounds.

We all know how easy it is for academics to quarrel with anybody's published research. If it's qualitative, it should have been quantitative. If it's quantitative, it is trival or it should have been published in the *American Economic Review* instead of a journal lower in the pecking order. The more sophisticated the administration and senior faculty, the more adroitly the game is played.

Still, when all this is said, it is mildly encouraging that neither the Reagan administration nor Congress has geared up for a determined national assault on subversives within the gates of our proudest universities. Not that the potential is not available. Former admiral, now senator, Jeremiah Denton heads his chamber's Internal Subversion Committee. Thus far the good senator appears more exercised about the erosion of teenage chastity than about unsound political tendencies on the campuses. We should fervently pray (voluntarily) that this challenging topic engages his energies for the remainder of his term. To date we lack a demagogue of McCarthy quality. This is not to deny that there are people in training around the country for the role, but no one has risen to public visibility.

Businesspeople are exceptionally sensitive to ridicule. The Reagan cabinet, a collection of millionaires, will on occasion retreat in the fashion of Agriculture Secretary John Block, who in the silly spring of 1982 first announced that members of screening panels that pass on research applications for funding by his department should be tested for loyalty to the GOP. Under fire from the scientific community, Block, within a week, reversed himself and graciously allowed scientists who also happened to be Democrats to serve.

Enough of foolish euphoria. Out there, dragons lurk. I come back to the role of money. Most discussions of academic freedom focus upon the context within which faculty operate or the interest of society in general in free discussion and diversity of opinion. There is another directly affected constituency—students. Assaults upon academic freedom acutely afflict students as well as their instructors. Students as well as university income suffer from the financial misfortunes of their families, so thoughtfully arranged by Reagan economic policies. Summer and part-time employment is increasingly hard to find. In a period of soaring general unemployment—the highest in four decades—public and private institutions are raising tuition and dormitory rentals considerably faster than general inflation has been rising.

A young person cannot enjoy the delights of academic freedom if financial exigency slams shut the campus gates. Such in fact is the situation of a steadily rising percentage of college-age young people. I quote on this theme Harvard's well-known extremist, Derek Bok. In his report to Harvard's Board of Overseers, President Bok wrote: "The Administration's proposals [he here refers to projected cutbacks in the availability of student loans] would further affect the quality of education by threatening the standards and even the survival of many colleges, not to mention their students."

Those who do enroll and graduate either have wisely chosen affluent parents or emerge bowed under a huge burden of debt. That burden in prospect shapes choices of program and vocational emphasis. The decline of graduate study, except in very narrowly defined areas, imperils primarily the humanities and the "soft" social sciences. Economists, notorious for their creation of a misleading but "hard" technique, are faring well. But the drift unmistakably is toward law, accounting, medicine, and business administration—all vocations where objectives are clear, financial rewards (at least in the past) substantial, and the bias of training is directed to the mastery of technique rather than the enlargement of comprehension of politics or society. Sad to say, the pursuit of vocation at the expense of liberal education is likely to result in smaller payoffs than those now current. Surpluses of lawyers, accountants, and even doctors now exist and are almost certain to increase.

Students continue to hope that they will grasp brass rings even as these diminish in number. The scramble for money and the decline of campus activism have led colleges to welcome back ROTC units summarily dismissed during the wild 1960s. For the first time since Vietnam, enrollment in ROTC units has exceeded 100,000. One can only sympathize. Student patriots are eligible for one of the 26,500 scholarships a generous Pentagon has funded. Eight thousand dollars is a sum unlikely to be ignored by either working-class or middle-class students.

Also scrambling for money, the faculty are doing more and more work for the military. Indeed the administration's 1983 budget calls for an additional $100 million to fund Defense Department support of university research. By and large, university administrators are practical folk, more involved in their budgets than the larger purposes of their institutions. Edward Blaustein, president of Rutgers, is typical of the breed. He has been quoted to the effect that Pentagon contracts have "nothing to do with weapons," for they "serve civilian needs no less than the Department of Defense needs." One wonders what the civilian "spin-off" of this Rutgers contract might be: thermo-stress in a gun barrel. Perhaps the civilian auspices will emerge under the auspices of your friendly police department.

Universities further narrow choices for both students and faculty by the way in which they trim their budgets. Take as illustration that excellent public institution, the University of Michigan. Last year it eliminated its geography department; its 1982 list of threatened specialties includes the schools of art, education, and natural resources, as well as the Institute of Labor and Industrial Relations, the Center for Continuing Education of Women, and the Institute for the Study of Mental Retardation and Related Disabilities. For the folks who run the computers, these are financially marginal activities, simply not cost-effective. Moreover, they serve the interest of constituencies that rarely contribute to university funds.

Pruning the curriculum obviously constricts student choice and, if, as I believe, choice is the essence of any kind of freedom, their academic freedom. I must at this juncture interpolate a word of explanation that goes to academic sociology. Faculty have allowed the elimination of unpopular courses and departments in part because they are frightened, also because only the Supreme Court thinks that faculty run their institutions, but finally because most university teachers, popular myths to the contrary notwithstanding, are imperceptibly more liberal than the population at large. I dare say that in my own field more economists voted for Reagan than for Carter or Anderson, let alone Barry Commoner, in 1980.

Substitution as well as curtailment is occurring. At Michigan again, the university is seeking a $7.2 million air force contract for robotics research. Here is a clear shift from attention to the needs and interests of unions, women, and the handicapped to steel-collared workers who never take coffee breaks, file grievances, or goof off on Mondays after hard weekends. Moreover, as Steven Emerson has pointed out in *The New Republic,* the American oil companies have been channeling Saudi funds through various financial laundries into universities to establish chairs in Islamic studies.[1] At Duke, the Saudis have sponsored an entire program of Islamic studies.

In general, donors get what they pay for. No militant Zionist, however glittering his credentials as a scholar of Arabic culture, will occupy a Saudi cum Aramco chair. Indeed, to be blunt about the issue, you really can purchase or rent faculty if you do it courteously. As David Noble, in an excellent *Nation* article, described the shift from government to business funding already underway in the Carter era, the way to co-opt the academics is the advice given by two students of regulation: "Regulatory policies increasingly are made with the participation of experts. A regulated firm or industry should be prepared whenever possible to coopt these experts."[2] How? One simply identifies the leaders in each relevant field and proceeds to hire them as consultants or advisers. This activity, our guides point out, demands a modicum of finesse. The experts must not recognize that they have lost objectivity and freedom of action.

The business community has taken to heart Irving Kristol's advice that they should be ideologically sensitive to the uses of the sums they contribute to universities. No shame at all, Kristol told the corporate community, in a little financial encouragement to campuses and individuals who are probusiness and display sympathetic comprehension of corporate needs. After all, the First Amendment does not require a corporation to support the research of, for example, the radical economists Sam Bowles or Herb Gintis. Rather, you might prefer to channel your money to the Virginia Polytechnic Institute, the University of Virginia, UCLA, or the University of Southern California, where Arthur Laffer holds forth.

Money corrupts, and lots of money corrupts lots of people. Gradually or not so gradually universities are focusing their activities where corporate dollars will flow. Recall that most scientists are quite conservative and of course business schools, law schools, and departments of economics traditionally have harbored few radicals. The interests of these specialties appear to coincide with those of students terrified that pursuit of nonvocational undergraduate majors will consign them to a career of fruitless search for employment.

This apparent convergence of faculty and student interests represents the most serious threat to genuine academic freedom and the narrowing of the ideological range of the university community. In this way it is worse, because it is less clearly outrageous, than cases of corporate executives or government officials pressuring deans and presidents to silence particularly vocal critics. The dirty work subsequently is performed by department chairpersons and senior colleagues.

We need to recall that freedom of expression in academe has always been more limited than outsiders comprehend. When the late Paul Lazersfeld examined the impact of McCarthyism upon universities, he discovered something both sad and interesting.[3] On the vast majority of campuses, McCarthy had no impact because faculty never had enjoyed free speech and they had been carefully selected for sound Americanism. In such places, academic freedom must have faintly resonated as a distant Ivy League hobby rather than a reality of life.

From these assorted phenomena, I draw some depressing general conclusions. Universities have always been vocational training schools, but in balmier days a specialist in Victorian novels, medieval art, Greek philosophy, any variety of history, or musicology could anticipate teaching the subject she or he loved to new cohorts of students. In the booming 1960s, university teaching was a favored path of social and occupational mobility for the bright sons and daughters of working-class parents.

The 1960s now appear to have been a rare exception to the usual stratification of higher education. We have returned or, at best, are moving toward a situation in which the progeny of the upper class have preferred access to medical, legal, and executive training programs because their parents can afford the costs of four years in appropriate undergraduate colleges. The faculty who survive and flourish in the new order or, better the old order restored, will be those who best prepare their students for elite professional education. Upon them will be showered the blessings of tenure, research grants, consulting fees, and the veritable affluence that some astute academics have achieved as entrepreneurs in activities as assorted as gene splicing, data processing, and economic forecasting.

My tone has been one of elegy instead of hope. But I cannot conclude without identifying some of the opportunities for resistance. In our last progressive period, the New Deal, progressive change was made politically feasible by a temporary coalition of the middle class and the working class. Much of the time both groups are antagonists rather than collaborators. But when times get sufficiently bad and home-owning middle Americans themselves feel the cold blast of economic calamity, they do, reluctantly, rethink their usual politics.

To his credit, Ronald Reagan has presided over the most effective economic program since Herbert Hoover. In his first two years, bankruptcies are running at 1930s levels, unemployment is higher than anyone under 55 can recall, home and farm foreclosures ominously mount, and proud home owners have discovered that the value of their major asset has been monthly declining. Reagan has violated the middle-class assurance that there is always money to be made in real estate.

The middle-class revolt is slow in coming. But there are signs and portents that it has tentatively begun. The preservation of social security benefits against evident administration designs to reduce them is a triumph of middle-class anger. So also is the damage control exercised by Congress over administration efforts to reduce student loans even more sharply than the administration did in 1981. This is, to repeat the cliche, a middle-class society. If the economy continues to behave as it has been (and I see no ground for optimism), a New Deal type coalition may well result.

Let me be clear. I do not rely upon the altruism of the prosperous. As the great English economist Alfred Marshall pointed out rather wistfully, self-interest is the strongest of human drives and altruism merely the highest. However, once the great sluggish middle class reaches the conclusion that Reagan is bad for their economic health and still more for the economic health of their children, the Reagan myth will dissolve and the hope of a new progressive era will approach political reality.

NOTES

1. Steven Emerson, "New Salaams to the Saudis," *New Republic* March 21, 1981.

2. David F. Noble and N. E. Pfund, "Business Goes Back to College," *The Nation,* September 20, 1980.

3. Paul Lazarsfeld and Wagner Thielens, Jr., *The Academic Mind* (Glencoe, Ill.: Frcss Press, 1958).

•7•

Academic Freedom: A Structural Approach

Stanley Aronowitz

The irony of the current crisis in higher education is that even as successive administrations in the 1970s and 1980s have reduced aid to colleges and universities, the importance of these institutions has grown in all spheres of society. In the 1920s, postsecondary education was reserved for two quite disparate groups: those destined to rule America's giant corporations or the state and those belonging to all social classes able to climb into the professions. For the vast majority—working class and old middle class alike—higher education was just not an option. Most factory jobs could be learned by on-the-job training, usually in a few weeks, or in the skilled trades by a prolonged apprenticeship, most of which could only be justified on economic or bureaucratic grounds, not on criteria derived from the requirements of the work itself. Shopkeepers acquired business acumen by imbibing tradition, or in more complex enterprises hired a small coterie of experts, mostly attorneys and accountants, to handle such issues as tax matters, bankruptcies, and mergers and consulted bankers and loan companies on investment decisions.

However, as Randall Collins has persuasively argued, we have entered a "credentialized society"[1] in the past 30 years. The degree or certificate may not train labor better to perform paid work; indeed, even in such professions as medicine, engineering, and law, most knowledge is acquired by performing tasks at the workplace. However, credentials have become a rite of passage, a prerequisite for civil service exams, a sign that a certain *process of formation* has taken place. In Pierre Bourdieu's terms, completion of a prescribed postsecondary course signifies cultural capital.[2] The new class of professionals and subprofessionals, most of whom are engaged in some form of wage labor, may not enjoy job security in an economy that seems to have entered a period of permanent technological revolution, mergers, rapid-fire business starts and almost as rapid failures, and massive regional and global shifts in capital location. These changes have required intellectual as well as manual labor to become increasingly mobile. For both, possessing cultural capital in the form of a credential becomes a code of legitimate formation. By "legitimate formation" I mean that the individual has gone through educational socialization that is recognized by employers and by the larger society as constituting adequate preparation for occupational status. It tells the employer that the applicant has endured at least the recognized rituals of initiation into the historically evolved occupations.

The academic system has replaced the old craft and professional traditions that were rooted in local geographic space or occupied a secure place in a status hierarchy. Since industrial society has obliterated these traditions, the problem became how to determine the suitability of a given worker for the job. Recall that the "journeyman's card" performed this function for the crafts and, contrary to received wisdom, professionals were not primarily certified until late in the nineteenth century by schools but by other professionals. Later, state certification was added through exams, most of which were written by those whose professional formation was, for example, through "reading" law, assisting senior physicians, or working for a self-employed professional (usually civil) engineer. As labor became mobile, following the movement of industrial capital, a new mechanism had to be found to assure employers of the technical and more importantly social competence of the prospective employee. The growth of the academic system for credentialing labor corresponds to the rationalization of production and its concomitant bureaucratization. It was the "objective" criterion invented to replace the tradition that certified competence on the basis of impersonal evaluation.[3]

As higher education became cultural capital, we see the passing of the "self-made" person—the autodidact who gained fame and/or riches by entirely individual means. (A partial exception to this rule is the entertainment/sports professions in which the academic system plays a smaller role. However, in recent years, musicians, actors, and directors receive more and more training in college departments, which have become primary recruiting grounds for Broadway and Hollywood; and football players are almost completely recruited from the college campus.) Now the term "self-made" connotes a person's ability to rise within a fairly well-established corporate or bureaucratic hierarchy. Because specific credentials are now overproduced (like most commodities), there is no correlation between the degree and obtaining a particular job; the degree, as I have stated, is merely a rite, a prerequisite, a sign of social and occupational formation. Therefore, individual worth is increasingly measured by the place of one's school in the academic hierarchy and his or her place within the school. Because even these prerequisites are no longer sufficient to ensure placement, landing a job becomes a sign of worth and presumed individual initiative. Of course, the reproduction of the ideology of status is made necessary, not by the facts of the academically linked labor market, but by that specific trait of American ideology, individualism. In contrast to many Western European countries where students travel through the centralized school system with an exquisite sense of collective fate, American schools are not only localized but the distinction between the private and the public is built into the status hierarchy. Furthermore, the grading system and the stress on individual achievement reproduces an ideology in which the student experiences his or her difference from all others. The two main points of distinction are presumed intelligence and the value placed upon hard work. In either case, students are encouraged to internalize their own responsibility for success or failure. (The kid was bright but fooled around too much, or, despite outrageous school behavior, the kid managed to get wonderful grades, proving that no matter what, "the cream always rises to the top.")

Since the content of most work is undergoing constant change, the higher the degree, the less specialized it becomes, regardless of the field. For example, possessing a degree from Harvard, Columbia, or Yale law school signifies nothing about the quality of the training of a particular candidate and even less the differential acquisition of specific knowledges relating to particular fields of the law. It merely constitutes a basis upon which leading corporations, major public agencies, and important law firms may recruit cadre. A Harvard degree is a *social* credential and has almost nothing to do with technical qualifications. It signifies the candidate has forged links with established networks and has achieved a grade necessary to obtain the degree. Because the corporate mode of industrial organization that dominates all organizations in our society is organized along both bureaucratic and hierarchical lines, the major qualification for a prospective employee is his or her generic understanding of the organization rather than specific kowledge. The lower one descends in the academic hierarchy, the more particular technical knowledges are constituted as qualifications, since the work performed is likely to be more specialized.

The academic system performs a second vital function: It reproduces the ideology of opportunity. Here I do not mean to suggest that "ideology" is merely false consciousness. Because credentials are necessary rites of passage to bureaucratic and technical labor, they connote important knowledge for a system in which knowledge is capital. It follows that attaining a degree presupposes possession of this cultural capital. The stress on educational credentials among racial and national minorities and women responds to the labor market. Even those among these groups who were able to "rise" to semiskilled jobs in the unionized monopoly sector in the 1940s and 1950s have lost their economic niches in the wake of the partial deindustrialization of intermediate technology industries such as auto, steel, and electrical manufacturing. Displaced from industrial labor, many have entered the academic system in order to qualify for jobs in the communications, financial services, and corporate administration professions associated with computers and other scientifically based technologies. Having arrived on the scene, they discovered what blacks found when they bought old houses in former Jewish and eastern European neighborhoods. During the first rain, the cellar flooded, the foundation eroded, and the walls and ceilings were termite-ridden.

Of course, the discovery that many universities had lost their groves and ivy to gypsy moths cannot deter the aspiration for postsecondary education. Credentials are the only game in town; especially in circumstances where the workplace is defined in terms of the manipulation of symbols to produce codes and signs rather than things. In a society where power and knowledge are ineluctably linked, achieving a degree replaces the high school diploma because it signifies knowledge of how systems work, more than specific technical knowledge (for which the student still requires substantial on-the-job training).[4]

I do not mean to imply that a basic background in mathematics and physical sciences is not needed for those aspiring to perform technical and scientific work. Nor can the vocabularies of the social sciences and their logical structures be dispensed with by people wishing to work in economics, human services, or social research. I am contending that these knowledges are generally available to the dedicated, disciplined autodidact, as much as law and medicine were during earlier periods of our history. Schools are miniature societies more than centers of technical and scientific education. In schools students learn how to operate within the historically evolved culture with particular modes of organization at different levels of the occupational and social hierarchies.

It is not necessary for students to "internalize" the organization to learn how to function within it, that is, to understand the boundaries of rule making and rule breaking. Of course, the more habitual these knowledges are, the less conflict is experienced by the worker. On the other hand, habituation is by no means the necessary condition for successful integration within large organizations.

This is an error common to Marxist and "bourgeois" social theorists concerned with processes of social reproduction. At one end, Talcott Parson's theory of socialization posits the coherent link between individual family and workplace as the necessary condition for functional completeness.[5] At the other, Herbert Marcuse's notion of technological society requires that its members become "one-dimensional," that is, lose their capacity for critical reflection.[6] The individuals in both theoretical paradigms are presumed social clones, however rebellious they may "feel."

These modes are reflections of tendencies in social thought that were dominant in the wake of the rise of rightist regimes in the 1930s. In the context of liberal and Marxist beliefs that fascism and other forms of totalitarianism were somehow external or conjunctural to the history of capitalism, the Frankfurt school insisted that the mode of social and sexual organization produced a new person fitted to the new order. This theory constituted a radical departure from the rationalistic proclivities of contemporary social and political theory. The Frankfurt school sought to explain social domination as a complex of economic, political, and ideological relations in which the transformation of culture was the crucial condition. Thus the imposition of a compulsory sexual morality was for Wilhelm Reich a characteristic of the mode of social reproduction, not merely a rule handed down from above to impose a regime of sexual repression.[7] The individual was always complicit in his oppression to the degree that the option of freedom was foreclosed by the repression of psychosexual needs generated from within as well as externally imposed. Similarly, Max Horkheimer and Marcuse argued that the blandishments of consumer society, particularly its spurious erotic satisfactions, were implanted in the psychic structures rather than being understood merely as the reward for performing prescribed work.

Parsonian theory asserts the symmetrical relationship between authority and individual action. Students of modern systems theory recognize him as a major predecessor. Parsons claims the fundamental continuity of society and culture as part of a more general theory of the evolution of living systems and argues that the distinctions among personality systems, cultural systems, and behavioral organisms are "merely functional." This position suggests that political and economic dimensions of society are the macrosocial side of a total system of which individual behavior is the microsocial aspect.

Social theory in the period between the First World War and the 1960s was obliged to explain the break of advanced capitalist societies with liberal society's tendency to posit the autonomous individual as the bedrock of social life. By arguing the systemic character of power/authority, that it was a function either of social evolution (Parsons) or the inevitable logic of capitalist accumulation and bureaucratic organization (Marx/Weber), social theory succeeded in abolishing the conception that authoritarianism within liberal society was anomalous.

Parsons subsumed the individual under the structural continuity between the individual, on the one hand, and family, work relations, and the state, on the other. The Frankfurt school argued from a utopian position that held up the possibility that people could understand each other perfectly. In order for this situation to come about, there would be no inegalitarian hierarchies or race, sex, or class. Later on, Jurgen Habermas was to call this "a public sphere" in which an individual in the community possessed communication competence.[8] Reich dispensed with the assumption of putative integrated civilization upon which the critique depended. He relied almost exclusively on the historical argument that capitalism distorted the psychosexual structure so that social character became self-repressive and externalized itself as fascism.

More recently, Pierre Bourdieu has invoked the category of "habitus" to explain the subordination of the worker to managerial authority, the student to the school administration, and, by extension, the child to the parents.[9] Like Parsons, he asserts the "specific effect of symbolic relations in the reproduction of power relations." Bourdieu speaks of symbolic "violence" as the characteristic relation of pedagogic communication which is charged with the transmission of something he calls the "cultural arbitrary" within a framework of legitimate authority. Although Bourdieu remains skeptical that the objects of the "cultural arbitrary," the students, are "free agents" such as those referred to in all social contract theories,[10] he does not submit to the view that pedagogic power is imposed by colonizing the unconscious. Power is imposed by a system of social domination by symbolic means through pedagogical authority; but its effectiveness in transmitting the "cultural arbitrary" is mediated by the strength of oppositional classes and movements: "The relative strength of the reinforcement given to the balance of powers between the groups or classes by symbolic relations expressing these power relations rises with the strength of various classes and the power of the market to confer higher value on the goods delivered by legitimate school authorities."[11] That is, as educational credentials become more central to determining whether an individual may gain access to jobs, goods, or economic security, the power of the educational system grows in the system of social domination. The converse is true as long as jobs paying relatively well can be procured without credentials, as in economies marked by technologies employing workers with little or no skill or professional formation.

Under current conditions, students accurately perceive school attendance as a means to enter the power system. To the extent that an oppositional group or class culture generates symbolic relations that constitute a counterlogic to the dominant "cultural arbitrary," students may "choose" to oppose the system of school-induced rewards by fighting authority. In effect, they respond to another authority system, one that places high social and economic value upon factory labor, street life, or participation in the underground economy, which is another labor market. Of course, students may not always be aware of the specific options they are choosing, but this is not the same as socialization or technological or psychosexual domination. This lack of understanding of the labor market is particularly acute when job recomposition is underway, and new definitions of work and their prerequisites have not yet become "common sense."

Further, the unintended consequences of refusing certain niches in the market system, those linked to school knowledges, for example, cannot exempt most of us from participating in the market system as such. The boundaries of opposition are framed by the system of wage labor, but there is no superior "rationality" associated with choosing to become part of the prevailing culture—hence the concept of "arbitrary" to connote a particular mode of participation.

In recent years, because the option of proletarian factory labor is increasingly foreclosed, alternatives to technical/scientific or bureaucratic labor have been similarly narrowed. This does not imply, however, that the technologized "arbitrary" is more than the most "logical" option given the international division of labor that has assigned certain functions to the United States in which administration and technical and scientific knowledge play important roles. Paul Willis has shown how students prepared themselves in English comprehensive high schools for factory labor by doing badly in school; in the Midlands region, traditional working-class symbolic relations were able, until the 1960s, to exert a powerful influence through producing an alternative cultural system, including a rationality of market value, among young people.[12]

Thus, we may reasonably conclude that the decline of the economic, social, and political weight of the working-class movements—trade unions, social clubs, neighborhoods—will tip the balance of power. These losses have specific historic preconditions in the patterns of capital accumulation, past struggles for hegemony at the workplace between capital and labor, the political triumphs of the workers' movement, and so on, but it is the weakening of an alternative cultural system that accounts for the growth of school enrollment among the underlying classes. Credentials are now recognized as the only possible way to enter the labor market system on favorable terms, except for the minority prepared to enter at its margins, spaces that often entail "nonlegitimate" economic relations.

Higher education is currently at an impasse. First, demand for college education has increased in the past two decades, especially among working adults for whom credentials have been identified, correctly, as the new condition of market survival in an increasingly uncertain situation. This rise of school attendance among the adult population that was recruited in the 1960s and the 1970s for public and corporate administrative employment has more than offset, at least in the large cities, the decline of the normal college-age population. These workers entered school on the heels of a successful struggle spearheaded by black and Hispanic students for "open admission" to institutions of higher education. Having established college and schooling as a "right," the hundreds of thousands of minorities and women who streamed into state institutions in the 1970s were soon followed by adults for whom such opportunities had in the past been unthinkable.

Without doubt, among the most important democratic achievements of the black freedom movement and the feminist movement of the 1960s and early 1970s was the hitherto unheard of policy adopted in many states that a college education was an entitlement. Students were admitted to schools without regard to their high school grades or test scores. The college was obliged, by this entitlement, to offer programs, often without credit, to students entering with "substandard" reading, writing, and calculating skills. In effect, open admission was, from the point of view of administration, a recognition that America had become a credentialed society and that the alternatives of factory and farm work, which implied a different set of norms, were rapidly disappearing as viable working-class options. The academic system was forced to accommodate a constituency historically considered beyond the pale of higher learning.

To be sure, University of California Chancellor Clark Kerr, the Carnegie Foundation, and other major educators and institutions recognized the inevitability of this change in the 1950s on the heels of sputnik-generated demands for an increased massification of higher education. The Kerr Plan provided for a three-tiered system that simultaneously provided for mass postsecondary schooling for those hitherto excluded while preserving the elite character of the major state universities, the private, northeastern Ivy League, and important regional campuses, such as Duke, Emery, Chicago, and Stanford. The junior college was transformed from a finishing school for young women destined to enter corporate or old ruling-class marriages into the "community" college, which became the repository of technical training for specialized skills. The four-year liberal arts college outside the major "multiversities" or the Ivy League remained an anomaly in the new system and seemed to lose its function. Engineering, teaching, medical technology, and industrial sciences were increasingly privileged in the "second" tier, as administrators and students perceived that the liberal arts, a curriculum traditionally reserved for preprofessionals, managers, and the intellectual elites, had no use in an increasingly technology-dominated society.

Consequently, the 1970s were marked by declining enrollments in nonelite liberal arts programs and concomitant dramatic expansions in technical training at the four-year colleges and the community colleges. In the process, the conflation of education and training has become the emblem of the new era in higher schooling.

Thus, the crisis of American higher education consists not only of its budget difficulties that have accompanied the world economic crunch but also in the contradiction between its traditional mision of providing the cadre for ideology, industrial, and service production and the new demand that it became a multilayered mass technical training institute. The market orientation of America's colleges and universities is the source of the crisis because, with the exception of a tiny group of elite schools, the function of the transmission of Western culture to society's political, economic, and ideological cadre has now been permanently displaced. Those fields traditionally associated with the liberal arts, particularly philosophy, history, and literature, have found themselves "technicized" in the majority of schools. They have become "breadth" requirements for engineers and business administration majors, subjects to be tolerated because they are not selected voluntarily. A sign that students no longer see reasons for choosing courses that acquaint them with the liberal tradition was the recent reimposition of a core liberal arts curriculum at Harvard University, one of the schools Kerr envisioned as the true repositories of academic learning. Administrators and faculty were concerned that not only had even the elite university become enslaved to the labor market but also that the signals students had received were distorted. No, said the faculty, large corporations want educated counselors, not only those trained in the law. It is not a waste of time to ponder Plato's *Republic* for Harvard or Columbia students, only for those at Los Angeles State College or Kingsborough Community.

The consequences of this situation extend far beyond the individuals involved to the sphere of international economics and are multiplied by the shifting position of the United States in the world order. The new conditions of international market competition place the national economy in greater jeopardy than at any time since the turn of the twentieth century. America can no longer rely on its scientific and technological superiority to rule the world or upon the magnitude of its capital resources. In recent years, government and corporate policymakers have discovered the importance of a sophisticated and literate labor force for setting the cultural environment for rapid capital accumulation. Although the extreme technicization of schooling was prompted at least partially by the student revolt of the 1960s, as well as by the economic downturn of the following decade, the attempt to bypass the need for broad cultural formation reduces the chance that the labor force will regain its productivity.

On a wider scale, the precipitous decline of cultural formation among cadre, not to mention the general labor force, makes it more likely that policymakers will resort to military options to solve international conflicts. Lacking the human resources to comprehend the enormity of the changes underway in the new world economic, political, and social orders, we are in danger of reverting to the most blatant use of force to solve our problems.

In this connection, I want to dispose of some popular left and liberal economic arguments. Conservative attacks on American higher education are motivated by their horror of the 1960s generation that made colleges the base for political and cultural opposition. The factor of a ballooning military budget should not be dismissed, but this was not the ground for the Nixon, Ford, or Carter cuts. The Carnegie Report of 1971, which already argued that there had been an "overproduction" of higher education facilities and services, was made in the context of the still powerful antiwar movement, as well as the report's anticipation of the coming economic crisis. Even though large liberal corporate foundations had encouraged the open admissions movement against educators for whom the "standards" of higher education would be unalterably eroded, by the early 1970s a certain scepticism had crept into organized liberal and conservative intelligence on these questions.[13] The target was not the community colleges or the major research universities, but the state-supported four-year liberal arts colleges for which there was no perceived function, since most of their students were destined neither for the professions or for management. These were major sites of the new minority and women students and the returning working adults, and became a surplus subsystem within academia. Their only function was to provide a credential, necessary to qualify labor for bureaucratic jobs, but not for an already "overexpanded" system.

Community and four-year colleges, especially those providing no specialized training or subprofessional credentials, are under attack in the 1980s both because social sciences and humanities have no *specific* function in the marketplace for mass technical and bureaucratic labor and because they "represent" the victory of minorities and women to gain access to the credential system. This is the basis of the conservative attack. Saving the nontechnical programs in colleges is a civil liberties struggle, with its implications for the struggle against sexism, racism, and anti-working-class bias in the university.

Of course, the fight to save these institutions is linked to the fight to save the liberal arts. For the liberal arts are not only the foundation of the bourgeois claim to be the inheritor of Western culture; they are also the condition for acquiring critical thinking in a society where the old labor, socialist, and radical public institutions that once provided these amenities have all but disappeared. That is, in the wake of the nearly complete transformation of the cultural balance of social power toward the technocratic classes, a new terrain of cultural struggle is within the universities, especially the battle for the traditional critical curriculum.

At the outset, it must be admitted that the demand for a new curriculum does not currently correspond to the economic and cultural perceptions of the majority of students, especially minorities and women. The degree to which their aspirations are dominated by labor market considerations can be measured by the proliferation of technical and business courses in higher education, the concomitant decline of liberal arts enrollments in most colleges, and the transformations of social sciences and humanities departments into service programs rather than having substantial student majors. With each passing year, English and history departments suffer budget cuts; when a professor retires he takes his job with him to Florida or Palm Springs;

in some cases, the absolute number of faculty lines in these departments is reduced by layoffs, even among tenured faculty, and, most
egregiously, graduate programs in these fields decline because they,
too, are subject to the shrinking market.

I want to argue that we have already lost an entire generation
(measured by ten years) of humanities scholars. Only those getting their
Ph.D.s from a major university, especially the Ivy League, the Big Ten,
and the University of California, can hope to find an academic job.
Furthermore, many graduates from these schools can no longer expect
to work in their field unless they are willing to take high school jobs (a
path fairly well trod in countries like France and Great Britain). Many
among the new academic surplus labor force are women. At the same
time, the veritable wage freezes imposed in many academic
institutions, the frequency of layoffs, and the shrinking of the number
of jobs have discouraged blacks and other minorities from choosing
these fields or almost any academic calling except administration and
technical and scientific occupations. Until the early 1980s, qualified
blacks able to enter elite universities chose law, medicine, engineering,
and practical sciences rather than risk less stable market situations,
such as the liberal arts professoriate. The partial exceptions, history
and economics, may be accounted for by the persistence of the black
tradition of cultural reclamation that has been deposited in the history
profession and the many jobs available outside the academic system for
economists.

However, the hardest hit have been women, for whom the
humanities and, more recently, the social sciences became important
entry points for professional opportunities during the dramatic
expansion of the academic system in the 1960s. The tenure system that
ensured a lifetime job for selected teachers has resulted in an aging
professoriate, overwhelmingly white and male. Given the economic
and ideological outlook of the 1980s, these tendencies will accelerate in
both the short and intermediate term. Because women are subject to
sexism which has excluded a fairly high number of them from the ranks
of the tenured in recent years, it is highly likely that their proportion of
the tenured faculty will diminish, even as the proportion of women
students rises at all levels of the academic system. Absent a strong
feminist movement that insists on the active implementation of
affirmative action programs, even the "normal" hiring practices in a
shrinking job market, will reduce women in teaching positions.

American ideology has always tied the struggle for social justice to
economic and institutional expansion. Americans have tended,
wrongly, to equate equality with equality of opportunity. The argument

is that only if the system grows can the excluded demand and get access to credential jobs and other cultural capital needed to enter the labor market on a more favorable basis. We have been less interested in programs of redistribution than in those that integrate women and minorities into an expanding market. However, during periods of economic downturn, which in America have been fueled by the rise of conservative ideologies that tend to legitimate exclusion using biological or cultural arguments that place responsibility on the victim, the discourses of exclusion subordinate the discourses of cultural and economic justice. We are now undergoing such a period. Discharged women faculty experience increasing difficulty persuading colleagues, students, and the media that they have been fired unjustly; radicals find that unsympathetic administrations are more willing to overrule favorable departmental tenure decisions. The late 1970s marked a new wave of antiradicalism on many campuses, and equally important a massive exodus by students from political and social concerns in the wake of unbearable pressures generated by the economic crisis, the practices of credentialism, and the increasing privatization of social life. To the extent which the student movement, including black and feminist organizations, constituted a "countervailing" power base against these tendencies in the late 1960s and early 1970s, it was able to impose its will on administrators, who nearly everywhere suffered a crisis of confidence.

I do not want to argue that the economic crisis was alone responsible for the changing political climate; ideological tendencies, particularly the rise of neoconservatism, which has displaced liberal hegemony among intellectuals, as well as many workers, were equally powerful in producing a new climate. The attack on the liberal arts gained momentum in part because its various fields had become havens for a new radical professoriate. Thus the conjuncture of various ideological with economic tendencies helps explain both the cutbacks in the university and the substantial number of politically and sexually motivated firings. Even as Marxists and other radicals gained increasing legitimacy within many fields, particularly history and sociology, they found themselves under severe counterattack from a defensive and embattled senior faculty that experienced its own intellectual bankruptcy while, at the same time, was under pressure from women and blacks to support affirmative action hiring at a time of job shrinkage.

These problems bring us flush against the contradictions of the tenure system and the pressures for ideological conformity in the academic system. Tenure has been under attack since the early 1970s. Conservative critics charge that the tens of thousands of dollars entailed in a single tenured academic job violate the pressing need to cut costs in social services. Academic administrators, encouraged by budget cuts, have replaced retiring faculty with a series of part-time employees whose combined salary is half that of the deposed senior professor, or, when the line is not "retired" with the professor, will hire an untenured, full-time professor. The new teacher earns much less than the retiree and may only occupy the job for one to six years after which he or she is obliged to look for another "temporary" position. In recent years the pool of adjunct and untenured teachers has expanded and the number of tenured faculty reduced.

These conditions, combined with the dramatic slowing of salary increases, have promoted many college faculties to seek and obtain union organization. In 1982, teachers in the largest academic system in the country, the California State University, chose a collective bargaining agent, the American Federation of Teachers (AFT) in a closely contested election with the AFT's competitor, the American Association of University Professors (AAUP) and the AAUP's ally, the National Education Association (NEA).[14]

Unions have won elections in such private universities as Boston University, Catholic colleges, and Yeshiva University. However, the prospects for new victories in this sector were considerably diminished by the Supreme Court decision in the Yeshiva case holding faculty of "mature" private universities to be supervisors because they share in decision making with the institutional administration.[15]

Naturally, the most notable absences from this record of union advances are the private research universities and the major state research institutions, such as the Midwest Big Ten members or the University of California. In these schools most faculty consider themselves part of the directorate of the academic system, clearly identified with the goals and policies of the administration and, more broadly, the state and corporations. To acknowledge that its traditional decision-making power has been progressively eroded both by the subordination of research to the various production markets, particularly the military, and by the increasing centralization of university management would degrade the status of the faculty. Many faculty members prefer to adhere to the ideology of intellectual autonomy that ignores the fact that research grants and facilities are made available only to those able to obtain grants from government agencies, corporations, and foundations. While in earlier times, faculty determination of tenure was tantamount to appointment, the new situation presents departments with a "higher" authority in the persons of deans, provosts, and college presidents who reserve the right to veto or reverse faculty decisions. Yet many of these professors are managers of their own research projects that often employ assistants and graduate students, have power over the careers of graduate students, and are the cadre from which administrators are recruited. As a result, the large research universities have, with almost no major exceptions, been exempt from unionization of their faculties.[16]

In the other systems, faculty unions have fought to maintain tenured positions against constant pressure from above to retire them. The union defends the institution as well because it holds that this is the only genuine way teachers can gain job security. At the same time, the tenure system has effectively excluded the new aspirants for academic positions at a time when jobs are scarce. The job scarcity affirms trade union resolve to uphold the system of institutional racism and sexism, despite union support for affirmative action programs.

But tenure was instituted to prevent state legislatures, other faculty, and outside groups from persecuting faculty for their political or intellectual dissent. Tenure was instituted to protect free inquiry, particulary radical inquiry, research and views that contradicted conventional wisdom. It was an institution that confined just cause for discharge after a tenure decision to misconduct of a personal nature or gross incompetence that may result in discrimination against students.

These are still good reasons to protect the minority that engages in oppositional inquiry. But the tenure system has been more often employed as a means to secure conformity among faculty and to exclude dissenters. Because teaching in universities is a good job, despite recent deterioration of working conditions and salaries, young and new faculty members are encouraged by the market conditions to become more ideologically and intellectually conservative, or at least to remain silent about their dissenting views. As a result of the pressure to conform, the American academy has become visibly less exciting, innovative, and important as a center of intellectual life since the late 1960s. This does not signify the decline of specific ideological tendencies. On the contrary, as I have already noted, Marxism has received a fairly warm reception in some fields, is tolerated in others to a degree unknown either in the 1950s or in the 1930s, but the price Marxism (as only one example of a radical "science") has been obliged to pay is that it must cloak its discoveries, methodologies and its culture in the guise of academic conventions. That is, Marxism has accomodated to the norms of academic life, not made its own way. To a large degree, this conformity is imposed on Marxism and other marginal perspectives by the norms of academic respectability. The Marxist economist must be adept, for example, in mainstream economics and will often try to present his or her position in the codes of the dominant paradigm in order to gain a hearing. Similarly, in philosophy, the past decade has witnessed an increasing outpouring of works purporting to demonstrate the commensurability of historical materialism with the canons of analytic thinking.

Analogously, those interested in feminist and black studies have survived to the extent that they conform to the same intellectual norms. The radical feminist who, nevertheless, works in the normal traditions of the historical profession has a better chance for tenure than the feminist who tries to develop a new theoretical paradigm of women's history that entails a critique on either methodological or ideological grounds of conventional narrative history and the absences therein—particularly women.

The arguments become fairly subtle. Some intellectual conservatives (that is, those for whom the positivist traditions of social science research, such hegemonic discourses as those of analytic philosophy or the new criticism, are obligatory norms for scholarship) argue that "women's" or "black" history are not proper objects of inquiry with methodologically valid sets of procedures for obtaining knowledge. These objects must be integrated into recognized disciplines, such as social, economic, or political history. Similarly, Marxist or "poststructuralist" literary critics still have a hard time in most English departments, even if they have wide acceptance in the relatively small and marginal comparative literature programs. Again, nonanalytic philosophers of the phenomenological, Marxist, or programmatic schools find difficulty getting jobs in this field, which is dominated almost completely by various schools of language philosophy. When the dissidents succeed, they are relegated to courses in "continental" or "history" of philosophy.

These examples demonstrate the degree to which academic departments refuse pluralist practices even as they oppose radicals on the same ground. Their dedication to normal science, in Kuhnian terms, is completely understandable; the problem is that they rarely tolerate those not engaged in research that conforms to the norms established by the "scientific community." Thus, exclusion from tenure is not often announced on overt ideological grounds, but on the quality of the research of the denied faculty member. The concept of "quality" is articulated in terms of a prefigured conception of normal science. Under these circumstances, overt political repression becomes unnecessary. Anyone engaged in theorizing or research who adopts an antipositivist perspective or defines an object of knowledge in terms that vary or oppose conventional definitions may find herself out in the cold. Under these conditions the liberal self-perception of the pluralistic academic system is preserved.

Some criteria for tenure are fairly arbitrary. Among them, the most egregious is the statement about whether a faculty member is a "congenial" colleague, helpful in matters concerning department administration, quiet and dependable at meetings, and good at faculty parties. The cultural conservatism of academics often masks deep ideological and intellectual differences with younger or minority colleagues. Even through the 1960s the biographies of faculty members tended to follow a few patterns. In general, most professors beat a straight line from high school, college, and graduate school. Networks established in undergraduate and graduate schools become, as for large corporation executives, the crucial foundation for recruitment to academic departments and have only been slightly altered by the "affirmative action," radical, and dissident professoriate. Graduation from a particular set of schools, a certain trajectory of career development, and the same intellectual interests are definite signs of probable congeniality. It is not that faculty consciously seeks clones in their young and new colleagues, but they have formed definitions of competence that are framed by well-trodden career paths, as well as race, sex, ethnicity, and intellectual orientation. This is the stuff of which intellectual sterility and political conformity are made. Only with the uncontrolled expansion of the academic system did marginal deviation from the established patterns become possible.

It is worth noting in this connection that recruitment below the elite schools reproduces the patterns of their more prestigious counterparts. Until the job crunch, a Yale graduate was regarded with suspicion if he or she applied to a community or state college unless the school was located in a desirable metropolitan area, such as New York, San Francisco, or Boston. Similarly, when I lived in San Diego and did not have an academic job, my application to a local state college was refused because the committee held it was unlikely I would stay. They argued that since I published more than the typical colleague at the school, I would feel "uncomfortable" in the surroundings. Thus, lacking counter hegemonic social movements, even a buoyant economy may not permit downward mobility even as it denies upward mobility to most women and minorities. The exceptions to this rule only verify this statement since few teachers in the Ivy League are graduates of universities not reputed to be at the cutting edge of research, and those coming from these universities are rarely found in community colleges or state liberal arts schools that recruit faculty in the image of their social function.

I want to conclude by posing a question raised indirectly in this article: From the point of view of the new relations of industrial and postindustrial society, is the curtailment of the academic system a rational policy? Obviously, for workers, women, and blacks, as well as political dissenters, the "givens" of American ideology point to a negative answer: Since American ideology cannot, at the moment at least, grant the need for redistributive justice and will only respond to pressures from below under conditions of expansion, those historically excluded from credentials must fight for expansion of, as well as space for, the critical curriculum. Under present conditions, the critical curriculum cannot achieve hegemony over the technical and technocratic orientation but must content itself with affirming pluralism in intellectual inquiry and hiring against the conformist tendencies that have gained the upper hand in mainstream instruction.

But what of those who wish to preserve the status quo? Are the current setbacks in the size and variety of higher education opportunities in their interest? In order to answer this question, I must recapitulate my argument:

1. In the absence of an alternative such as the romance of the factory or the streets that animated prior generations of working-class kids for whom college was not only unattainable but also undesirable because it prepared them for becoming part of the system's apparatus, today's workers are obliged to get credentials on penalty of dead-end jobs, lower pay, and economic insecurity.

2. Getting a degree is no substitute for a critical education, which is barely available in most schools and, in the nadir of the student, women's and black freedom movements, is not likely to remain an option.

3. The distance between the new student and the old faculty, each of which has been formed in a radically different cultural and social context, is becoming greater. Thus, the quality of credentialed education is declining, but students learn about authority through being subjected to pedagogic "violence," a knowledge that prepares them for bureaucratic work.

4. From the point of view of systemic reproduction, the elite university finds itself in serious trouble, mainly because its own uncritical traditions, its technocratic orientation, and the market orientation of students who failed to get the message not to worry conspire to produce a degraded educational and intellectual environment. Tenure has reduced the innovative possibilities of the universities of this type, but the most important problem remains the canon of normal science which inhibits a "scientific" revolution able to comprehend the new world economic and cultural order and provide students with adequate preparation for that order. In other words, the old culture, which is not being transmitted to the new generations, still grips the professoriate. On the one hand, this culture must be transmitted; on the other hand, it

must be overcome within teaching and learning, in research, and in policy formation. Technocracy as ideology is unable to generate a culture that lives with the ambiguities of the transition already underway because it reduces problems to types of instrumental rationality.

Taken together these problems suggest, not planned shrinkage, but a bold program of academic renovation similar to the program that motivated the expansion after 1957. Radical critics of the academic system who have linked it to the labor market have pinpointed only one side of its current role in society. Among its other functions the complex of ideas and practices that constitute ideology production, politically and economically directed research in scientific and technological fields, and the state are vital not only to maintain the prevailing order, but also to solve pressing systemic problems. If Jurgen Habermas is right, that modern societies need not only knowledges for the creation of new productive forces to ensure their development but also learning mechanisms to revolutionize their communication competence and to solve new problems that lie outside economic rationalities, then the university, which has become broadly responsible for intellectual renovation, must itself be changed. To the extent that the academic system is confined, and confines itself, to producing technical knowledge, to that extent society itself is deprived of social and cultural knowledge of which power is, in part, constituted. Thus, the formation of a critical cadre able to span a wide area of political, cultural, and social knowledge is an absolutely essential condition for crisis management. The conservative ideology that currently dominates our leading universities combined with the political and class-motivated cutbacks at all levels of the academic system, is clearly opposed to the long-term interests of the system, and, it may be argued, is not even consonant with its short-term interests.

Let me give a single example: Business journals, economists, and the daily press have agreed that among our most pressing economic problems is productivity. In the new circumstances of the world economic order, productivity is intimately tied to knowledge as much as it is to the surplus extracted from manual labor. Just as the Reagan administration and its predecessors unwisely curbed research and development activities that were not linked to the military, so American industries have suffered serious setbacks in advanced technological industries where knowledge production is central. Needless to say, universities have been the main contractors of government-sponsored military basic research and have been the major losers in the current retrenchment. By subjecting university programs, faculty, and facilities to the market system, America is losing the capacity to respond to those problems not subject to market solutions—for example, the growing ideological and political isolation of the United States in world affairs, not only from the third world, but from its erstwhile allies in Western Europe. As United States economic power diminishes, Americans need different skills and understanding to deal with an increasingly interdependent world. This political sophistication was, to be sure, not needed in the postwar era, when United States economic power outweighed its sad parochialism. The American academic system is the only place where a new generation of serious scholars of the world economy, diverse political systems, and different cultures can be educated.

Of course, this article is not intended to advise the corporate establishment or the political directorate concerning shortsighted education policies. I merely wish to remind liberal and radical critics that the fight to expand educational opportunity is not only oppositional; it may correspond to the system's interest, and some who occupy the commanding heights of political and economic power may recognize this.

A program that fights to expand opportunities for credentials is necessary but not sufficient to defend the interests of those historically excluded. Equally important is to enrich the composition of the professoriate with those whose dissidence consists in their will to carve pedagogic space for critical education. This project entails an ambiguous struggle for the traditional liberal arts in the wake of their marginality and new curricula that expose students to the academic system as an object of social and intellectual inquiry. These must be seen in the context of a larger project to deconstruct the hegemonic categories of social and scientific thought. To achieve this program, a new student movement would have to be created. This is the last paradox of liberal and radical practice: There is virtually no likelihood that substantial elements of the powerful will recognize their own self-interest in saving the academic system from decay. On the other hand, those who must save it will help not only themselves but their antagonists.

NOTES

1. Randall Collins, *The Credentialed Society* (Berkeley; University of California Press, 1978).

2. Pierre Bourdieu and Jean-Claude Passeron, *Reproduction in Education, Society, and Culture* (Los Angeles: Sage Publications, 1979).

3. A possible objection to this assertion might be that even in large universities, especially graduate programs, students are subject to the tutelage and ultimate judgment of a single adviser. However, the adviser himself is certified by the academic system; his right to certify others is a privilege conferred impersonally. The degree is not signed by the adviser alone but also by the administration of the university, which reserves, at least putatively, the ultimate authority over the process.

4. I am not claiming that the diploma is entirely superseded by a bachelor's degree. The diploma is still a prerequisite for many public sector jobs and clerical positions in the private sector but is no longer a sufficient credential for technical and administrative occupations. Postsecondary education of some kind has become the sine qua non of these jobs.

5. Talcott Parsons, *Essays in Social Theory* (Glencoe, Ill.: Free Press, 1958).

6. Herbert Marcuse, *One Dimensional Man* (Boston: Beacon Press, 1964).

7. Wilhelm Reich, *The Imposition of Compulsory Sexual Morality* (New York: Farrar Straus & Giroux, 1971).

8. See Jurgen Habermas, *Communication and the Evolution of Society* (Boston: Beacon Press, 1980), pp. 30–X77.

9. Pierre Bourdieu, *Outline of a Theory of Practice* (Cambridge: Cambridge University Press, 1980).

10. Here social contract theory refers to those perspectives in which the subjects of social domination accept their situation as part of a larger agreement with those in power. Bourdieu, the Frankfurt school, and Reich, among others, argue that the process by which authority establishes itself entails a transformation of the largely unconscious, habitual processes of everyday life.

11. Bourdieu, *Reproduction*, pp. 141–176.

12. Paul Willis, *Learning to Labour* (New York: Columbia University Press, 1981).

13. Alain Touraine, *The Academic System in American Society* (New York: McGraw-Hill, 1971).

14. By June 1983, neither union had received final certification because of more than 500 challenged ballots, enough to swing the election to the AAUP. However, the stunning victory for faculty unionism is unmistakeable: Of 14,000 votes, only 2,500 were "nonunion." Similar victories were won by AAUP at Rutgers and Wayne State universities. The AFT represents faculty and some staff at the City University of New York and the faculty in the New York State University system.

15. *National Labor Relations Board versus Yeshiva University*, 444 U.S. 672 (1980).

16. The recruitment of administrators from faculty ranks is rapidly receding in importance as the academic system has increasingly adopted the corporate managerial practice of recruiting professional managers for high university positions. In many cases, even when administrators hold formal academic credentials these serve as legitimating fig–leaves for a professionalized management.

·8·

The Rise of Corporate Politics and the Decline of Academic Freedom

Michael Useem

The start of the 1980s has been a period of extraordinary political transformation in the United States. The effects have been as profound for higher education as anywhere. College programs oriented toward human services are being closed and engineering colleges opened, campus activism is giving way to student careerism, and university budgets are being acutely squeezed between spiraling administrative costs and declining state support. This chapter will suggest that such changes and crises are posing grave threats to the traditional mission of the university, to freedom of the academy in the broadest form. It will also argue that a root cause of this transformation is a new and more intensive form of business-political mobilization.

THE CHANGING ECONOMY AND CULTURE OF HIGHER EDUCATION

The economic conditions facing the nation's several thousand colleges and universities and some ten million students have significantly worsened during the past several years. Government support for students is in sharp decline. The national administration is

Appreciation is extended to Craig Kaplan, Jerome Karabel, the National Emergency Civil Liberties Committee, and the National Science Foundation (SOC77-06658).

requesting less than $5 billion in student aid programs for 1983, down from nearly twice that amount in 1981. Government support for university research is on a less precipitous but nonetheless downward slope as well. If President Ronald Reagan's recommendations prevail, federal underwriting of university research will drop in constant dollars between 1981 and 1983 by nearly 10 percent. In addition, the composition of the diminished overall budget is undergoing rapid restructuring, perhaps faster than during any other period of change in federal research priorities. The research budget of every federal agency, with the sole exception of the Department of Defense, is being reduced. The budget for Health and Human Services is down by 11 percent in 1982 compared to 1981, the Environmental Protection Agency by 60 percent, and the Department of Labor by 100 percent. By 1983, Labor is slated to have no research programs at all. At the same time, the Defense Department's budget is up by 14 percent. As a result, while universities received 11 percent of their federal research budget from the Department of Defense in 1980, by 1983 the share from Defense is projected to reach 15 percent.[1]

National support for higher education is ebbing, and public financing of colleges and universities in many states is in even faster decline. State tax revenues have been severely depressed by the prolonged economic recession, leading to frozen budgets for higher education and even major reductions. In 1982, academic hiring was temporarily suspended throughout the University of California system; emergencies were declared in Minnesota and Washington, with consequent efforts to terminate numbers of academic appointments and programs; and the state of Michigan was unable to provide its largest public institution, Michigan State University, with the final quarterly installment of state funds, forcing the university to borrow in the commercial market until the new fiscal year.

Although the crisis of state revenues and funding is far more advanced in some regions than others, nearly all states are anticipating declining support for higher education. A survey of state governors, chairs of state education and appropriation committees, and state higher education executive officers in the fall of 1981, for instance, found a broad consensus that state appropriations will continue their path of decline. Three-quarters predicted that state funding would lag inflation, and two-thirds expected colleges and universities to suffer further cuts in personnel, capital outlays, and academic programs.[2]

The transformation in the political culture of American higher education has been nearly as pronounced as the change in its political economy. "I am in the university to acquire skills which I will need in order to survive in the world, and not to resolve the great problems of society," comments one university senior in response to a recent national survey.[3] He would have spoken for a silent minority on campus a decade earlier; now he represents a seeming majority. Half of the 1,500 students surveyed in this study wanted their university education limited to technical competence and career training. Student concern with self-development and personal advancement is ascendent; engagement in social problems and political issues is descendent. More broadly, fueled by the national administration's coolness toward scholarly inquiry and critical thought, antiintellectual values have taken on new life both off and on campus.

INSTITUTIONAL ACADEMIC FREEDOM

These adverse developments in the economic and political environments of higher education are impinging on the core programs and organization of the academic system. The effects include the following:

Unequalizing access: College and university tuition rates have been rising far faster than inflation. Private university tutition, for instance, increased by 15 percent in one 12-month period ending in early in 1982, while the inflation rate itself stood at 8 percent. Combined with declining federal and state assistance for attending college, the barriers to entry for the sons and daughters of poor and blue-collar families are becoming higher than ever. "Class-blind" admissions policies, never entirely blind in any case, have been publicly abandoned by several institutions in response to the new economic reality. And, as is the case whenever economic hurdles are raised, racial minorities are disproportionately affected.

Unequalizing quality: For those who are admitted and can afford to attend, the disparities in experience are widening as differences between institutions expand. The "prediction for the 80's," according to a headline description of one study of the finances of higher education, is simply that "rich colleges will get richer," while others will be scrambling to survive.[4] The quality of an institution has lasting effects on its graduates' employment opportunities, and thus the greater inequality among institutions will further heighten disparities in the life experiences of those who are able to complete their education.

Narrowing of curriculum: The liberal arts, humanities, and social sciences are in retreat, while vocational programs, engineering, business, and military science are advancing.

Reduction of research: Basic research is in decline as the chief source of extramural funding, the federal government, reorients its priorities. Fundamental research in virtually all fields is affected, but especially distressed is scholarly work in those disciplines in the social sciences and humanities with the strongest traditions of critical inquiry and concern for the human services.

Responsiveness to industry: The acute financial needs of some institutions and faculty have facilitated a new openness to business priorities, particularly in the engineering and scientific fields. Colleges and universities are increasingly looking toward the private sector for support; so, too, are faculty members whose stagnating salaries are turning private consulting into economic necessity.

These new threats to academic freedom at the institutional level have not precluded problems at the individual level. Dissident faculty continue to face special problems at the time of reappointment and tenure. But the new pressures on institutional academic freedom, although more impersonal, may at the same time be more extensive in scope and lasting in outcome.

Being an active feminist can still be an unknowledged grounds for an unfavorable university tenure decision. Yet recent gains by far larger numbers of women at the same institution, activist and non-activist alike, may be entirely reversed as the institution moves its resources into engineering and management, divisions with few women faculty, and extracts the same from humanities and education programs, areas with large numbers of women. Racial minorities, whatever their political profile on campus, face similar circumstances. Their strongest enclaves—black, Chicano, and Native American studies programs—have been first targets for austerity-minded decision makers.

True, politically troublesome faculty are at times harassed. But they are relatively small in number compared to those whose intellectual and teaching opportunities are being closed by institutional shifts in response to the changing environment. Those reluctant to accept weapons research contracts, teach unthreatening subjects, or avoid political visibility need not be cajoled. Rather, support for nondefense work will be in short supply, programs that raise critical questions will be eliminated, and disciplines and departments with notable records of agitation will be isolated.

The current threat to academic freedom thus could not be more fundamental in consequence but also more different in exercise from the targeted attacks on academic dissidence in the past. The scope and means of the threat to institutional academic freedom, however, are not isolated phenomena. They are part of the historic redefinition of the role of the public and nonprofit sectors that the Reagan administration is so effectively promoting. To understand the transformation of higher education, therefore, it is important to reflect on the rise of this administration and the constellation of political and economic forces that it represents. The national administration leads, but its capacity to do so depends on a broad consensus among those institutions and organizations upon whose power that of the administration itself ultimately resides.

THE ORGANIZATION AND CONDITION OF AMERICA BUSINESS

Drawing on a study that I recently completed on business political activity in the United States and Great Britain, I will suggest that an important source of this consensus and its elevation to a national political mandate are to be found in the changing social organization of the business community and the adverse economic conditions it has faced in recent years. This study included extensive interviews with some 150 business leaders in New York, Boston, and London, and intensive analysis of a number of quantitative information profiles of large corporations and their senior managers.[5] The results of the study suggest that the unprecedented reversal of the fortunes of the public and nonprofit sectors, higher education included, are in part the product of the decline of the economic position of large companies and, at the same time, an increasing capacity of the business community to respond politically to its growing adversity. I will describe this capacity first and then turn to the adversity.

The heightening of business political capacity depends, first of all, on the diminishing number of significant actors. Economic resources are slowly but inexorably being concentrated in fewer corporate hands, facilitating the formation of a common political culture and social organization among those directing corporate activities. The share of total manufacturing assets held by the 200 largest manufacturing firms, for instance, has been increasing by 0.5 percent annually since the turn of the century, and there is no sign of any slackening in recent decades. The top 200 are now in control of approximately three-fifths of all manufacturing assets.[6]

Indicative of the overall level of concentration and the opportunities it can present for political coordination, a single business association with fewer than 200 members, the Business Roundtable, brings together those who are responsible for corporate decisions affecting a large portion of the economy. The 196 chief executive officers who participate in Roundtable deliberations on public policy are collectively responsible for firms whose annual revenues are in the aggregate equivalent to nearly half of the U.S. gross national product. Thus, the great bulk of the private economy is now overseen by those managers of just several hundred large corporations.

Accompanying concentration, particularly in recent years, has been product diversification, paced by the so-called "conglomerates" but pursued to varying degrees by most firms as well.[7] Not only are large enterprises in control of a dominant and still expanding share of all economic activity, but most are also increasingly familiar with a range of disparate market conditions, labor forces, and business climates. The extent of this diversification is illustrated by changes in a sample of more than 270 *Fortune* 500 firms between 1949 and 1974. The percentage of companies in a largely single line of business declined from 42 to 14. Conversely, the percentage of corporations involved in several related or unrelated lines of manufacturing grew over the same period from 30 to 63. Only 1 in 20 of the companies could be considered conglomerates in 1949; 1 in 4 could be so classified by 1974.[8] Diversification has meant that firms now have better appreciation for one another's problems and policy needs, for they face more similar market circumstances than ever before.

The fortunes of large corporations are also increasingly interdependent. Networks of economic relations among the largest firms are becoming more inclusive of all companies, and among the most significant trends is the rise of intercorporate ownership. The share of all corporate stock owned by other companies, especially financial institutions, has been steadily rising in recent years, reaching more than a third of the total by the mid-1970s.[9] Although still a minority fraction, the high concentration of corporate investments has meant that the top stockholders of most large companies are now other, primarily financial, corporations. Typical of the present-day ownership profile is that of Mobil Oil Corporation, the fourth largest American industrial firm. Of the top ten shareholders in 1973, possessing in the aggregate some 20 percent of the voting rights for Mobil, nine are other corporations, all but one banks or insurance companies.[10] This transformation in stockholder composition is evident in the shareholder profile of virtually all major firms.[11] The orphans and the widows have been swept away by the institutions.

The intercorporate ownership network now incorporates nearly all large companies, and it is little based on purely particularistic ties between pairs or small cliques of firms. Some intercorporate ownership does reflect an interest on the part of one corporation in pressuring, co-opting, controlling, or even acquiring another company or set of firms. But the bulk of such shareholding is the product of investment strategies that treat large blocs of companies as largely equivalent; the acquisition of stock in one enterprise rather than another is most typically the product of a return-on-investment decision and does not reflect an anticipated exchange of products or some other specific relationship between the firms. The structure of the intercorporate network of ownership, in short, is both inclusive and diffuse. Diffuse signifies the network is spread widely rather than concentrated within small cliques. The rise of this network in the past few decades has created a context in which decisions taken by large companies are necessarily of concern to many other large corporations. The same is true for political factors that may retard the growth of company profits. Corporations not directly affected by a problem confronting a single firm or sector nonetheless may have their own prospects dimmed by virtue of the indirect dependency. Political challenges to one become, in attenuated but real ways, of concern to all.

To this ownership interdependency is added a managerial interdependency. The most important strand is the network of shared directorships, often called the interlocking directorate. This network is constituted of those company directors who simultaneously serve on the boards of two or more large companies. It is not a network, however, whose members are detached from the practice of running business. Approximately three-quarters of the outside directors of a typical large firm are themselves top managers, often chief executives of still other large companies.[12] As in the case of the economic network, the directorship network encompasses nearly all important corporations, and it does so in a dispersed fashion favorable to collective political action.

The scope of the network is apparent in studies of the number of large companies that are tied together in a single lattice by the shared directorships. Two early studies provide indicators that probably underestimate present-day inclusiveness: According to a 1962 analysis, nine-tenths of America's 1,131 largest companies are directly or indirectly linked in one encompassing network; another of the 797 largest firms in 1969 reports a still higher degree of inclusion.[13]

Like the ownership network, the directorship network is not only inclusive but diffusely structured as well. In previous work on the interlocking directorate, it has generally been viewed as not diffusely organized. Rather, shared directorships have been seen as an instrument for cementing ties between specific pairs or cliques of firms. Sharing a director is a device to ensure cooperation as firms buy and sell products or extend credit to one another.[14] Studies of changes in the directorship network, however, suggest that this is not the main reason they are formed. When ties in the network are broken acci- dentally, as when a multiple director dies or retires, they are rarely repaired in the same way. New ties do form, but not between the same pairs or cliques of firms,[15] If the ties had been intended to coordinate small groups of firms, their accidental severance should have instead been followed by quick repair.

The interviews with the senior executives reveal that the interlocking directorate is indeed not reducible to a set of particularistic ties between firms. Rather, most ties are the product of an entirely different corporate consideration. Companies are anxious to place their senior managers on the boards of other firms, not to secure some exchange with those firms, but rather to ensure that their managers remain fully abreast of the changing corporate environment and practices of other corporations.[16] These are not the ties that bind, but that inform.

CORPORATE POLITICAL LEADERSHIP

The unplanned consequence of the inclusive and diffusely structured interlocking directorates is the formation of a communication network with special political capacities. This network, termed here the inner circle, consists of the limited number of senior managers of the nation's largest firms who are also involved in the affairs of other large corporations. It is opportunely situated. Its foundation on economic and social networks diffusely transcending the major companies ensures that its members are more unified than other business leaders, for the inner circle shares a special culture, informal acquaintanceship, and common tradition more developed than anywhere else within the business community. It is rooted in interests that go far beyond the parochial concerns of individual firms or industrial sectors.[17] These characteristics enable the circle to act, albeit in a highly imperfect fashion, as a politicized leading edge for all large corporations as a bloc.

Political leadership by the inner circle takes various forms. Its members are disproportionately on the numerous councils and boards that provide formal counsel to the national government, move into the top ranks of the major business associations most directly involved in the promotion of public polices on behalf of all large business, and join the front ranks of the contributors to national political parties and candidates. In 1976, for instance, only 3 percent of the managers of large American corporations served on an advisory committee to a U.S. government agency (such as the National Industrial Energy Council of the U.S. Department of Commerce), whereas 11 percent of those in the inner circle held such an appointment. Similar participation ratios are also obtained for leadership positions in the preeminent business associations, notably the Business Roundtable, Business Council, Committee for Economic Development, and Council on Foreign Relations.[18] The inner circle is also at the forefront of business outreach to higher education. Business trustees of colleges and universities are drawn heavily from the ranks of the inner circle. Moreover, while corporate executives who serve on governing boards generally raise more money for their institution than do nonbusiness trustees, those in the inner circle are far more successful at it than their other business colleagues. The best single predictor of the amount of financial support that new trustees will bring to their institution is whether they travel in the inner circle.[19]

DECLINING COMPANY PROFITS AND
RISING GOVERNMENT REGULATION

The inner circle constitutes a leadership group for the entire large business community. By virtue of the intercorporate networks on which it is formed, it has the organizational ties and general vision of business needs that permit it to represent effectively the broader political concerns of business. The inner circle was not formed to do this, but it can do so as an unanticipated consequence nonetheless. The formation of the inner circle has thus provided business with the capacity to act if need be, and the adversities it faced in the 1970s have led it to do so.

Two distinct challenges confronted the business community in the 1970s. The challenges were widely felt, they did not permit individual solution, and thus they generated the kind of shared grievance that so often is the final trigger behind collective political mobilization. One of the challenges was economic, the other organizational, but both led to a search for political solution. The economic problem was the broad decline in company profits, a trend that left few companies unaffected. The organizational grievance was the rise of cross-industry government regulation. This, too, had an impact on virtually all large companies.

The 1970s were a period of downwardly sloping profits for American business. Martin Feldstein and Lawrence Summers, for example, examined pretax rates of return for nonfinancial U.S. companies, examining the ratios of domestic profits to assets. The annual corporate profit rate averaged 12.5 percent at the end of the 1940s, 11.8 percent in the early 1950s, and 10.8 percent in the late 1950s. The movement in the 1960s was modestly upward, peaking in the middle of the decade at nearly 14 percent in 1965. Thereafter it declined, however, reaching unusually low levels in the mid-1970s. Indeed, lower profit rates were recorded than in any other period since the Second World War. The average annual rate for the first half of the 1960s was 11.2 percent; the second half, 12.2 percent. But performance for the first five years of the 1970s declined to an average 8.1 percent and for the next two years to 7.4 percent.[20] Extending the estimates further, Feldstein and two colleagues found the profit rate in 1979 to be lowest in two decades, save the recession years of 1974–75.[21]

Similar trends appear if various alternative measures of profit levels are used instead. After-tax returns on capital, for instance, have been gauged by David Holland and Stuart Myers since 1947, and they, too, find that compared with the 1960s, the 1970s were years of very poor performance.[22] After-tax profits averaged 7.5 percent in the early 1960s, up from the 6.1 percent of the 1950s, and it reached 9.0 percent in the late 1960s. But after that it declined considerably, dropping to 6.0 percent in the early 1970s and 5.9 percent between 1975 and 1978.

The rise of cross-industry government regulation in the 1970s added to the sense of shared adversity within the business community. Although industry-specific regulation has often served to fragment business, regulatory agencies and programs created in the 1970s achieved much the opposite because of their universally experienced impact. Managers of companies in diverse industries found little common cause in dealing with industry-specific regulatory agencies, but they did find much to share in their unhappy experience with the newer, functional agencies. Moreover, industry-specific regulation was usually developed with some degree of industry cooperation, while general regulation has been far more adversarial in origin and implementation.[23] At the forefront of the new, overarching regulation are the Occupational Safety and Health Administration (OSHA), the Equal Employment Opportunity Commission (EEOC), and, above all, the Environmental Protection Agency (EPA).

The disparate growth rates of the specific and general regulatory programs are reflected in the expenditure trends of the key agencies. Between 1974 and 1979, the annual outlays of the EPA more than doubled, rising from $232 million to $552 million. Similar growth rates of near or more than 100 percent are observed for four other cross-industry agencies—the Occupational Safety and Health Administration, Equal Employment Opportunity Commission, National Labor Relations Board, and the Securities and Exchange Commission. The aggregate expenditures for these five agencies increased more than twofold during this six-year period, from $432 million in 1974 to $945 million in 1979. For the industry-specific regulatory agencies, however, the 1970s were a period of less bullish growth. The total expenditures for the four largest agencies—the Civil Aeronautics Board, Federal Trade Commission, Federal Communications Commission, and Interstate Commerce Commission—grew by only 50 percent, climbing from near $200 million to just under $300 million. Moreover, the outlays of the general regulatory agencies rose substantially faster than did overall government spending or business itself. By the end of the decade, the great majority of federal regulatory expenditures were devoted to the general rather than the specific agencies.[24]

The cost of general government regulation to large companies was widely believed to be massive, although few of the managers that I interviewed could cite a specific cost figure for their own firm. An overall estimate comes from a study by an accounting firm of the direct impact in 1977 of six general regulatory agencies and programs, including OSHA, EEOC, and EPA, on 48 large companies, all members of the Business Roundtable. Using company-supplied data, this evaluation found a total annual cost of $2.6 billion, of which three-quarters stemmed from EPA regulations alone.[25] The total annual burden of both industry-specific and general cross-industry government regulation has been estimated for all companies to run as high as $100 billion or more although the tenuous assumptions underlying such a calculation dictate cautious interpretation.[26]

Executives of large corporations reported the growth of an awareness that all were experiencing increasingly burdensome federal demands and that a joint counteroffensive was long overdue. One senior manager of a large metals producer observed that across the business community "there is a better understanding of common objectives now, certainly on the tax situation, on OSHA, on pollution, and on regulation in general. Everybody finds that the costs escalate."

POLITICAL MOBILIZATION

The formation of classwide organization linking virtually all large business firms, and the emergence of a distinct and autonomous leadership element positioned to understand and represent their common political interests, had considerably improved the political capacity of the business community by the late 1970s. The rise of general government regulation and the prolonged decline of corporate profit in this same period added the urgent sense that this capacity should be applied. As a result, recent years have been marked by significant intensification of corporate political activity.

Few senior business leaders ever enter the political fray as candidates themselves. Only 6 percent of the chief executive officers of more than half the 800 largest firms surveyed in 1975 had been elected to public office, although better than 90 percent indicated they would like to see business executives more active in electoral politics.[27] Less visible political activity is far more widespread, though, according to a Conference Board survey of 400 chief executives of large enterprises in 1979. Nearly half had publicly endorsed candidates for political office since becoming chief executive, and an equal proportion had actively campaigned or served as a fund raiser for a candidate.[28]

Company activity has become widespread as well, and it has taken diverse forms. Nonproduct advertising increased sharply during the 1970s. By one estimate, such spending by large U.S. companies and trade associations reached nearly $500 million in 1977, up from less than half that in 1971, although the growth rate may have slowed in more recent years.[29] Most nonproduct advertising is designed to promote company recognition or reputation. But one in five of the major American companies now devote resources to the advocacy of neither product nor image but company views on contemporary political and social issues.[30] Newspapers and magazines with wide and influential readerships are the favored vehicle for such corporate "aditorials."

"Forsaking our religious heritage, not only in our schools, but everywhere," is a root cause of America's critical problems, according to Tiffany & Company. It is this, not inflation, that is responsible for our "accentuating crime, immorality, greed and selfishness." Renowned for its jewelery but less for its economics, Tiffany nonetheless gave its costly advertising space in the The New York Times to a diagnosis of the U.S. "national calamity" rather than its fine silverware.[31] The range of messages in the corporate aditorial is as diverse as contemporary politics. Smith Kline Corporation, a major pharmaceutical standing midway on the Fortune 500 list of top manufacturers, allocates a generous share of its national media budget neither to promoting Contac pills nor Sineoff, nor even to expressing company philosophy on the proper role of government. Instead, it buys space to permit featured intellectuals to express themselves on issues of moment. The title of one advertisement appearing in Newsweek and elsewhere is indicative: "To afford lasting gains in quality of life, we must renew America's aging industrial base, concludes distinguished sociologist Amitai Etzioni." Professor Etzioni's views on reindustrialization occupy more than two full pages of advertising space.[32] Dresser Industries has reproduced a lengthy interview with a black South African woman opposed to withdrawal of U.S. corporate investments, requiring two pages in the *Wall Street Journal*.[33] W. R. Grace & Company extensively advertises its views of proposals to alter the U.S. personal income tax rates.[34] Union Carbide uses its space to report the results of a national survey it commissioned on public attitudes toward government and the economy.[35] And of course Mobil Oil Corporation has long played a leading role in this field, devoting its regular place in a number of periodicals to its views on a nearly limitless range of social and political questions, some with exceedingly faint bearing on Mobil operations.

Corporate money has also been increasingly bestowed on organizations, such as the American Enterprise Institute, whose purpose is to improve the political climate for business. And companies have intensified the use of the electronic and print media to communicate their ideas on how to restore corporate growth, ideas that have generally focused on reducing the interference and cost of the public sector. Education is rarely targeted specifically, but neither is it exempt from cuts when the public is urged to press for reductions in taxes and nonmilitary government spending. The feeling is widespread in higher management circles that companies should be more aggressive in communicating this message. More than half of the top officers of 400 large corporations surveyed in 1979 felt that they should take their "views on public policy issues" to "the people" through personal and media appearances.[36] "Glib and glamorous spokespeople for the left have often succeeded in capturing the greatest share of attention while most business executives haven't yet mastered the necessary techniques," laments Willard C. Butcher, the successor to David Rockefeller as president and chief executive of Chase Manhattan Bank, but "we can't withdraw and whine over biased reporting. We have a right and obligation to hit back." His call is one that increasing numbers of business executives are heeding. "We must take our message directly into American homes, to the people, to the ultimate deciders of our society's fate. We need nothing less than a major and sustained effort in the marketplace of ideas."[37]

Perhaps the most significant area of expanding corporate political activity is in the field of political action committees. Direct corporate financing of political campaigns and candidates is prohibited by law, but companies are permitted to form internal political action committees (PACs) that solicit funds from upper management and channel it to campaigns and candidates deemed friendly to the company or business philosophy. Business monies flowing through PACs exhibited explosive growth during the 1970s Fewer than 100 corporate PACs were in operation during the 1972 election; by 1980, the number exceeded 1,100. By contrast, the number of labor political action committees exhibited only modest growth, rising from 200 to near 300 by the end of the decade.

The divergent growth curves for corporate and labor PACs are evident as well in their aggregate funding level. In 1968, corporate and business-related committees are estimated to have spent $1.4 million on candidates for national office, while national labor committees distributed $7.6 million to House and Senate candidates. A decade later, business committees contributed more than $17 million to federal candidates (another $20 million went to other campaigns); but labor spending on federal campaigns had risen to only $10 million (an additional $8 million was spent on other candidates). While political action committee underwriting of Democratic candidates rose twofold between 1972 and 1979, support of Republican candidates more than tripled. Since the parties themselves decreasingly financed the campaigns of their own candidates during this same period, PACs acquired special salience for aspiring politicians. During the 1978 campaign, for instance, the two parties directly and indirectly provided $11 million to candidates for national office, while PACs gave $35 million. In 1980, the PAC contribution to House and Senate campaigns rose to $55 million, approaching a quarter of the total congressional campaign receipts of $252 million.

Corporate PAC activity is highly concentrated among the nation's largest companies. Nearly half (45 percent) of the 821 corporate committees active in the 1978 election campaign were of firms among *Fortune*'s list of the 1,300 largest enterprises. And it is among the very largest that the committees are most often found: Of the manufacturing firms ranked in size between 501 and 1000, 34 had formed a PAC, but of the 500 top manufacturers, 202 had an operative PAC. And of the 100 largest, 70 sponsored a PAC. Moreover, PAC expenditures were far greater at the top of the *Fortune* list: The committees of firms in the second 500 industrials disbursed under $2,000 on average; those near the bottom of the top 500 contributed $6,000 each; the PACs of the ten largest industrials provided $70,000 each.[38]

THE CONSEQUENCES FOR HIGHER EDUCATION

The mobilized business community has targeted government regulation and social spending, and more generally the high and seemingly unproductive costs of many areas of government and nonprofit activity, as the first source of its declining fortunes. Under the broader banner of reindustrialization and economic revitalization, it has actively campaigned for reductions in the cost of doing the public's business. The concentration and diversification of large companies, their increasing ownership and directorship interdependence, and the formation of an overarching informal social organization within the business community have all facilitated this mobilization. The long-term decline in profit rates and upturn in federal regulation have added special impetus and power to it.

It is the success of this program to curb the growth of the public sector that has been a critical ingredient behind the declining condition of higher education in the 1980s. The political thrust, electoral victory, and continued commitment of the Reagan administration to moving resources from the public sector to the private are in no small part a product of the intensified and new forms of corporate involvement in politics. The squeeze on the private sector has thus been successfully shifted onto the public and nonprofit sectors as well. Higher education has been among the many casualties as a result, an outcome not explicitly intended but a certain by-product nonetheless.

Many business leaders are of course distrustful of the political values and many of the programs in higher education. They believe that the university system is partly to blame for the antibusiness and progovernment public mood that had come to prevail in the 1970s. "Why do we contribute money to institutions that graduate our foes?" wondered one industrialist, reflecting a mood prevalent in certain business quarters.[39] The humanities and social sciences in particular are perceived by some to foster values antithetical to the premises of capitalism. A senior manager of one firm offered that "nineteen out of the top twenty graduate departments of economics are hostile to free enterprise," Chicago being the twentieth.[40] Various programs to transform this intellectual and political culture have been suggested, and a few tried. The chairman of a major corporation recommends the route of discretionary funding: "Corporate support should be channeled to those who speak out for limited government and those who stress the importance of individual liberties. Conversely, I believe that corporate support should be denied to those who favor a collectivist society under limitless government."[41] Some companies have moved to screen more carefully where their philanthropy is directed. And seminars and educational materials for faculty who wish to learn more about free enterprise are now more freely available. Business leaders concerned to effect change at this level have generally preferred the carrot to the stick. Very few openly advocate the dismissal of dissident or antibusiness faculty. They prefer, instead, to follow Irving Kristol's simple advice that "businessmen or corporations do not have any obligation to give money to institutions whose views or attitudes they disapprove of."[42]

Such attitudes can translate into issues of academic freedom at the individual level, although more often in positive than negative form. Rather than urging the dismissal of faculty unfriendly toward business, companies prefer to provide universities with money to establish endowed chairs in free enterprise and programs for the study of government regulation. Whatever the effects on higher education, however, they are modest by comparison with the consequences of the general reductions in public support for higher education. Individual threats to academic freedom are more visible and angering, but the institutional threats are more profound and lasting.

The programmatic changes in higher education are not a product of a spontaneous public disaffection with academe's traditional functions. Nor are they simply an inchoate response to a period of economic stagnation. Rather, the changes are in part a product of a broader redefinition of the balance between the public and private sectors sought by the national administration and the institutions on which its power resides. Among the most important of these supporting institutions are the large corporation and the intercorporate networks that have drawn them together. Business has many internal disagreements, of course, and it is frequently opposed to policies pursued by the Reagan administration. But on the issue of revitalizing capitalism through a shrinkage of the public sector, there is considerable consensus. Moreover, the drive to reduce it may be further intensified as corporate profits appear to be continuing their downward slide well into the 1980s. Unless there is a strong economic recovery and a significant countermobilization by other political constituencies, the years ahead may well remain very problematic for the preservation of institutional academic freedoms.

NOTES

1. "Two Year Drop Seen in Campus Research Aid," Chronicle of Higher Education, March 24, 1982.

2. Robert L. Jacobson, "Officials See State Funds for Colleges Lagging Over the Next 3 Years," Chronicle of Higher Education, March 17, 1982.

3. Jack Magarrell, "American Students Seek Survival Skills, Not Social Conscience, Interviews Show," Chronicle of Higher Education, April 7, 1982.

4. Malcolm G. Scully, "Prediction for the 80's: Rich Colleges Will Get Richer," Chronicle of Higher Education, January 13, 1982.

5. This study is reported in Michael Useem, "The Social Organization of the American Business Elite and Participation of Corporation Directors in the Governance of American Institutions," American Sociological Review 44 (1979): 553–72; Michael Useem, "Corporations and the Corporate Elite," in Annual Review of Sociology, ed. Alex Inkeles et al. (Palo Alto, Calif.: Annual Reviews, 1980), Vol. 6, pp. 41–77; Michael Useem, "Business Segments and Corporate Relations with American Universities," Social Problems 29 (1981): 129–41; Michael Useem, "Classwide Rationality in the Politics of Managers and Directors of Large Corporations in the United States and Great Britain," Administrative Science Quarterly 27 (1982): 199–226; Michael Useem, The Inner Circle: Large Corporations and Business Political Activity in the U.S. and U.K. (New York: Oxford, University Press, 1983); Michael Useem and Arlene McCormack, "The Dominant Segment of the British Business Elite," Sociology 15 (1981): 381–406.

6. R. Marris, Theory and Future of the Corporate Economy and Society (Amsterdam: North-Holland, 1979).

7. Mark Green and Andrew Buchsbaum, The Corporate Lobbies: Political Profiles of the Business Roundtable and the Chamber of Commerce (Washington, D.C.: Public Citizen, 1980), p. 68.

8. R. P. Rumelt, Strategy, Structure, and Economic Performance (Cambridge, Mass.: Harvard University Press, 1974); R. P. Rumelt, "Diversity and Profitability," Working Paper MGL-51, University of California, Los Angeles, 1977; T. C. Honeycutt and D. L. Zimmerman, "The Measurement of Corporate Diversification: 1950–1967," Antitrust Bulletin 21 (1976): 509–35.

9. David M. Kotz, Bank Control of Large Corporations in the United States (Berkeley: University of California Press, 1978).

10. Corporate Data Exchange, Stock Ownership Directory: Transportation (New York, 1977), pp. 224–25.

11. Ibid.; Corporate Data Exchange, CDE Stock Ownership Directory: Agribusiness (New York, 1978); Corporate Data Exchange, CDE Stock Ownership Directory: Banking and Finance (New York, 1980).

12. Louis Harris and Associates, A Survey of Outside Directors of Major Publicly Owned Corporations (New York, 1977).

13. James Bearden, William Atwood, Peter Freitas, Carol Hendricks, Beth Mintz, and Michael Schwartz, "The Nature and Extent of Bank Centrality in Corporate Networks," paper presented at the Annual Meeting of the American Sociological Association, 1975; Peter Mariolis, "Interlocking Directorates and Control of Corporations: The Theory of Bank Control," Social Science Quarterly 56 (1975): 425–39.

14. Michael P. Allen, "The Structure of Interorganizational Elite Cooptation: Interlocking Corporate Directorates," American Sociological Review 39 (1974): 393–406; Jeffrey Pfeffer and Gerald R. Salancik, The External Control of Organizations: A Resource Dependence Perspective (New York: Harper & Row, 1978).

15. Thomas Koening, Robert Gogel, and John Sonquist, "Models of the Significance of Interlocking Corporate Directorates," *American Journal of Economics and Sociology* 38 (1979): 173–86; Donald Palmer, "Broken Ties: Some Political and Interorganization Determinants of Interlocking Directorates Among Large American Corporations," paper presented at the Annual Meeting of the American Sociological Association, 1980.

16. Useem, "Classwide Rationality."

17. Michael Useem, "The Inner group of the American Capitalist Class," *Social Problems* 25 (1978): 225–40; "Business Segments."

18. Useem, "Social Organization."

19. Useem, "Inner Group"; Useem, "Business Segments."

20. Martin Feldstein and Lawrence Summers, "Is the Rate of Profit Falling?" in *Brookings Papers on Economic Activity*, no. 1, ed. Arthur M. Okun and George L. Perry (Washington, D.C.: Brookings Institution, 1977); see also William D. Nordhaus, "The Falling Share of Profit," in *Brookings Papers on Economic Activity*, no. 1, ed. Arthur M. Okun and George L. Perry (Washington, D.C.: Brookings Institution, 1974).

21. Martin Feldstein, James Poterba, and Louis Dicks-Mireaux, "The Effective Tax Rate and the Pretax Rate of Return," National Bureau of Economic Research, 1982.

22. Daniel M. Holland and Steward C. Myers, "Profitability and Capital Costs for Manufacturing Corporations and All Nonfinancial Corporations," *American Economic Review* 70 (1980): 320–25.

23. Kim McQuaid, "Big Business and Public Policy in Contemporary United States," *Quarterly Review of Economics and Business* 20 (1980): 57–68; Edward S. Herman, *Corporate Control, Corporate Power* (New York: Cambridge University Press, 1981), pp. 172–84.

24. Murray L. Weidenbaum, *The Impact of Government Regulation* (St. Louis, Mo.: Center for the Study of American Business, Washington University, 1978).

25. Arthur Andersen, *The Study of Government Regulation* (New York: Business Roundtable, 1979).

26. See Comptroller General, *Government Regulatory Activity: Justification, Processes, Impacts, and Alternative* (Washington, D.C.: General Accounting Office, 1977); Robert DeFina, *Public and Private Expenditures for Federal Regulation of Business* (St. Louis, Mo.: Center for the Study of American Business, Washington University, 1977); Data Resources, *The Macroeconomic Impact of Federal Pollution Control Programs, 1978 Assessment* (Washington, D.C.: Council on Environmental Quality, 1979); Mark Green and Norman Waitzman, "Costs, Benefit, and Class," *Working Papers for a New Society* 7 (May–June 1980): 39–51.

27. Charles G. Burck, "A Group Profile of the Fortune 500 Chief Executive," *Fortune*, May 1976, pp. 173ff; and information furnished by *Fortune* magazine.

28. David G. Moore, *Politics and The Corporate Executive* (New York: Conference Board, 1980).

29. J. S. Henry, "From Soap to Soapbox: The Corporate Merchandising of Ideas," *Working Papers for a New Society* 7 (May–June 1980): 55–57.

30. Association of National Advertisers, *Current Company Practices in the Use of Corporate Advertising* (New York, 1982).

31. Advertisement, *New York Times*, July 31, 1981, p. A3.

32. *Newsweek*, September 1980.

33. *Wall Street Journal*, February 26, 1981, pp. 12–13.

34. *New York Times*, March 12, 1981, p. 26.

35. Union Carbide, *The Vital Consensus: American Attitudes on Economic Growth* (New York, 1980).

36. Moore, *Politics and the Corporate Executive*, p. 47.

37. Willard C. Butcher, "Going Public for the Private Enterprise System" (New York: Chase Manhattan Bank, 1980).

38. Edwin M. Epstein, "The Emergence of Political Action Committees," in *Political Finance*, ed. Herbert E. Alexander (Beverly Hills, Calif.: Sage Publications, 1979); Edwin M. Epstein, "Business and Labor Under the Federal Campaign Act of 1971," in *Parties, Interest Groups and Campaign Finance Laws*, ed. Michael J. Malbin (Washington, D.C.: American Enterprise Institute, 1980); Edwin M. Epstein, "The PAC Phenomenon: An Overview," *Arizona Law Review* 22 (1980): 355–72; Herbert E. Alexander, "Corporate Political Behavior," in *Corporations and Their Critics*," eds. Thornton Bradshaw and David Vogel (New York: McGraw-Hill, 1981); and John R. Mulkern, Edward Handler, and Lawrence Godtfredsen, "Corporate PACs as Fundraisers," *California Management Review* 23 (Spring 1981): 49–55.

39. Quoted in Leonard Silk and David Vogel, *Ethics and Profits: The Crisis of Confidence in American Business* (New York: Simon & Schuster, 1976).

40. Ibid.

41. Robert H. Malott, "Corporate Support of Education: Some Strings Attached," *Harvard Business Review* (July–August 1978): 133–38.

42. Irving Kristol, "On Corporate Philanthropy," *Wall Street Jounrnal*, March 21, 1977.

III
Employment Perspectives: Editors' Note

In few areas is the issue of who does the work so bound up with not only the quality and the content of the endeavor but also with the social role of an institution, as in higher education.

If our educational system is to perform its legitimating function in terms of perpetuating the myth of equal opportunity (and to some much lesser extent, create a reality of upward mobility), it must itself serve as an exemplar. It must judge performance on the merits, be accessible to all, and encourage advancement—and all without discrimination. Evelyn Hu-DeHart graphically illustrates the failure of higher education in this regard for women and minorities. In her essay she describes her own experiences as a minority woman faculty member and analyzes some of the general problems women and minorities face in the academy. She also discusses her views on the failure of affirmative action to rectify the situation.

Jean Elshtain cautions those seeking to address parts of this problem by pressing the educational structures to take seriously the commitment to equality to be wary of sacrificing the "authority" of the university. In her article she draws a distinction, which she says many ignore, between "authority" and "domination" and argues that the "authority" of the academy is crucial to the maintenance of intellectual vitality and critical thought. She makes this point in a response to a number of the positions taken by Hu-DeHart and by Ellen Schrecker. In the course of her presentation, Elshtain also reiterates the arguments advanced by Piven and Ollman regarding the importance of intellectual space on the campus and strongly asserts that scholarship and academic excellence must be advanced and not undermined by arguments couched in terms of academic freedom.

The issues addressed by Hu-DeHart and by Elshtain are obviously made more difficult by virtue of the economic situation. According to Emily Abel, economic problems coupled with demographic changes have resulted in the exclusion of large numbers, men as well as women and minorities, from regular academic careers. They either work as poorly paid and insecure part-time teachers or else leave the academy altogether, often, it seems, laboring under the misconception that they will find jobs in business or government that will utilize their academic training. As a result of this, Abel writes, not only are large numbers of young scholars exploited and forced to live marginal economic existences, but possibly more importantly, many creative minds are lost to disciplines that must be expanded and developed.

•9•

The Employment Crisis
in
the Academy
Emily K. Abel

Since the early 1970s, an increasing number of people qualified to teach humanities and social sciences in colleges and universities have been unable to find regular academic employment. Like vast numbers of other Americans, they are discovering that academic credentials no longer can be converted automatically into occupational success. This essay will discuss both the causes of the collapse of the job market in higher education and the implications of this employment crisis for academic freedom.

Many displaced academics entered graduate school during the late 1960s and early 1970s when it was widely assumed that the golden age of higher education would last forever. The graduate student body more than tripled between 1960 and 1975, growing from 314,000 to 1,054,000.[1] In 1970 alone almost 30,000 people received Ph.D.s, and by 1976 the annual rate had risen to 34,000.[2] In fact, more than 25 percent of all Ph.D.s in the humanities ever awarded in the United States were conferred during the 1960s and over 44 percent during the following decade.[3]

However, by the mid-1970s, demographic trends and the fiscal crisis of the state began to result in a contraction of higher education. Although the number of undergraduates burgeoned throughout the 1960s and early 1970s, enrollment growth peaked in 1972,[4] and many observers began to warn that the size of the college-age population would plunge during the 1980s.[5] Moreover, like other large institutions, colleges and universities have been beset by financial problems. Their expenditures grew rapidly during the 1970s as a result of increases in faculty salaries and the rising cost of utilities and supplies.[6] At the same time, because of the deepening recession and "tax revolts," federal and state aid to higher education has been reduced sharply.[7]

Although all human services currently are under siege, higher education may be especially vulnerable. In the mid-1970s, government officials, educators, and members of high-level commissions began to speak with anxiety about the "overeducated work force." Labor unrest, absenteeism, and high turnover rates were attributed to the dissatisfaction of educated workers whose expectations of meaningful and well-paid jobs outstripped the possibilities of obtaining them. The potential dangers emanating from workers with college degrees were the special focus of concern.[8]

Although the production of new Ph.D.s continued to increase throughout the 1970s, fewer positions were available for them. Only 16 percent of all humanities Ph.D.s in 1969 were still seeking employment at the time they received their degrees, whereas a third of the 1979 cohort had not found work by graduation.[9] Furthermore, success in obtaining an initial appointment no longer was a guarantee of permanent academic employment. A growing proportion of faculty positions were nonladder, temporary jobs, which terminated automatically after one to three years.[10] And tenure became increasingly difficult to attain. For one thing, the requirements for tenure and promotion were raised; one or even two books were demanded by schools where previously a few articles had sufficed. Moreover, an increasing number of colleges and universities instituted tenure quotas.[11] Thus, some junior faculty fulfilled all the requirements but still were denied tenure. In the late 1970s, the Modern Language Association warned that only a small fraction of all recent Ph.D.s in English and foreign languages could expect to make lifelong careers of college teaching.[12]

Long-term projections of the academic job market are even more sobering. Although predicting social phenomena is an inexact art at best, most forecasters have been convinced that, throughout the 1980s, teaching jobs will be obtained by only a tiny proportion of the scholars who seek them.[13] One of the gloomiest projections is offered by William G. Bowen, who anticipates that between 1980 and 1995 there will be 100,000 openings for new faculty in all disciplines, the same number as were filled during the three peak years of 1965–67. During these 15 years, about 450,000 new Ph.D.s will be awarded.[14]

Doctorates in the humanities and social sciences are in a particularly vulnerable position. The primary employment of Ph.D. recipients in these fields traditionally has been college teaching.

Although more than half of the Ph.D.s in the physical and life sciences entered nonacademic employment in 1974, 70 percent of the doctorates in the social sciences and 85 to 90 percent of those in the humanities obtained academic positions.[15] Most Ph.D. candidates in the latter fields still focus their expectations exclusively on college teaching.[16] Moreover, these disciplines already have suffered from dramatic shifts in student interest. The proportion of all undergraduates majoring in vocational and professional programs grew from 38 to 58 percent between 1969 and 1976; by contrast, the percentage majoring in the humanities dropped form 9 to 5 percent and in the social sciences from 12 to 8 percent.[17] The surveys of college freshmen conducted annually by Alexander Astin indicate that these disciplines will not recoup their losses in the near future. Six percent of the students entering college in the fall of 1980 expected to concentrate in accounting, 8 percent in business, and 9 percent in engineering. However, just .9 percent expected to major in English, .6 percent in history, .4 percent in sociology and a mere .1 percent in anthropology.[18]

The academic job crisis also falls most heavily on such groups as women and minorities, who traditionally have been underrepresented on university and college faculties.[19] The impact of the collapse of the job market on women has been documented particularly well. Although women as a percentage of Ph.D.s soared during the 1970s, their share of faculty positions did not grow commensurately. Women alone were responsible for the increase in doctoral degrees awarded during the 1970s. The number of men receiving Ph.D.s fell from 25,890 in 1970 to 23,658 in 1978. By contrast, the number of women Ph.D. recipients more than doubled, growing from 3,976 to 8,473.[20] The percentage of women among new doctorates in the humanities rose from 20 percent in 1967 to 39 percent in 1979.[21] However, just as women bear the brunt of unemployment and underemployment in the work force generally, so women academics are affected disproportionately by the job crisis in higher education. In 1979, women doctorates were two to five times as likely as their male counterparts to be unemployed, and they were five times as likely to be employed part time.[22] The fraction of women Ph.D.s who were given terminal, nonladder appointments was almost twice as high as the proportion of men.[23] Finally, women who do secure tenure-track jobs are far less likely than their male colleagues to attain tenure.[24]

The consequences of the employment crisis in higher education thus extend beyond the lives of the individuals affected. Although increasing numbers of observers have begun to bemoan the "lost generation of scholars," few have noted that the voices of particularly large numbers of women and minorities will be silenced. Throughout the late 1960s and 1970s, scholars from these groups enriched a wide range of disciplines by challenging previously unexamined assumptions and introducing new perspectives. The departure of large numbers of women and minorities thus may skew the future development of scholarly inquiry.

THE ACADEMIC PROLETARIAT

Ph.D.s in the humanities and social sciences who are unable to secure regular academic appointments often accept positions that seriously restrict their autonomy. Many became part-time, temporary teachers.[25] The number of part timers in colleges and universities throughout the country began to grow during the 1960s as these institutions sought to cope with soaring enrollment, but the greatest increase of part-time instructors occurred after enrollment had peaked. The use of part-time faculty in colleges and universities was recommended in 1972 by the Carnegie Commission in order to retain "flexibility" during a period of declining or shifting enrollment.[26] Within the next four years, the number of part-time teachers at four-year institutions jumped 73 percent, from 120,000 to 208,000. During the same period, the number of full-time faculty rose by only 18 percent, from 380,000 to 448,000.[27] By 1982, part timers constituted about a third of all faculty in institutions of higher education.[28] They tend to be concentrated in the schools established to accommodate groups previously denied access to higher education. Part-time teachers represented 51 percent of the faculty in community colleges but only 24 percent of the staff in four-year colleges and universities in 1977.[29] Adjuncts are expected to constitute between 38 and 45 percent of the total faculty in academic institutions and 70 to 80 percent in community colleges by 1985.[30]

By hiring large numbers of part-time faculty, colleges and universities have adopted employment practices common in the economy at large. The part-time work force in the United States swelled during the 1950s and 1960s and continued to grow at a slower, though steady, pace throughout the 1970s. In 1980, part-time workers constituted 23 percent of the total labor force.[31] Most part-time jobs are located in the "competitive sector" of the economy, consisting of small retail and service industries, where conditions of work differ dramatically from those in the "monopoly sector." Whereas employees in monopolistic industries typically enjoy relatively high salaries, opportunities for advancement, and job protection, "secondary workers" receive lower pay, have no clear channels for promotion, and lack security of employment.[32] In every respect, part-time faculty positions resemble work in the competitive sector. Although no academic job can be equated with marginal employment in industry, the basic structure of part-time work in colleges and universities is similar to that of jobs in auto repair shops, cleaners, restaurants, and neighborhood grocery stores.

For example, the wages of part-time teachers generally are lower than those of tenure-track faculty.[33] Part timers are paid between 25 and 35 percent less per course than their full-time colleagues.[34] Furthermore, because adjuncts rarely receive either promotions or increments for inflation, this differential tends to increase over time.[35] Very few part timers are eligible for fringe benefits. About 50 percent of adjuncts teaching at least half time receive some retirement coverage, 19 percent are entitled to workers' compensation, and 21 percent are covered by some form of health insurance.[36] But most teach less than 50 percent at any one institution.[37] Just 40 percent of adjuncts working less than half time have access to retirement coverage, 9 percent to workers' compensation, and a mere 5 percent to medical benefits.[38]

Just as employers in business and industry avoid training their marginal workers, so colleges and universities invest few resources in part-time faculty. Only about 15 percent of all postsecondary institutions provide formal orientations for part-time teachers and just 20 percent furnish new adjuncts with information about either students or pedagogy.[39] In most cases, faculty handbooks are not available.[40] More seriously, part timers lack access to research support; very few are reimbursed for travel to professional meetings, and virtually none are eligible for paid research leaves.[41]

Moreover, part-time academic positions are dead-end, not entry-level, jobs. Only a small proportion of part timers can advance in either rank or salary.[42] Also, although department chairs occasionally encourage adjuncts to believe they have secured a "foot in the door," the two sectors of the teaching staff are kept distinct; part timers rarely are promoted to the ranks of the full-time faculty.[43] In fact, teaching part time at one institution does not increase the likelihood of securing a regular position at any other; only a tiny fraction of all part timers who apply for tenure-track positions find them.[44] Like secondary workers in general, adjuncts find themselves consigned to a random series of part-time jobs.

It is true that part-time faculty in higher education have obtained advanced degrees and other secondary employees are unskilled workers. Nevertheless, gas station attendants and short-order cooks who do bring specific skills to their jobs find that their talents go unrewarded. Similarly, part timers often complain that employers routinely discount their achievements and efforts. For example, most are paid a flat fee regardless of academic credentials, publication record, or prior teaching experience. Furthermore, they are discouraged from developing courses in their fields of expertise and very often are relegated to introductory courses.[45] Finally, although their classes frequently are cancelled just prior to the beginning of the semester, or even after a term already has started, they almost never are reimbursed for time spent preparing syllabi or teaching materials.[46]

But by far the most serious complaint of part-time teachers is their lack of job security. Only 15 percent of part timers are even eligible for tenure.[47] At most colleges and universities, they are subject to being bumped by full-time faculty, and at virtually all institutions their jobs are conditional on enrollment.[48] Like other secondary workers, they are temporary labor. About three quarters of all part timers are appointed for only one term at a time; just 5 percent have jobs lasting more than a year.[49] Some administrations specifically discourage adjuncts from believing that they have any claim to reappointment. At one institution where I taught, the vice president cautioned department chairs against allowing any part-time faculty to become "entrenched." Ironically, affirmative action procedures also have undermined whatever frail security part timers have obtained. At many schools, hiring is confined to the part-time ranks, and the administration seeks to demonstrate compliance with federal guidelines by "recycling" adjuncts. Hence, the upper echelons of the faculty remain white male preserves and part-time appointments become revolving doors.

Part timers also lose their jobs first during retrenchment. Because their contracts terminate automatically at the end of each term or year, an administration that wants to reduce labor costs can simply refrain from reappointing part-time staff. Thus, even part-time teachers who have taught regularly at a particular school for several years may disappear without being counted in layoff statistics. One must read between the lines of reports that speak of "cancelling classes," "cutting sections," or "reassigning full-time faculty."[50]

The haphazard manner of recruitment also reduces the security of part-time teachers. At many institutions there are no set times for filing applications and no specific criteria governing selection. Thus, the recruitment process often appears completely capricious. The absence of the elaborate rituals surrounding the appointment of tenure-track faculty serves to underline the point that part timers are casual laborers and readily expendable.

Because adjuncts have an extremely tenuous hold over their jobs, they easily can be purged when they introduce unpopular opinions into the classroom. A recent attack on the Women's Studies Program at California State University, Long Beach, provides a case in point. Like many women's studies programs, this one was staffed almost exclusively by part-time teachers. The classes of some tenured women faculty were cross-listed with the women's studies offerings, but part timers were responsible for the bulk of the core courses. Even those part-time faculty who had taught in the program each year since its founding in 1972 were not considered regular members of the academic community. Not only were they appointed only one semester at a time, but they were ineligible to serve on campus committees and thus did not interact with most other professors; as a result, the program remained marginal to the university. In 1982, the director of the program did have a full-time position, but her appointment also was temporary, not tenure track.

The vulnerability of the program was heightened by its political orientation and pattern of governance. Although Long Beach State is located just one mile from Orange County, most of the staff defined themselves as radical or socialist feminists, and they pointed with pride to their close ties to the women's community. Believing that activism must be integrated with scholarship, they used experience in the women's movement as one criterion for the selection of new faculty and encouraged students to participate in women's groups. The program also attempted to substitute collective decision making for the traditional hierarchical pattern. Although the director alone was entrusted with responsibility for curricular and personnel decisions, she formulated policy with the help of a steering committee, composed of all women's studies faculty, and she insisted that at least one member of this committee attend her meetings with deans.

The administration was in a bind. Because class size was high, the deans had an interest in safeguarding the program. State funding at all California state universities is tied directly to enrollment and, as we have seen, demographic projections warned of an imminent drop in the number of 18- to 22-year-olds. The deans thus understandably were reluctant to dismantle any program that continuously demonstrated its ability to draw students. Nevertheless, the views espoused by women's studies faculty were anathema to virtually all administrators.

An incident in the spring of 1982 provided the administration with an opportunity to restructure the program. Two women from a local Fundamentalist church visited several classes and then filed complaints with the president of the university, charging that the program exhibited a disturbingly prolesbian and pro-Marxist bias.

Right-wing state legislators furnished support to these women. The administration responded by firing two part-time teachers and replacing the director with a tenured faculty member whose politics clashed sharply with those of the rest of the women's studies teachers.

NONACADEMIC EMPLOYMENT

The other option for unemployed Ph.D.s is to find nonteaching jobs. In fact, the number of doctorates entering alternative employment has risen sharply. Whereas 8 percent of humanities Ph.D.s who received their degrees between 1934 and 1968 worked outside higher education in 1977, 20 percent of the 1975–76 cohort had found nonacademic jobs by that date.[51]

This is the solution to the job crisis most widely endorsed by senior academics. True, some have advocated that the number of new graduate students be restricted. Just as other professionals have established their monopolies by regulating entry, so some tenured teachers have recommended that no new graduate programs be founded, that some of the existing programs be dismantled, and that others restrict their intakes.[52] But the self-interest of professors lies in maintaining the size of their graduate enrollments. A steady stream of graduate students enables them to teach their own specialties. As teaching assistants, graduate students release senior professors from the burden of staffing undergraduate courses and grading exams and papers. The time saved can be spent on activities that enhance their professorial reputations and thus, indirectly, earning power. Moreover, professors who do succeed in placing proteges improve their own standing in the profession. Finally, university faculty, like members of other professions, acquire prestige partly on the basis of the status of the clients they serve. Professors in large graduate departments attain higher esteem than faculty members who teach only undergraduate courses, notwithstanding the current emphasis on basic skills. Thus, graduate faculty face a dilemma. Their own privileges rest on contributing to the "overproduction" that has led to the erosion of the status of their profession as a whole.[53]

Because many academics are unwilling to control supply, the more popular remedy is to encourage surplus doctorates to seek alternative employment, primarily in business and government. Proponents of alternative careers frequently portray business as the new frontier; although the number of jobs in higher education is contracting rapidly, opportunities in business are said to be virtually unlimited. An anthropologist writing in the newsletter of the American Anthropological

Association encouraged "enterprising" doctorates to "carve out new domains of employment."[54] A book on careers published by the American Sociological Association urged displaced academics to explore "the unexploited . . . labor market."[55] Similarly, the director of an association of historians spoke of corporations as the "untapped area" for members of her profession.[56]

Publications of the various professional associations also present case studies of Ph.D.s employed outside academia who can serve as role models for disappointed job seekers. For example, the *Anthropology Newsletter* frequently includes a column entitled "Profile of an Anthropologist," which features members of the profession holding nonteaching jobs. The upbeat tone of the October 1979 column is representative. Although a young anthropologist had "considered nothing other than academic employment" while working on her Ph.D., she realized she would be forced to alter her goals when her first foray into the academic job market proved unsuccessful. Initial contacts with anthropologists employed by government agencies convinced her that a job in the civil service could be challenging and satisfying, and she "pursued federal employment aggressively." Within a few months, she found a position that suited her. Soon afterward, she was able to move to Washington, D.C., and to a better job by following "the same aggressive methods." Happily employed as a government anthropologist, she has few regrets about her move away from academia.[57]

The same revivalist optimism—listen and heed and you too can be saved—is contained in articles written by Ph.D.s themselves in the publications of the Modern Language Association. In one, a veritable Horatio Alger story, a man described his experiences after leaving his family behind in order to look for work in a new city. At first his search yielded nothing more promising than a temporary job loading newspapers on a truck, and his lodgings consisted of a furnished room in which he slept with two other men. He became so discouraged that he began to fear for his sanity. Nevertheless, he persevered and eventually found an editorial job on a business journal. He counseled academics who follow his example to remember that, although "they face a struggle, . . . talent and resourcefulness are not long denied an opportunity."[58] The recurrent message to unemployed academics is that the search for nonteaching work may be long, frustrating, and discouraging, but plenty of satisfying and worthwhile jobs exist for people who are determined, aggressive, and eager for a challenge.

Proponents of nonacademic employment also seek to upgrade the image of nonteaching jobs in order to enhance their appeal. Jobs that academics traditionally have viewed with disdain now are touted as honorable pursuits for new Ph.D.s.[59] Recent doctorates are urged to stop romanticizing academia. Universities are no purer than any other social institution; they serve similar ends and operate in similar ways. Moreover, Ph.D.s are told, university and college professors increasingly have been compelled to emulate the techniques of profit-making enterprises; at many institutions, faculty members advertise their courses before the beginning of term and adapt their lectures, syllabi, and grades to student preferences.[60]

But, it is stressed repeatedly, Ph.D.s who seek jobs in government and business are not just pursuing self-interest. Like many of the actions taken by members of professions on their own behalf, the movement into nonacademic employment is couched in the language of altruism. Doctorates bring with them the qualities of mind and character that enabled them to succeed in academia. They are determined, hardworking, resourceful people who have a high level of verbal and analytic skills and an extensive body of knowledge upon which to draw.[61]

In fact, it is asserted, the benefits that derive from employing Ph.D.s extend beyond the specific companies that hire them. Because doctorates can exert an "uplifting" effect on the organizations they enter, their employment will be good for society at large. Although some advocates of nonteaching jobs exhort displaced academics to cease exaggerating the distinction between higher education and the surrounding society, others wax eloquent about the possibility of infusing business and government with the values of academia. The claims held out for doctorates in the humanities are particularly exalted. According to Dorothy G. Harrison, the "dispersion of their scholarly talent throughout society" will result in the "enrichment of commercial or public activities."[62] Ernest R. May envisages an "increase in the sensitivity" of government and business "to the values and needs of the people whom they affect."[63] Paula Backscheider, a professor of English, urged her colleagues to "learn to rejoice" as their students "infiltrate" the world around them: "I think we will feel better about Gulf Oil and Westinghouse and the Center for Government Research when we know that the people who work there share some of our values, our education, and our delights."[64]

Many activities have been designed to facilitate the entry of Ph.D.s into nonacademic careers. For example, several universities have established special summer sessions to retrain doctorates in the humanities and social sciences for management positions in business and industry. The first of these programs was Careers in Business, organized by the Graduate School of Business Administration at New York University in 1977. Within a few years, the University of Virginia,

UCLA, the University of Texas, the University of Pennsylvania, and Harvard University had emulated that model. Lasting between four and twelve weeks, the programs at these various universities provide classes in marketing, accounting, finance, and business organization; help students develop business résumés; introduce them to representatives of the business community; and arrange internships and job interviews.[65]

All the academic associations endorse these "retooling" programs, but their own activities have been directed toward manufacturing demand for academic expertise and redesigning graduate curricula in order to prepare students for employment outside universities. Thus, the American Sociological Association has placed renewed emphasis on applied sociology. In 1979, it established an ad hoc committee on Professional Opportunities in Applied Sociology, which has sought to enhance the prestige of applied research, strengthen the links between academics and practitioners, and examine the training required for positions in industry, research organizations, and consulting firms.[66] The American Anthropological Association has taken steps to improve its relationship with the Society for Applied Anthropology, reserved two seats on its executive board for practicing anthropologists, and established a Committee on Anthropology as a Profession, which, among other goals, seeks to explore and expand employment opportunities in the field of applied anthropology.[67]

Although the humanities lack the same tradition of applied work, members of these disciplines have adopted similar techniques in order to enlarge job options for new scholars. English departments have instituted courses in technical writing and actively encouraged Ph.D. recipients to establish writing programs for corporate executives.[68] Philosophers have campaigned for the inclusion of philosophy courses in the high school curriculum.[69] A subcommittee of the American Philosophical Association's Committee on Placement deals specifically with nonteaching jobs; it recommends that unemployed Ph.D.s find positions in academic administration.[70] Historians have developed the new field of applied or public history which they view as, perhaps, a partial solution to the career difficulties of young historians. The first public history programs were established at the University of California, Santa Barbara, and at Carnegie-Mellon University in 1976. Four years later, more than 50 colleges and universities were teaching courses in such aspects of public history as archival management, historical preservation, museum curatorship, and scholarly editing.[71] During the same period, a new national journal, The Public Historian, was launched, and public historians began holding annual conventions.[72] In 1979, the National Council on Public History was founded to coordinate the work of public historians and publicize their activities.[73] Public historians also enjoy a close relationship with the National Coordinating Committee for the Promotion of History, an association sponsored by the major professional associations for historians, which disseminates information about positions for historians outside universities and seeks to generate demand for the services of historians in both public and private enterprises.[74] The ultimate goal of public historians is "the establishment of an historical office in every organization of significant size."[75]

Many public historians seek to democratize both the creation and study of history. Freed from the need to write works of history that satisfy the narrow definitions of scholarship imposed by many tenure committees, they have produced documentary films, photographic exhibits, and popular articles. Some of these newer history projects have been undertaken in conjunction with both community and trade union groups. All reach a wider audience than traditional scholarly articles.

Nevertheless, the public history movement also illustrates the difficulties confronting those who seek to send unemployed Ph.D.s into nonteaching jobs.[76] First, the optimistic assertions that myriad opportunities await historians who venture outside higher education to seek employment may be greatly exaggerated. Museums, libraries, local history societies, and historic preservation projects all are plagued by severe shortages of funds. Furthermore, even were they able to hire additional staff, they might not grant priority to applicants with advanced degrees in history. The recent attempts to carve out new domains for academic historians have generated considerable resentment among the people already employed in these fields.[77]

Partly by default, many proponents of public history now look to business as the source of new jobs.[78] Both the National Council on Public History and the National Coordinating Committee are waging campaigns to demonstrate that the expertise of historians can be of value to business. One of their most widely publicized examples is Wells Fargo Bank, which established an historical office with a staff of 13 to administer the corporate archives, arrange exhibits in the bank's mini-museum, collect and evaluate Wells Fargo memorabilia, and conduct research for both legal cases and public relations. Their long-range plan is to write a book-length history of the bank.[79]

But there are a number of drawbacks to sending surplus historians into corporations. First, the direction of historical studies could well be distorted. During the past decade, large numbers of historians have radically altered our notions about what is significant in history. Whereas earlier generations of historians explained historical change by focusing on the lives of a few celebrated individuals, social historians turned their attention to groups such as women, ethnic minorities, and workers. Should the historical profession succeed in its aim of placing an historian in every major corporation, history writing might revert to the elitism that previously characterized it.

Furthermore, although bold claims are being advanced for the value of historical analysis to corporations, institutional constraints may well intervene. In fact, most articles exhorting historians to find employment in the private sector contain a basic contradiction. Although they claim that business requires the broad perspective and deep understanding of historians, they also insist that the behavior and attitudes of university-trained historians must be reshaped. In order to fit into corporate settings, academics need to learn to work as members of teams,[80] to meet deadlines,[81] to answer questions posed by others,[82] and to create products that are suited to the demands of their employers.[83] These requirements would involve a total reorientation of historians, transforming them from intellectuals into technicians.[84] As other essays in this volume demonstrate, it would be wrong to draw a dichotomy between the "pure" research conducted in universities and the "tainted" research carried out under corporate auspices. Research priorities of university professors frequently are determined by outside interests. Nevertheless, historians employed by corporations would lack even the minimal independence university-based researchers currently possess.

For example, historians working as team members in business settings would be collaborating, not with academics from other disciplines whose analyses could enrich their own, but rather with businesspeople, whose emphasis on practical results is antithetical to the basic aims of historical inquiry. The premium placed on efficiency and speed in corporations would further undermine historians' autonomy. Historians customarily work without time constraints, not simply because they are concerned with "looking up every source," as one advocate of public history snidely put it, but also because they seek to understand the ramifications of their findings and to relate them to a broader context.[85] Working under strict deadlines, few historians would be able to ponder the theoretical implications of their research.

The requirements that practicing historians answer questions framed by others and hold themselves accountable to their employers rather than to the broad academic community are even greater threats to their independence. Many who would channel historians into business believe that the promulgation of a code of ethics would guarantee the integrity of these historians,[86] but such confidence is unwarranted: Numerous studies have documented the irrelevance of written codes to the behavior of the professionals they are supposed to regulate.[87]

Nevertheless, some proponents of public history go so far as to claim that works of history produced directly under corporate auspices could be more objective than those of university-based academics. Ignoring everything that has been written about the crucial role of outsiders in research, they contend that staff historians would gain "the perspectives and understanding" that come only from "operating inside a corporation."[88] In addition, they assert, corporate historians would be able to document their studies more thoroughly than any other scholars. Here the argument approaches sophistry. They declare that corporate executives understandably are outraged by the "sensationalism" of most academic histories of business and therefore are justified in closing their archives to scholars. Because historians hired by corporations would endorse the activities and goals of private enterprise, they would be permitted to examine any records they chose and thus would be in a position to write the first truly impartial institutional histories.[89] The defects of this argument are readily apparent. First, demanding a prior commitment to particular conclusions totally invalidates the scientific claims of any research. Second, were corporations sincerely interested in obtaining accurate accounts of their pasts, they would open their archives to scholars of diverse political persuasions.

Clearly, it is vital that displaced academics reassess the skills they possess and transfer them directly to other, more remunerative fields. But we should recognize the social costs of channeling large numbers of teachers and scholars into careers in business and industry and seek alternative employment that responds to genuine social needs. We also should work to improve the status and conditions of part-time academic positions. Because the job crisis in higher education stems from political decisions as well as demographic trends, it is necessary to challenge government policies that place defense before social services. Finally, we should make explicit the connections between the collapse of the academic job market and larger problems of work and unemployment in this society and participate in movements that address these broader issues.

NOTES

1. National Center for Education Statistics, *Digest of Education Statistics* (Washington, D.C.: Government Printing Office, 1979), p. 96.

2. Ibid., p. 123.

3. National Research Council, *Employment of Humanities Ph.D.s: A Departure from Traditional Jobs* (Washington, D.C.: National Academy of Sciences, 1980), p. 7.

4. National Center for Education Statistics, *The Condition of Education* (Washington, D.C.: Government Printing Office, 1978), p. 102.

5. See, for example, Allan M. Cartter, *Ph.D.'s and the Academic Labor Market* (New York: McGraw-Hill, 1973).

6. *Condition of Education*, pp. 142–43.

7. Janet Hook and Kim McDonald, "First Effects of U.S. Budget Cuts Beginning to Hit Many Colleges," *Chronicle of Higher Education*, December 2, 1981, p. 1; Jack Magarrell, "Serious Financial Problems Facing States Portend a Lean Year for Public Colleges," *Chronicle of Higher Education*, February 17, 1981, p. 1; Jack Magarrell, "Falling State Revenues, Cuts in Payrolls Bring Hard Times to Public Institutions," *Chronicle of Higher Education*, February 10, 1982, p. 1; Jack Magarrell, "Public Colleges in Michigan and Ohio Troubled by Further Efforts to Reduce State Spending," *Chronicle of Higher Education*, April 7, 1982, p. 8.

8. See Carnegie Commission on Higher Education, *College Graduates and Jobs* (New York: McGraw-Hill, 1973), p. 5; see *Work in America, Report of a Special Task Force to the Secretary of Health, Education and Welfare* (Cambridge, Mass.: MIT Press, 1973), pp. 134–38.

9. Lewis C. Solmon, Laura Kent, Nancy L. Ochsner, and Margo-Lea Hurwicz, *Underemployed Ph.D.'s* (Lexington, Mass.: Lexington Books, 1981), p. 20.

10. Modern Language Association, "A Statement on the Academic Job Market in Language and Literature" (n.d.).

11. Charlotte V. Kuh, *Market Conditions and Tenure for Ph.D.s in U.S. Higher Education*, Carnegie Council on Policy Studies in Higher Education, Technical Report no. 3, July 1977; Roy Radner and Charlotte V. Kuh, *Market Conditions and Tenure in U.S. Higher Education: 1955–1973*, Carnegie Council on Policy Studies in Higher Education, Technical Report no. 2, July 1977; Roy Radner and Charlotte Kuh, *Preserving a Lost Generation: Policies to Assure a Steady Flow of Young Scholars until the Year 2000*, Carnegie Council on Policy Studies in Higher Education, Report, October 1978, p. 2.

12. Modern Language Association, "Statement on the Academic Job Market."

13. Cartter, *Ph.D.'s*; R. G. D'Andrade, E. A. Hammel, D. L. Adkins, and C. K. McDaniel, "Academic Opportunity in Anthropology, 1974–90," *American Anthropologist 77*, (December 1975): 753–73; Stephen Dresch, "Educational Saturation: A Demographic-Economic Model," *AAUP Bulletin 60* (October 1975): 239–46; Luis Fernandez, *U.S. Doctorate Faculty After the Boom: Demographic Predictions to 2000*, Carnegie Council on Policy Studies in Higher Education, Technical Report no. 4, April 1978; Richard B. Freeman, *The Over-Educated American* (New York: Academic Press, 1976); Solmon et al., *Underemployed Ph.D.'s*, p. 1.

14. William G. Bowen, *Graduate Education in the Arts and Sciences: Prospects for the Future, Report of the President* (Princeton, N.J.: Princeton University, 1981), pp. 19–20.

15. Allan M. Cartter, "The Academic Labor Market," in *Higher Education and the Labor Market*, ed. Margaret S. Gordon (New York: McGraw-Hill, 1974), p. 301.

16. Lewis C. Solmon, Nancy L. Ochsner, and Margo-Lea Hurwicz, *Alternative Careers for Humanities Ph.D.s* (New York: Praeger, 1979), p. 54.

17. Verne Stadtman, *Academic Adaptations: Higher Education Prepares for the 1980s and 1990s* (San Francisco: Jossey-Bass, 1980), p. 3.

18. *Chronicle of Higher Education*, January 28, 1980, pp. 4–5.

19. See National Research Council, *Career Outcomes in a Matched Sample of Men and Women Ph.D.s* (Washington, D.C.: National Academy Press, 1981); see National Research Council, *Employment of Minority Ph.D.s: Change Over Time* (Washington, D.C.: National Academy Press, 1981).

20. National Center for Education Statistics, *Digest of Education Statistics* (Washington, D.C.: Government Printing Office, 1980), p. 102.

21. Solmon, et al., *Underemployed Ph.D.'s*, p. 127.

22. National Research Council, *Career Outcomes*, p. 8.

23. Ibid., p. 46.

24. Ibid., p. xvii.

25. National Research Council, *Employment of Humanities Ph.D.'s*, p. 33.

26. Carnegie Commission on Higher Education, *The More Effective Use of Resources: An Imperative for Higher Education* (New York: McGraw-Hill, 1972), p. 113.

27. *Digest of Education Statistics*, p. 104.

28. David W. Leslie, Samuel E. Kellams, and G. Manny Gunne, *Part-Time Faculty in American Higher Education* (New York: Praeger, 1982), p. 19.

29. Howard P. Tuckman, Jaime Caldwell, and William Vogler, "Part-timers and the Academic Labor Market in the Eighties," *American Sociologist* 13 (November 1978): 185.

30. Ibid.

31. *Special Labor Force Report 244* (Washington, D.C.: Department of Labor, Bureau of Labor Statistics, 1981), p. 7.

32. Richard Edwards, *Contested Terrain: The Transformation of the Workplace in the Twentieth Century* (New York: Basic Books, 1979), pp. 163–99; see also Robert E. Roemer and James E. Schnitz, "Academic Employment as Day Labor: The Dual Labor Market in Higher Education," *Journal of Higher Education* 53 (1982): 514–31.

33. There is no uniformity among the salaries of part-time faculty. Adjuncts earn the most at universities, somewhat less at four-year colleges, and the least at community colleges; however, even within one type of institution, their wages vary significantly. Howard P. Tuckman and Jaime Caldwell, "The Determinants of Variations in Earnings among Part-Time Faculty," in *Part-Time Faculty Series*, Howard P. Tuckman, William D. Vogler and Jaime Caldwell (Washington, D.C.: American Association of University Professors, 1978), p. 55.

34. Tuckman, Caldwell, and Vogler, "Academic Labor Market," p. 187.

35. Leslie et al., *Part-Time Faculty*, p. 31; Tuckman, Caldwell, and Vogler, "Academic Labor Market," p. 192.

36. Tuckman, Caldwell, and Vogler, "Academic Labor Market," p. 187.

37. In fact, some institutions that provide fringe benefits to adjuncts teaching more than 50 percent are careful to ensure that most part timers work less than half time.

38. Tuckman, Caldwell, and Vogler, "Academic Labor Market," p. 187.

39. Leslie et al., *Part-Time Faculty*, p. 81–82.

40. Ibid, p. 103.

41. Ibid, p. 84.

42. Ibid, p. 78; Tuckman and Caldwell, "Variations in Earnings," in *Part-Time Faculty Series*, p. 66.

43. See Leslie et al., *Part-Time Faculty*, p. 44.

44. Howard P. Tuckman, Jaime Caldwell, and William D. Vogler, "Part-Time Employment and Career Progression," in *Part-Time Faculty Series*, p. 82.

45. Seventy-five percent of adjuncts in community colleges teach introductory courses, 52 percent in four-year colleges, and 40 percent in universities. Howard P. Tuckman and William D. Vogler, "The 'Part' in Part-Time Wages," *AAUP Bulletin* (May 1978): 71. In the California State University and College system in 1976, 45 percent of the

classes taught by part timers were lower division courses, compared to only 31 percent of those taught by full-time faculty. Office of the Chancellor, California State University and Colleges, *Task Force on Temporary Faculty* (December 1977), Appendix II, p. b.

46. Leslie et al., *Part-Time Faculty*, p. 78.

47. Ibid, p. 49.

48. Ibid, pp. 88–89.

49. Tuckman and Vogler, "Part-Time Wages," p. 74.

50. Because administrators generally do not release information about the number of part timers they employ, reliable information about the dismissal of adjuncts rarely is available. Nevertheless, government officials in California reported that 7,000 part-time community college faculty, or just under one-quarter of all adjuncts in the system, lost their jobs immediately after the passage of Proposition 13; the number of full-time teachers declined only 2 percent. Chancellor's Office, California Community Colleges, "Summary of Proposition 13 Impact on Community College Programs, Students, Faculty, and Finance" (January 1979), p. 3.

51. National Research Council, *Humanities Ph.D.'s*, p. 51.

52. See John Algeo, "After the Fall: Some Observations on Graduate Curricula," *Profession 78* (New York: Modern Language Association, 1978), pp. 16–18; H. M. Blalock, "Comment," *American Sociologist* 13, (November 1978): 219–20; Ward Hellstrom, "Academic Responsibility and the Job Market," *Profession 80* (New York: Modern Language Association, 1980), p. 24; Quentin M. Hope, "Notes on the Profession," *Employment and the Profession*, Special Joint Issue, Bulletins of the Association of Departments of English and the Association of Departments of Foreign Languages (September 1976), p. 19; Paul Kay, "The Myth of Nonacademic Employment: Observations on the Growth of an Ideology," *American Sociologist* 13, (November 1978): 216–19; Marilyn Williamson, "Give Them More Than They Seek," *Employment and the Profession*, p. 27; Neal Woodruff, "Only Connect," *Employment and the Profession*, pp. 73–76.

53. Algeo, "After the Fall," pp. 18–19; Hellstrom, "Responsibility," pp. 24–25; Hope, "Notes," p. 20; Stuart Tave, "The Guilt of the Professor," *Profession 79* (New York: Modern Language Association, 1979), p. 25; see David G. Brown, *The Mobile Professors* (Washington, D.C.: American Council on Education, 1967), p. 120.

54. Steve Barnett, quoted in "Profile of an Anthropologist," *Anthropology Newsletter* 21 (April 1980): 6.

55. Sharon K. Panian and Melvin L. DeFleur, *Sociologists in Non-Academic Employment* (Washington, D.C.: American Sociological Association, n.d.), p. 35.

56. Comments of Arnita Jones in "First National Symposium on Public History: A Report," *The Public Historian* 2 (Fall 1979): 13.

57. "Profile of an Anthropologist," *Anthropology Newsletter* (October 1979): 20.

58. Richard H. Bamble, "Hitch Your Wagon to a Star: Confessions of a Postacademic Job Seeker," *Profession 80*, pp. 20–23.

59. See Woodrull, "Only Connect," p. 77.

60. Interview with June Millett, Placement Officer, August 1980.

61. See Paula Backscheider, "Into All the World," *ADE Bulletin* 68 (Summer 1981): 17; Kenneth W. Haas, "The Value of a Professional English Education," *Employment and the Profession*, p. 62; see also Rita D. Jacobs, *The Useful Humanists: Alternative Careers for Ph.D.s in the Humanities* (New York: Rockefeller Foundation, 1977), p. 21.

62. Dorothy G. Harrison, "The Nonacademic Job Market," *Employment and the Profession*, p. 68.

63. Ernest R. May, "Nonacdemic Career Possibilities," *Employment and the Profession*, p. 72.

64. Backscheider, "All the World," p. 19. For a discussion of similar arguments employed to convince community college students to enroll in vocational programs, see

Fred L. Pincus, "The False Promises of Community Colleges: Class Conflict and Vocational Education," *Harvard Educational Review* 50 (August 1980): 332–61.

65. Interview with Patricia Katsky, Program Coordinator, Careers in Business for Ph.D.s, UCLA, August 1980; interview with Ernest Kurnow, Director, Careers in Business, New York University, New York, December 1980; Jill Felzan, "Retooling the Historian: Careers in Business Programs," *The Public Historian* 3, (Summer 1981): 133–43.

66. Interview with Howard Freeman, Chairman, Ad Hoc Committee on Professional Opportunities in Applied Sociology, American Sociological Association, Los Angeles, May 1981; interview with Russell Dynes, Executive Director, American Sociological Association, Washington, D.C., December 1980; American Sociological Association, *Footnotes* (February 1980): 7; (August 1980), p. 20; (December 1980), pp. 1–4; see also Beverly Watkins, " 'Applied' Sociologist Find Gaps in Training for Non-Academic Jobs," *Chronicle of Higher Education*, September 10, 1979, p. 12.

67. Interview with Robert Cimino, Director, Departmental Services Program, American Anthropological Association, Washington, D.C., December 1980; see Rayna Rapp, "Focusing on Non-Traditional, Non-Academic Anthropology: History, Science, Politics, Ethnics," Paper presented at the annual convention, American Anthropological Association, Los Angeles, November 1981.

68. Interview with Kirschner; see Andrew D. Turnbull, "Wanted: Humanists to Write Computer Manuals," *Chronicle of Higher Education*, October 20, 1982, p. 23.

69. Janet Hook, "Students of Popular Culture Try to Recruit Philosophers," *Chronicle of Higher Education*, January 6, 1982, p. 9.

70. American Philosophical Association, *Proceedings* 51 (August 1978): 761.

71. Nina Kressner Cobb, "Necessity Was the Mother: The Institute for Research in History," *The Public Historian* (Spring): 78. However, some of these programs are at the undergraduate, not the graduate, level.

72. See G. Wesley Johnson, Peter N. Stearns, and Joel A. Tarr, "Public History: A New Area of Training, Research and Employment," American Historical Association, *Newsletter* (March 1980): 7.

73. See "Formation of the National Council on Public History," *The Public Historian* (Fall 1979): 83.

74. Arnita Jones, "The National Coordinating Committee: Programs and Possibilities," *The Public Historian* 1(Fall 1978): 49–60; interview with Page Miller, Director, National Coordinating Committee for the Promotion of History, Washington, D.C., December 1981. For an analysis of demand creation in the field of law, see Richard L. Abel, "Toward a Political Economy of Lawyers Services," *Wisconsin Law Review* (1981): 1117–87.

75. Robert Kelley, "Public History: Its Origins, Nature, and Prospects," *The Public Historian* 1 (Fall 1978): 22.

76. Two articles that criticize some aspects of the public history movement are Howard Green, "A Critique of the Professional Public History Movement," *Radical History Review* (Fall 1981): 164–71 and Ronald J. Grele, "Whose Public? Whose History? What Is the Goal of a Public Historian?" *The Public Historian* (Winter 1981): 40–48.

77. See Jerry George, "Take a 'Public Historian' to Lunch," *History News* (May 1979): 1; Green, "Critique," pp. 165–66.

78. See, for example, Kelley, "Public History," p. 22.

79. Harold P. Anderson, Comments, in "First National Symposium on Public History: A Report," *The Public Historian* 2 (Fall 1979): 50–52; Anderson, "The Corporate History Department: The Wells Fargo Model," *The Public Historian* 3 (Summer 1981): 25–29; Janis MacKenzie, "Wells Fargo and Company: Banking on the Past," National Coordinating Council Supplement no. 25. Of course, Wells Fargo may well be unique. Although these historians perform a wide range of services, the impetus behind the establishment of an

historical office was a desire to enhance the image of Wells Fargo as an institution with a long and distinguished pedigree. Other private enterprises may well have far less incentive to hire a staff of historians. See Richard Forman, "History Inside Business," *The Public Historian* 3 (Summer 1981): 49; Albro Martin, "The Office of the Corporate Historian: Organization and Functions," *The Public Historian* 3 (Summer 1981): 11; Robert W. Pomeroy, "Historians' Skills and Business Needs," *The Public Historian* 1 (Winter 1979): 8; Ernest Swiger, Jr., "Historians and Corporate Consulting," *The Public Historian* 3 (Summer 1981), p. 101.

80. Comments by Anderson, p. 52; G. Wesley Johnson, "Editor's Preface," *The Public Historian* 1 (Fall 1978): p. 7.

81. See "First National Symposium," p. 41; Lawrence Degraaf, "Summary: An Academic Perspective," *The Public Historian* 2 (Spring 1980): 60; *Outside Academe: New Ways of Working in the Humanities* (New York: Haworth and Institute for Research in History, 1981), p. 30.

82. See Johnson, "Editor's Preface," p. 8; Kelley, "Public History," p. 18; see also Edward D. Berkowitz, "The Historian as Policy Analyst: The Challenge of HEW," *The Public Historian* 1 (Spring 1979): 17.

83. See "First National Symposium," p. 41; Degraaf, "Summary," p. 69.

84. For the distinction between intellectuals and technicians, see Alvin W. Gouldner, *The Future of Intellectuals and the Rise of the New Class: A Frame of Reference, Theses, Conjectures, Arguments, and an Historical Perspective on the Role of Intellectuals and Intelligentsia in the International Class Contest of the Modern Era* (New York: Seabury Press, 1979).

85. DeGraaf, "Summary," p. 69.

86. See Johnson, "Editor's Preface," p. 9.

87. See Abel, "Political Economy."

88. Forman, "Business," pp. 44–45.

89. See Comments by Anderson, p. 52; Forman, "Business," p. 44; Barbara Benson Kohn, "Corporate History and the Corporate History Department: Manufacturers Hanover Trust Company," *The Public Historian* 3 (Summer 1981): 36; W. David Lewis and Wesley Phillips Newton, "The Writing of Corporate History," *The Public Historian* 3 (Summer 1981): 65–67.

•10•

Women, Minorities, and Academic Freedom

Evelyn Hu-DeHart

As an Asian woman teaching Latin American history who used to direct a women's studies program, I am a double token and serve multiple functions. My university and my department, one would think, should be rather pleased with me. But these very same conditions of my person and my work also contribute to my lack of confidence, not in myself, but in the university, where, despite my usefulness and my achievements, my chances for long-term academic security and freedom under the current system are in question. Not only is my individual career at stake, but what I represent personally as a role model and what I do in my teaching, research, and community activities are in peril in these economic and politically conservative times. I will develop in this chapter an historical and contemporary analysis of the experience and prospects for women and minority professionals in American colleges and universities, occasionally using myself and other colleagues for purposes of illustration, and conclude with a few suggestions for action.

Actually, my data speak more to the issue of women academics, both white and minority, and less to the experience of minority men. There are several reasons for this slant. First of all, there has been considerable research and thinking done on the subject of women academics in the last decade. Much of the study on women does not distinguish between white and minority women, because our experiences seem to have more in common than they diverge. Of course, minority women often do suffer from the double discrimination of race and sex, although, ironically, for affirmative action statistical purposes, as in my own case, we can be very useful and even sought after on the hiring and entry level. Thus, although a minority woman, I have found more to identify with in the collective of women on campus, regardless of race or ethnic origin, than in the collective of minorities.

One problem of minority identification is that the status encompasses so many different groups, blacks, Asians, Hispanics, Native Americans, each with a distinct historical experience and record in academe. Furthermore, certain types of minority men, notably Chinese and Japanese, have fared so well in strong, prestigious, and well-paid disciplines, such as mathematics, the natural and physical sciences, and engineering, that they do not, in fact, face the issue of underrepresentation. There is no comparable positive experience for any group of women, except in the case of teachers and women's colleges, and in traditional female departments such as nursing and home economics, where the pay and the status are generally low.

In other minority groups, such as black and Hispanic, while there is still serious underrepresentation, the men have progressed considerably farther than the women, for the simple fact that they are, after all, men in an institution designed for men.[1] Related to this, society in general and the university in particular have responded much better in attitude, if not in fact, to the civil rights issue of race discrimination than sex discrimination, which is probably more complex and certainly more threatening to the almost exclusively male power structure of the university. Furthermore, due to the larger number and wider distribution of women in society and on campuses, as opposed to the greater segregation of various minority groups, men in general have simply found it more difficult to come to terms with sexism and sex discrimination.[2]

The key issue I wish to address, then, is the gross and worsening underrepresentation of women in American academe, one that gets progressively worse as we move up the ranks. Given the large and growing number of women in graduate school and among recent Ph.D.s, this is a disturbing phenomenon that needs examination, explanation, and correction. Differences between women in general, and minority men notwithstanding, much of what I have to say about the obstacles facing women can be readily generalized to include minority men. Even as I focus on women, I shall make these connections whenever relevant.

THE STATUS OF WOMEN IN ACADEME

In 1978, the American Association of University Women published an update of its 1970 report on the status of women in academe. The new report was based on data gathered in 1976. The study's findings are not at all encouraging and echo similar findings in other studies made in the 1970s. It revealed that women have made no progress in the six intervening years, comprising in 1976 as in 1970 no more than one-fourth of college and university faculties. Moreover, this figure of 25 percent is misleading, for it does not immediately indicate the skewed distribution of women within all ranks of the faculty. The truth is, "Women are more likely to occupy positions in the lower ranks, to be without tenure, or to hold positions not even on the tenure ladder, for example, part-time faculty members, instructors, lecturers and non-teaching personnel." Even at the women's colleges, contrary to a widely held popular notion, women are concentrated in the lower ranks and do not comprise even half of the faculty. More specifically, full-time faculty women account for only 8 percent of full professors, 16 percent of associate professors, 28 percent of assistant professors, and 49 percent of instructors; only 16.5 percent of all tenured faculty are women. The larger and more prestigious the institution, public or private, the fewer the women. At all institutions, there are more women holding part-time than full-time appointments.[3]

In absolute terms women have gained ground during the postwar educational boom. In relative terms, however, women have lost ground, even as they have entered and completed graduate programs leading to the Ph.D. degree in ever larger numbers.

Two points need emphasizing. One, women are still largely to be found in women's colleges and in traditional female disciplines and departments. Hence, with more women entering academe, they tend to cluster in areas and schools where women already dominate. By the same token, men continue to prevail in traditional male departments, especially in large private and public universities where research and graduate training take place, and accordingly, where there is the highest pay, prestige, and faculty power. Two, women are more subject to "marginal" appointments, those on "soft" money, irregular, nonladder (that is, with no prospect of promotion up the ranks and ultimately toward tenure consideration), fringe, underprivileged, and underpaid. Some scholars have convincingly applied Braverman's "logic of deskilling" to explain this dichotomy between men and women academic professionals. Braverman observed that in professional work there tends to develop a split "between prestige jobs with good pay, autonomy, and opportunities for growth and development and a new class of more routinized, poorly paid jobs with little autonomy and which are unconnected by promotion ladders to prestige jobs in the profession."[4]

During this century and especially after World War II, more women have entered graduate school and earned the highest degrees. We have witnessed the manifold expansion of American higher education with corresponding increased opportunities for training and careers in academe. And, more recently, the civil rights and women's movements have promoted, specifically with affirmative action, the elimination of sex and race discrimination in hiring and promotion. These signs of progress notwithstanding, and contrary to all expectations, women have actually suffered status decline rather than improvement in academe.[5]

There is one further gross inequity between men and women in academe: Women faculty continue to experience considerable wage discrimination. In the history profession, for example, a 1981 report found that "the average woman historian earns $3,000 a year less than her male counterpart."[6]

THE IMPERFECT MERITOCRACY

The foundation of the academic system, in hiring as well as retention and promotion, is the merit principle—that is, individuals are sought, hired, and promoted strictly on the basis of individual talent and achievements. Moreover, this meritocracy supposedly functions in a fair, consistent, and unrestricted manner. Thus, all those who move up through the ranks are unquestionably deserving, and those who do not are simply personal failures.

If one accepts this assumption regarding the meritocracy, it follows then that women (and most minorities) are underrepresented in academe because (1) there are numerically not enough qualified women candidates for the hiring pools, and (2) the available women candidates just do not measure up to men in terms of qualifications. Women, this argument goes on to point out, take themselves less seriously professionally, lack professional commitment and ability, publish less, and are generally less capable. In short, they are "less ambitious, . . . less productive, . . . earn their advanced degrees later in life than males, and . . . are more casual about their careers."[7] One could almost hear white male department heads and deans sigh in frustration—if only there were more well-qualified women to hire, they would have gladly done so.

To test the validity of these assumptions, that the meritocracy exists and works, recent studies have examined closely the premises cited to explain women's low representation and low status. They found little evidence to support such contentions. One study of 20,000

PH.Ds reports women to be superior to male counterparts on all measures and in all specializations: brighter by any index than men and equal in productivity in terms of books and articles published. It concludes, "Controlling factors relevant to rank, tenure, and salary, sex remains the critical variable between the status of women and men faculty."[8]

When statistical controls measuring academic ability or scholarly achievements are not applied, women academics as a group are less productive professionally than men as a group. Researchers looking into this situation suggest that the reason lies not in women's innate intellectual inferiority but rather in the pattern of their professional activity: proportionately many more women than men are heavily involved in areas such as nursing and education, where teaching, rather than research, prevails, and many more women than men are concentrated in the heavily teaching-oriented ranks of assistant professors, lecturers, and instructors—these latter two without even much access to research facilities, grants, and release time to be more productive.[9]

Regarding the question of quantity, the number of women doctorates far outstrips their success at being hired and promoted. In 1974–75, for example, Princeton, Yale, and Harvard had only 2.7 percent women associate or full professors, up from 1 percent five years earlier. Yet these same elite institutions trained proportionately many more women than they were willing to hire from each other. As early as 1962–63, 16 percent of their doctorates were granted to women. The truth is, the women who do not drop out of graduate school and do not drop out of the job market "are self-selected for commitment as well as ability."[10]

Going beyond quantity and quality, researchers have found other inhibitors to women's progress through the academic career. They have discovered that, indeed, men are able to compete more successfully in the meritocracy as it is set up, not because they are inherently superior to women, but because the system is tailored for the traditional white male with his traditional wife and supportive children who stay out of his hair "when daddy is working." Most women, especially married women with children, simply do not find this image of the career culture and family applicable to their personal situation. Much like men in corporations and the ministry, male academics have in fact a "two-person single career"—that is, their wives take up certain unpaid responsibilities to further the husbands' career, from entertaining colleagues to enhance their collegiality, to domestic work and child care to foster a stable, happy family environment, to helping with research, typing, and even writing.

We need only read the prefaces to most academic monographs written by our male colleagues to take note of this phenomenon. On the other hand, few women professors enjoy the social and research/secretarial assistance of a husband in their professional work.

Career and family conflicts, therefore, are mostly characteristic of women and thus considered "women's problems." These are, then, not proper considerations within the traditional meritocratic academic system. For the women, "[I]t is *her* problem to choose between a few prepackaged options: being a housewife, or professor, or trying to piece together a collage of wife, mother and traditional career."[11]

Not surprisingly, then, most women who have chosen to enter this traditional male career have also chosen to forsake the thought of having a family, because, sadly, that seems to be the choice forced upon them by the system. Most conclude that it would be impossible to assume the additional burden of a "double day" and still try to finish their degree, land a job, and advance in their career. One recent study shows that fewer than half of women academics are married, compared to almost 90 percent of the men. About one-third of the women in academe have children, compared to more than two-thirds of the men, and those women tend to have fewer children than men with families. Moreover, married women are substantially less likely to achieve tenure than unmarried women, who are still less likely to earn tenure than married men with children.[12]

THE FAILED PROMISE OF AFFIRMATIVE ACTION

Affirmative action is one of those peculiar creations that is at once both more and less than what it should be. To its detractors in the university, it threatens to lower standards and destroy the meritocracy as it now stands. To those who wanted to believe in it, mostly women and minorities, it promised to strengthen the merit principle but has sadly failed to deliver. Part of its failure, I must admit, is probably our own fault, because we did not immediately see through its political limitations and therefore formed unrealistically high expectations of its ability to bring about significant changes. Simply put, affirmative action may have opened some doors for women and minorities to enter academe, but it has done very little to establish more equitable bases for competition within the meritocracy. For women, it has merely allowed more women to compete with traditional men in the traditional career pattern. Thus, ironically, we are witnessing the status decline of women precisely when affirmative action has been in operation. The fact of the matter is that affirmative action has done nothing at all to facilitate the upward mobility of women in the academic system, their promotion into the tenured ranks and into high-level administration where important governing and curriculum decisions are made.

At best, affirmative action has addressed only the more blatant forms of discrimination on campuses, such as in housing, athletics, and printed matter. "To a much lesser degree is attention devoted to the more subtle forms of discrimination such as recruitment and hiring practices, promotion policies and procedures, and financial assistance. . . . Many collegiate institutions have not been able to move beyond simple correction of noncompliance to push plans and programs that will compensate for past and present discrimination or to prevent recurrence of discrimination in the future."[13] Their compliance has been more perfunctory than substantive.

One dubious achievement of affirmative action has been to sensitize white male administrators to overt racist and sexist language and practices, so as to appear more attuned to fair play and to the interests of women and minorities. Furthermore, in an insidious manner, one familiar ploy of some compliance officials is to pit minorities against women, leading them falsely to think that they must compete for the same small "slice of the pie."[14]

Affirmative action officers and affirmative action programs have yet to challenge the basic structure of inequity built into the meritocratic system. There is no reason why a system that has traditionally been flexible regarding the work needs of the male professor—by providing leaves of absences for research, reduced teaching load upon assumption of administrative duties, joint and part-time appointments for senior faculty—cannot be equally flexible in providing for the special needs of the female professor.[15]

Yet few affirmative action programs have raised, for example, the issue of role conflicts women may face between career and family. As a rule, they do not address problems such as maternity leave and child care, in short, the special needs and interests of women that may, at certain times in their lives, slow down or inhibit career advancement. They do not question the fact that while university administrators are accustomed to dealing with male professors who suffer a variety of ailments, from nervous breakdowns to alcoholism, most are downright insensitive to women's demands for a clear policy guideline regarding pregnancy.

In my own case, when I had my second child in 1979, my provost denied me a maternity leave, because he did not "believe in them." Hence I resumed my teaching duties one week after giving birth. When I had my first child in 1975, I did not even know enough to ask for a maternity leave. As it turned out, the provost had violated a recently enacted act of Congress that ruled that maternity must be included within any employer's disability leave policy. Every year I know of a few white male colleagues who have taken up to six months of paid disability leave due to depression or nervous breakdown; I know few women colleagues who are married, fewer still who have small children, and none who has taken a paid maternity leave.

There are two interesting perceptions of affirmative action functions and goals, both of which turn out to be false. One, to those who wanted to believe in it, it promised that, finally, women and minority academics would be allowed to go as far as their talents and ambitions permit. The other, which can be labeled the "white male backlash," is that affirmative action will destroy the meritocracy, because it will force academic institutions to hire unqualified or less qualified women and minorities in place of better qualified candidates, presumably white and male. Among prestigious individuals who warned of this danger was Philip Handler, past president of the American Academy of Sciences. This charge rests on the assumptions mentioned above, that there are not enough excellent women and minority candidates to meet the quota forced upon the academies. Unfortunately, some women and minorities have internalized the suspicion of inferiority and suffer from what black woman historian Nell Painter has aptly termed the "stigma of affirmative action."[16]

TOKENISM AND THE SUPERWOMAN

Perhaps the most tangible results of affirmative action chipping faintheartedly and ineffectually at the meritocracy are the twin phenomena of "tokenism" and the "superwoman."

Tokenism, or the superficial representation of sexual, racial, or ethnic minorities, has many manifestations. It means that as the token woman or minority or both rolled into one, she is called upon to serve on more committees than is the usual. This may make the committee look good, but often takes away precious time from the woman to devote to her work and family, if she has one. There is great pressure on her to accept all such committee assignments, for if she declines she may be subject to charges of lack of cooperation with affirmative action, not to mention lack of collegiality and devotion to community service. Yet, when promotion time comes, it is unclear how much credit she receives for this extra service.

Tokenism also means the perpetuation of stereotypes, regarding the way we look and the way we act. As long as we are tokens and hence numerically insignificant, we cannot provide the variety of images and behavior patterns to erode the popular fixed notions of how a woman intellectual should look and act. It means that women and minorities are permitted less individuality in the day-to-day interaction with students and colleagues and in their work habits. Brilliant but tactless and sloppy men are far more readily accepted as colleagues than equally brillant but aggressive and outspoken women and minorities. A token is in itself a stereotype.

At the same time, there are some serious burdens and responsibilities to being one of a few women or minority-group members on a college faculty. As the one woman or the one minority, or both in one, all eyes are on our behavior and our performance. We cannot afford a single mistake, and if we slip or fail, we affect the reputation and future prospects of the entire group or groups that we personally represent. In short, far from lowering standards, a higher standard of performance is imposed upon us, and we carry the burden of proof for ourselves and others like us. No similar pressure befalls the white male colleague. Whoever heard the remark: "We gave a white male a chance, and look how it worked out!" When we fail, we fail for all women and all minorities, but when a white male fails, he simply fails as an individual. On the other hand, given the nature of tokenism, it is questionable whether a successful woman or minority paves the way for others.

Besides heavier committee service, being a woman and minority probably entails more time spent on counseling, particularly of women and minority students. In addition, because women and minority members of a department often happen to be the younger members, and likely to be more socially and politically aware than the older faculty, they are sought out more frequently by students who can identify better with their age and attitudes. Whether we like or or not, whether we feel comfortable or not, we as minorities or women fill the function of role models, and I think we have an obligation to assume this responsibility and to speak frankly about our experiences. I was first awakened to this responsibility when, during my second year of teaching, a senior woman told me she took my course on the Cuban revolution not so much because she was interested in Cuba, but because she did not feel she could graduate from college without having had at least one woman professor, in order to validate her own sense of self-worth. Since then, I have become much more conscious of what I, as a woman professor, mean to many of my students and that my importance to them lies in much more than any course material I may impart to them in the classroom.

Finally, speaking professionally, what does it mean to be a token, to be that one woman or minority in a department full of white males? It means in most cases that we are not the beneficiary of what one of my woman colleagues in biology graphically labels the "greenhouse effect." That is, being the one woman or minority entering the system, with no woman or minority colleague on the senior level, we often have no "patron" to nurture, groom, and otherwise guide us through a system where there are few written rules, but many do's and don'ts, to give us inspiration and encouragement, to serve as role models for us. We are not part of the "old boys" who go out for beer and baseball on the weekends, to develop the kind of "collegiality" that in fact figures prominently in promotion considerations, but that remains one of the most subjectively measured unwritten criteria.

The superwoman is that woman professor, particularly one who is married and has children, who apparently manages both career and family well despite all odds. She also allows the system to claim that, indeed, if the woman is sufficiently qualified and motivated, the meritocracy works for her. "Qualified," however, as many women have found out, means "only the best in the field." During the preparation for an academic career, from graduate school on, women less motivated, committed, or capable have selected themselves out, compared to the male candidate whose path is relatively easier. As the woman academic Constance Carroll pointedly argues: "You must be better qualified than the men, . . . more articulate, . . . more aggressive, . . . have more stamina to face inevitable setbacks, have more patience, since you will advance more slowly, and above all, remain feminine and not appear threatening."[17]

Being a superwoman is a double bind in more ways than one. To other women, she serves as a role model, but at the same time, she sends out a discouraging message, that unless other women measure up to her super abilities and stamina, they might as well forget about pursuing an academic career. Unlike the career pattern for men, there is little room at the top for a less than super woman. In a few high ranking women, unfortunately, tokenism and especially the superwoman image, which they have internalized uncritically, have created the "queen bee" syndrome, which means they become essentially nonsupportive of other women in the profession.

Another double bind for the potential superwoman is that she treads a very precarious line. Her superior qualifications can easily backfire among more insecure senior male colleagues in a position to evaluate her for promotion.

TENURE: ACADEMIC FREEDOM OR ACADEMIC REPRESSION?

At the heart of the meritocracy is tenure; at the heart of tenure is freedom of inquiry and protection from persecution. Just as women and minorities do not object to the principle of merit, similarly they uphold the principle of academic freedom. But just as they have also begun to question the meritocracy as it is actually practiced, so too they are beginning to have doubts about tenure and the tenure process as currently conducted. Putting it bluntly, if having tenure guarantees academic freedom, some of those without tenure, especially women and minorities may be experiencing some form of academic repression, or at the very least, little or no protection of freedom of speech and more subtly, denial of freedom of inquiry.

First of all, the fact that the meritocracy in fact is not race- and most certainly not sex-blind, but actually plays favorites, denies a large group of people the right to compete in the academic system. The repercussion goes deeper than individual careers. By maintaining women and minorities at best at token levels, the system perpetuates a wide variety of stereotypes, including the subtly negative one of the superwoman. For unless woman and minority academics form a "critical mass"—a just and fair proportionate representation—there is little chance of eliminating these negative images. The underrepresentation of women and minorities also denies women and minority students especially, but also the white male students, sufficient role models, at a time when society and education actively promote the ideal equality of race and sex.

I suggested earlier that tokenism is better than nothing, but we are in danger of even losing that dubious honor. The demographic decline of college-age students, as well as the economic constraints beginning in the mid-1970s, come at a time when many departments in colleges and universities across the country are practically "tenured-in," that is, faced with a large, tenured, white male faculty. If these departments have women or minority members, these tend to be clustered in the few untenured slots. So these assistant professors are coming up for tenure just at a time when tenure has become all but impossible. Caught in the retrenchment are some white male colleagues, to be sure, but the fact remains that disproportionately more women and minorities are "last hired" and hence will suffer more from being "first fired."

The tendency toward more conservative rather than innovative trends during times of economic and social crises can be seen also in how the budget ax falls. The reluctance to tenure even extremely well-qualified junior faculty is matched by the tendency to cut or drastically reduce the budget of certain departments and programs. Here is where women and minority faculty are adversely affected to yet another disproportionate degree. In the case of women, the absolute gains they have made in the last several decades have to a large extent been in traditional female departments, where a considerable number of the few minority (black) women academics can also be found. As mentioned earlier, women faculty have fallen in status in traditionally male departments, so that they are stratified horizontally by rank as well as vertically by department. With the female departments enjoying far less prestige and power, it is not surprising, then, that these tend to be areas where economic cuts are made when administrators face smaller budgets. Similarly, minority faculty, men and women, also tend to be located in less prestigious areas, including fields where teaching and community activities are important.

The recent budget recommendations of the provost of the University of Missouri are a good illustration of what is happening. He proposed the elimination or severe cutbacks in the following programs: library and informational science, public and community services, education, home economics, and nursing. Not only will some of these programs, serving a large number of women and minority students, be adversely affected but of the faculty slated to lose their jobs will be 7 of the 34 full-time black faculty, or more than 20 percent of their ranks, and 35 of 406 full-time women faculty, or nearly 9 percent. Within the powerful medical school, one of the areas slated for elimination is the medical dietetic and food systems program, where all ten faculty members due to lose their positions are women, one of them black. In discussing his reasons for recommending the termination of this program, the dean bluntly pointed out to its woman director: "You know you don't have as much clout as physicians do."[18]

Within humanities and social science disciplines and programs, there is also a clear pattern of distribution of women and minority faculty members. First of all, as stated earlier, most of them are clustered near the lower and nonladder ranks. But beyond that, women and minorities are more visible in the recently created, nontraditional, often interdisciplinary programs, such as women's studies, black studies, urban studies, and other ethnic and minority studies and within the established disciplines of history, political science, sociology, language and literature, more prominent in ethnic and third world areas of research and teaching.

There are clear historical reasons for this pattern of interest. Because these newer programs were generally created in the 1960s and early 1970s, they are less established, less controlled by traditional white male faculties and traditional methodologies, and nence were more open in terms of career opportunities and ideology to women and minorities. But women and minorities simply did not enter these new fields of inquiry because there were more job openings. They often made a conscious, political decision when they entered graduate school to pursue these studies, because they came of age academically during the great social awakening of the 1960s and 1970s. It is natural that many women and minority students found these areas of inquiry more relevant and compelling; in fact, many probably formed part of the grass-roots movements to put these new studies on the college curriculum.

The new and the interdisciplinary programs are more vulnerable than traditional departments for a variety of reasons. They have a predominantly untenured, women and minority, faculty, which is often heavily part time as well. To many senior male colleagues in traditional disciplines and deans who felt pressured into supporting the emergence of these new programs, they continue to be less than legitimate and their scholarship suspect. Actually, because they are still in the process of developing, they often entail more work, and more creative work, for their faculties. They are often more teaching-oriented, especially on the undergraduate level, many having not yet developed plans for graduate programs. Many started on "soft" money and still operate on extremely limited budgets. Women's studies on my campus, which grants a B.A. degree, depends largely on a part-time and graduate student teaching staff and operates on a measly budget of a few thousand dollars a year. Women's studies and urban studies both have had untenured faculty as directors, and black studies is currently directed by an untenured black faculty. I know of no other programs or departments with similar circumstances.

The repression against these faculties and their areas of inquiry is more subtle than blatant discrimination and is currently carried out under the guise of retrenchments and budget trimming and through the use of the tenure system. By subtle, I mean that administrators do not have to acknowledge that they intend to target certain areas and programs for perpetual second-class status within the system. They can accomplish this goal simply by applying the tenure process in a traditional, nonflexible way.

Tenure, in most universities, is judged according to the three stated criteria of teaching, community service, and publications. Many faculty members in nontraditional interdisciplinary areas have considerable difficulty in gaining a favorable tenure review. Although they often spend a disproportionate amount of time in course development and student contact (and frequently have trouble locating good texts and reading material because these do not yet exist in abundance), their perhaps more "informal" style and nontraditional classroom methods are sometimes questioned. They are often assumed to be less rigorous and less demanding of their students. Most of all, they run into difficulty with publications, not necessarily because they publish less but because they may not publish that traditional monograph, or they publish in journals with less established reputations or circulation. My colleagues in women's studies, black studies, and other ethnic studies undoubtedly know what I mean.

Some woman studies faculty have testified to what their association with that area has cost them in terms of being rewarded. They feel caught in an unfair double bind not of their own creation. They are asked by administrators to develop a curriculum and a degree program in this area, because of grass-roots student pressure. Then, when review time comes, they are told they have not published enough and their efforts toward developing the new program practically discounted. I know one woman whose original field was American political history. Her department encouraged her to develop the first women's studies program on her campus. Then, in her fourth year, her contract was not renewed, on grounds that she had deviated from the field for which she was originally hired, and she had not published enough in that field.

Feminist historian Estelle Friedman's case at Stanford University also illustrates these problems. Author of a prize-winning book on women's prison reform and winner of prestigious teaching awards, she was supported by a majority of her department but twice denied tenure in 1982 by the university's division of humanities and science. The review committee cited deficiency in her "quality of mind" as the reason. One of four women faculty members who set up Stanford's path-breaking feminist studies program, Friedman has also directed the program and, by 1982, was the only one left on campus of the original four. Not only would her departure be a serious blow to feminist studies at Stanford but the dean refused to consider her contribution to the formation and development of the program in the tenure decision.[19]

Compounding the difficulty for women and minority faculty in new and interdisciplinary programs is the fact that many of them do not even have the benefit of peer review, a foundation of the traditional tenure process, because there is no core of tenured faculty in their departments to conduct such a review. Hence they are subjected to a universitywide tenure review committee that, even if it does its work conscientiously, does not understand the work under scrutiny and, most importantly, cannot follow through a positive recommendation with a strong department backing, another foundation of the traditional tenure process.

Finally, faculty in new, less than legitimate programs often have to fight for the survival of their programs. This kind of campus activism—by insisting, for example, that the study of women has a rightful place in a university curriculum—can also lessen one's chances of career advancement.[20]

The traditional merit system explains in part why women academics seem to encounter more problems attaining tenure. As two women lawyers, examining the question conclude: "The difficulty of validating the 'merit' approach in promotion and tenure decisions is reflected in the university's inability to define academic performance. The elements to be considered in making reappointment or tenure decisions as recited in faculty handbooks are generally so vague as to justify any interpretation applied by the faculty committee." Typically, they continued, there is no set weight accorded the three general criteria, nor is it clear what is the minimal level of performance required in each area. Another impediment they found is the shroud of secrecy surrounding meetings in which tenure and promotion are discussed.[21] There is the now celebrated case of the male sociology professor in Georgia who preferred to go to jail rather than disclose his decision at the tenure review of a female colleague who was denied promotion. He claimed he was denied his academic freedom when a judge forced him to disclose his decision. Of course, one could argue that if his decision was based solely on merit considerations, he should have been able to defend his position as a rational one, whatever it was.

CONCLUSION

All young faculty—with a disproportionate number of women and minorities—are in a crisis because of the drastic curtailment of tenure promotions on most campuses today. Tenure is an all-or-nothing only game in town. In the humanities and social sciences, for most of the young faculty denied tenure, it is highly unlikely that they will receive a secure academic appointment anywhere else. It usually spells for them the end of a career.

Beyond the loss of personal careers, the current tenure crisis implies other serious consequences:

1. The gradual disappearance of women and minority faculty on the full-time staff is a very real possibility. These are the professors who can

serve as role models for many of our women and minority students. Only full-time faculty have access to power within university governance and influence decisions regarding curriculum, work conditions, and other issues. From their high ranks are recruited the deans and upper administrators. The crisis for women and minorities occur just when they thought they were beginning to build a "critical mass" across college campuses; instead, they see that incipient mass in danger of being decimated.

2. Beyond this danger, women and minority faculty are to a large extent involved with teaching and research in new, nontraditional, often interdisciplinary fields, which have yet to gain full legitimacy within the university power structure. Many of these programs came into existence as a result of grass-roots organization and pressure from undergraduate and graduate students, community activists, and young faculty. The struggle to preserve these programs is a continuing one. In part because they are new, they have a largely untenured and often heavily part-time faculty, and hence have less clout within the university community. Their faculty members often have to become activists for their programs, in addition to performing their regular academic duties. Finally, they are often at a disadvantage when evaluated for tenure on traditional bases, and when reviewed not by a panel of peers, but by others, usually established white males from traditional disciplines who may have formed a priori reservations about the legitimacy of their scholarship.

In summary, women and minority faculty suffer disproportionately from the tenure crunch, leading to the conclusion that there is a kind of both de facto race and sex discrimination in academe. There exists also a subtle kind of academic repression against certain areas of inquiry, largely represented by these same women and minority professors. Even within more established humanities and social science departments, those faculty associated with less mainstream areas such as women's history, Afro-American history, or third world history, are often women and minority, nontenured, and hence more vulnerable, both in their persons and in their fields.

In short, under the current meritocracy and tenure system, which is far from the ideal its supporters claim it to be, there is very little academic freedom for the untenured. And if things do not change, most of the women and minority academics are not likely to be tenured and will never enjoy any academic protection. If we are not vigilant, we may soon find both women and minority professors, as well as nontraditional areas of inquiry, effectively eliminated from our campuses, which will then revert back, unfortunately, to the bastions of traditional white male supremacy that they had once been.[22]

SOME SUGGESTIONS FOR ACTION

The only solution to the present crisis lies in organization and collective action. I would like to suggest that all women and minority faculties on college and university campuses form caucuses, if they have not already, separately or together. Second, each caucus should gather the facts about women and minority faculty members, carefully delineating their numbers, ranks, distribution, and salary, if available; then, by department and school, make a careful comparison with their white male colleagues. The next step is to call attention to these facts by widely publicizing them. Update the data frequently and monitor the progress of each woman and minority, particularly those coming up for tenure. If we go our individual ways, we will simply be chewed up by the system and deemed personal failures, and we will never begin to make meaningful changes.

The above steps are the easy ones. More difficult, particularly in these politically conservative and economically restrictive times, is to force open the debate on the meritocracy and tenure system. No one, least of all women and minorities, who as a group are probably better qualified and more motivated given the obstacles they have had to overcome, argues against or wants to destroy the merit principle. What we do question, however, is whether a fair and consistent merit system has indeed functioned on most campuses. As one perceptive observer said way back in 1974: "Good affirmative action programs honor the merit principle because the goal of equal employment opportunity *is* a merit system and the means of its attainment must be consistent with that goal." Moreover, this same observer argued, "In the academy itself, tenure is on its way to becoming a job rights system for the protection of mediocrity rather than the right of free inquiry. And, except for the first tenure decision made too early in the professor's professional career, academe has little stomach for the hard choices."[23]

In opening up the debate on a real meritocracy, one which is color- and sex-blind as well as nontradition-bound, we must insist that it take into consideration such valid issues as women's role conflicts and the demands placed on faculties developing new programs, as well as the proper criteria for evaluating their efforts and accomplishments.

NOTES

1. Constance M. Carroll, a black woman academic, has found that the increase in academic employment since 1970 has been far greater for black men than for black

women. Constance M. Carroll, "Three's a Crowd: The Dilemma of the Black Woman in Higher Education," in *Academic Women on the Move,* ed. Alice S. Rossi and Ann Calderwood (New York: Russell Sage Foundation, 1973), p. 179. Lora H. Robinson, "Institutional Variation in the Status of Academic Women,' in Rossi and Calderwood, *Academic Women,* p. 212; Malcolm G. Scully, "Part-Time Teachers: Many Are Angry," *Chronicle of Higher Education,* January 20, 1975.

2. For a discussion of her personal ordeal with sex discrimination litigation against a university and an account of the general difficulties with sex discrimination suits, see two books by Joan Abramson: *The Invisible Woman: Discrimination in the Academic Profession* (San Francisco: Jossey-Bass, 1975), and *Old Boys, New Women. The Politics of Sex Discrimination* (New York: Praeger, 1979).

3. Suzanne Howard, *But We Will Persist. A Comparative Research Report on the Status of Women in Academe* (Washington, D.C.: American Association of University Women, 1978), pp. 6, 9, 22.

4. Michael J. Carter and Susan Boslego Carter, "Women's Recent Progress in the Professions, or, Women Get a Ticket to Ride After the Gravy Train Has Left the Station," *Feminist Studies* 7 (Fall 1981): 478.

5. Pamela Roby, "Institutional Barriers to Women Students in Higher Education," in Rossi and Calderwood, *Academic Women,* p. 37; Patricia Albjerg Graham, "Status Transitions of Women Students, Faculty and Administrators," in Rossi and Calderwood, *Academic Women,* p. 163; Carter and Carter, "Women's Recent Progress," pp. 481–82; Michelle Patterson and Laurie Engleberg, "Women in Male-Dominated Professions," in *Women Working, Theories and Facts in Perspective,* ed. Ann H. Stromberg and Shirley Harkess (Palo Alto, Calif.: Mayfield, 1978). Marion Kilson, "The Status of Women in Higher Education," *Signs* 1 (Summer 1976): 935–38; found that the proportion of tenured women faculty dropped from 17 percent in 1971–72 to 13 percent in 1974–75, that among women faculty, while 44 percent had tenure in 1971–72, only 27 percent had tenure in 1974–75, while for men the proportion dipped slightly from 59 to 57 percent; Mary Frank Fox, "Sex, Salary and Achievement: Reward Dualism in Academia," *Sociology of Education* 54 (April 1981): 81.

6. Karen J. Winkler, "The Status of Women in the Historical Profession," *Chronicle of Higher Education,* January 12, 1981 (this is a summary of the 1980 update of the 1970 "Rose report" issued by the Committee on Women Historians of the American Historical Association).

7. Leigh Bienen, Alicia Ostriker, and J. P. Ostricker, "Sex Discrimination in the Universities: Faculty Problems and No Solution," *Women's Rights Law Reporter* 2 (March 1975): 4; Judith P. Vladeck and Margaret M. Young, "Sex Discrimination in Higher Education: It's Not Academic," *Women's Rights Law Reporter* 4 (Winter 1978): 65; Emily Abel, "Collective Protest and the Meritocracy: Faculty Women and Sex Discrimination Lawsuits," *Feminist Studies* 7 (Fall 1981): 505; Abramson, *Invisible Woman,* pp. 69, 84.

8. Judith Hoch and Thomasine Kushner, "Alma Pater," *International Journal of Women's Studies* 4 (1981): 261; Laura Morlock, "Discipline Variation in the Status of Academic Women," in Rossi and Calderwood, *Academic Women,* p. 292; Helen S. Astin and Alan E. Bayer, "Sex Discrimination in Academe," in Rossi and Calderwood, *Academic Women,* p. 339.

9. Bienen, Ostriker, and Ostriker, "Sex Discrimination in the Universities," pp. 7–9.

10. Ibid., pp 6, 9.

11. Arlie Russell Hochschild, "Inside the Clockwork of Male Careers," in *Women and the Power to Change,* ed. Florence Howe (New York: McGraw-Hill, 1975), pp. 67–68.

12. Hoch and Kushner, "Alma Pater," p. 262; Patterson and Engelberg, "Women in Male Dominated Professions," p. 286. In another sample, it was found that 57 percent of

women and 100 percent of men are married; Tana Slay and Ann McDonald, "Female Professors, Male Professors. Career Development: Attitudes, Benefits, Costs," *Psychological Reports* 48 (1981): 311.

13. Howard, *But We Will Persist*, p. 10.

14. Carroll, "Three's a Crowd," p. 183.

15. Graham, "Status Transitions of Women Students," p. 168; Patterson and Engelbert, "Women in Male-Dominated Professions," p. 287–88.

16. Nell Irvin Painter, "Hers," *New York Times*, December 10, 1981.

17. Carroll, "Three's a Crowd," *Academic Women*, p. 182.

18. Dale Singer, "Missouri U. Deans Defend Programs Slated for Cuts," *St. Louis Post-Dispatch*, May 2, 1982.

19. Anne C. Roark, "Tenure: Feminist Scholar's Rejection Raises Sex-Discrimination Issue," *Los Angeles Times*, January 29, 1983; Karen Winkler, "Feminist Professor v. Stanford. A Tenure Test Case," *Chronicle of Higher Education*, February 16, 1983, pp. 5–6.

20. Theresa Guminski Turk, "Women Faculty in Higher Education: Academic Administration and Governance in a State University System, 1966–1977," *Pacific Sociological Review* 24 (April 1981): 223–24; Abel, "Collective Protest and the Meritocracy," p. 509.

21. Valdeck and Young, "Sex Discrimination in Higher Education," pp. 65–66.

22. Emily Abel, "The Academic Job Crisis: Some Possible Responses," *Women' Studies Newsletter* 8 (Fall/Winter 1980): 5, essentially asks the same question: "While it is certainly true that the halcyon days of the sixties have ended, and that many institutions are suffering from financial constraints, we also have to ask why the first programs to be eliminated would need to be those serving women, minorities, and low-income people, thus wiping out the gains made by these groups during the 1960s. Why must cuts be felt disproportionately by faculty at the bottom of the academic hierarchy? In other words, we should recognize the extent to which attempts to cut women's studies programs may serve as a means of subverting our ultimate goals: to gain a legitimate place in the college curriculum for the study of women and to increase the proportion of university professors who are women."

23. Brewster C. Denny, "The Decline of Merit," *Science*, December 6, 1974.

·11·

Reflections on Academic Freedom, Equality, and Excellence

Jean Bethke Elshtain

I intend to raise some disquieting questions. I shall do so from the standpoint of a political theorist concerned with the philosophic foundations of our political and scholarly points of view. Specifically, I shall position myself against shibboleths widely and unthinkingly shared by an important segment of critical and left-wing opinion in America. These shibboleths, baldly put, may be cast as follows: (1) Academic freedom for individual scholars is largely a sham and has been historically. (2) The autonomy or freedom of academic departments serves, and has served, to legitimate repression in the hands of a narrow, undemocratic "oligarchy."[1] (3) Women and minority persons should be compensated for past discrimination in ways that may require overriding "qualitative" distinctions.[2] (4) The pursuit of excellence and an insistence on canons for scholarly achievement are either in direct conflict with the pursuit of academic equality, a smoke screen to justify ideological hegemony, or themselves inherently inegalitarian. I here overstate what I shall position myself against but not, I think, by very much. Having said this, I do not draw the conclusion, nor should the reader, that any one individual with left or radical views clings rigidly to the full cluster of positions I have summarized. Nevertheless, they are "in the air" and often go unchallenged.

As I explore points 1 through 4 I hope to excavate the unspoken premise that underlies much received left opinion, namely, that the authority now lodged in academic departments or, for that matter, in

161

individual scholars is suspect, perhaps illegitimate, and must in any case be demystified. This suspicion of personal authority and its subsequent covert or explicit repudiation locks much left-wing and "progressive" thinking solidly in the camp of that mainstream liberalism it presumes to counter. This should become clear as I move through my argument.

The first question is, on the one hand, historical—Has academic freedom in any meaningful way served to protect dissent and dissenters in the past?—and, on the other, theoretical—Is there some alternative framework to that which now exists that would better nurture and protect dissent and dissenters? The historical question presents the empirical claim that academic freedom has often, if not without exception, served to provide a surround within which scholars could pursue matters as they deemed fit whatever their politics or, alternatively, that the academy has behaved in consistently craven and obsequious ways and academic freedom has failed to protect dissent at many, if not all, critical points in our history. In order to adjudicate the historic accuracy or inaccuracy of these two views, one requires concrete evidence. For the sake of argument, I shall accept the bleak side of the story told by others in this volume concerning the bad record of the American academy in this matter.[3] But does this strike a blow against individual academic freedom itself—or should it? Too often those who paint the past in somber hues collapse the abuse to which the academic freedom ideal has been subject to the notion that liberal academic freedom is almost bound to be bogus, a smoke screen deployed in a manipulative and ideological fashion.

To be sure, understandings and definitions of academic freedom expand or constrict with the Zeitgeist, for academics, like the Supreme Court, pay close attention to the election returns. But to portray the freedom of individual scholars in a manner that holds that freedom up for ridicule and suspicion is a dangerous business. Dangerous not just because it may backfire and undermine just claims by radical academics that their freedom as scholars is being abridged but, further, because such demystifying, hard-nosed talk from the left only serves to deepen what might be called our culture's "deauthorization" of the human person, the erosion of our status as individual "authors" with particular claims and "authorities" of one sort or another (whether as scholars and teachers, parents, or whatever).

This delegitimation is part of the historic project of liberalism in its Weberian, bureaucratic form—that is, in its modern incarnation. To castigate cynically academic freedom as a weapon deployed self-servingly by those in power serves in the long run to undercut the possibility that radical scholars may speak *with* and *from* that authority that should be theirs if they have engaged in honest scholarly endeavors. To the extent that the scholar is delegitimated, his or her academic freedom having been shown up as a cover-up, to that extent we erode the claims any scholar, including the radical, may have upon our attention and our political conscience. I shall return to this general theme in my discussion of the pursuit of excellence.

Before I turn to a second challenge to received opinion in the matter of academic freedom as departmental autonomy, let me indicate, should the too brief comments above have left any doubts, that I do not defend academic freedom from a narrowly strategic design. My defense is not lodged in an imperative that dictates my need for academic freedom in order that I might, in turn, dictate a specific ideology to my students in my classroom. In other words, I am not countering conservative or liberal cynicism—to the extent it exists—with my own. The arguments of those who insist that the classroom must be connected in some immediate link to the "outside struggle" are troubling. For the "test" of whether the classroom has "worked" or not, whether the inoculation has taken, becomes student behavior outside the classroom. Conceiving of the classroom in instrumental terms, with the explicit political aim of turning out students as products of a particular sort, radicals join hands with the celebrants of the "new practicality." This "new practicality" is deeply antiintellectual. It aims to gear students for the "real world" of the market, to offer vocationalism as a way to meet student "needs." That the "real practicalist" is the market does nothing to sunder the underlying philosophic union of the two positions. In their insistence on behavioralistically observable results they are brothers and sisters under the skin. For each group—with each defending academic freedom as a strategy to pursue its would-be ends—the classroom is important primarily because it can be deployed to other, specifiable ends: The teacher has bigger fish to fry. This all too easily legitimates antiintellectualism even as it promotes a crude utilitarian ethic.

The only pedagogically and morally sound defense of academic freedom for individual teachers must be to protect and nurture the element of intellectual surprise and unpredictability in classrooms and in scholarly research. This element is lost if the classroom is directly politicized and geared toward ends the teacher knows best; for example, my positions have changed over a semester through exchanges with students, through questions put to me, through problems I have unexpectedly posed to myself as I made implicit views explicit. If I entered the classroom with the left-wing analogue of Edmund Burke's little platoons in my head this could not happen for I would want to mold my students into politicos of one sort or another.

Those who seek academic freedom in order to mobilize the young for a given doctrine or ideology believe, in the final analysis, in control, not change. They seek, not so much to help what is most distinctive, hence potentially revolutionary, about every unique student emerge as that student reveals herself or himself through language as a form of action, but to produce consensus with a prepackaged dogma. My defense of individual academic freedom, then, is made in order to protect the give and take of argument, to sustain the tension between the teacher's authority (which cannot, *pace* some simplistic arguments, be reduced to terms of power), and to explain how that authority may be exercised even as a dialogue of equal interlocutors is nourished. This tension and complexity is quashed by ideological certitude, but it is part of what the classroom is when it is at its best. To see the vocation of teaching in this light requires a defense of individual academic freedom as an intrinsic, not an instrumental, good.

Just as individual academic freedom has come under fire, or has been defended in ways that erode its legitimate raison d'être, so the freedom or autonomy of academic departments has been questioned.[4] That is, the right of academics, constituted as departments, to make decisions concerning their own has come under fire as just another way individuals perform the police function of their repressive social order. They "do the dirty work" so the higher-ups need not deny tenure for spurious reasons that may cloak a political end, or refuse to hire someone who might shake things up on the grounds that he or she is "unqualified." Again, there is much truth to this indictment and to the abuse that the right or autonomy of departments to make hiring, firing, tenure, and merit decisions is subject. I grant this, yet I find that traditional right a vital one that must be sustained. Although it is subject to abuse, there is nothing intrinsic in guarantees of departmental autonomy that requires repressive outcomes. Such outcomes are one possibility, but so are others.

For example: I come from a university that has a "critical mass" of radical political economists on the staff of its economics department, a department that has expanded rapidly and in a generally radical or critical direction. In this situation the department's guarantee of autonomy might well serve in protective ways to provide a barrier against outside pressures—though there are none at present—whether from some future central administration or, say, from a state legislature worried about radicals inculcating the Commonwealth of Massachusetts' youth. I am simply making the modest point that the freedom of departments cuts a number of ways. That this autonomy has often failed to protect the individual academic freedom of unpopular members does not mean that it must thus fail. It is unwise for the left to oppose this autonomy outright, particularly in the absence of clear-headed proposals on how to structure the situation so that fair and protective rather than ill-considered and repressive outcomes are more likely. At work in many critiques of departmental autonomy, an underlying subtext, if you will, is that assault on personally visible authority I have already noted above and to which I shall return.

One suggested alternative to what is construed as the arcane feudal system of departmental decision making is for faculty to "organize collectively to protect the individual rights of all."[5] But what new principles should guide faculties thus collectively organized? What new structures must emerge? Must departmental autonomy give way altogether before the new order? Given the minority status of women, minorities, and radicals, why would a collective organization, in some automatic way, guarantee their protection and their voice? Might they not be subjected to a "tyranny of the majority" within such a collective situation with fewer opportunities to make their case than at the more personal level of the department?

These questions push us directly into consideration of shibboleth three—that women and minority persons must be compensated for past discrimination in ways that may require overriding "qualitative" distinctions. Those who subscribe to the view that the academy can and must be an instrumentality for retributive justice are often strong advocates of the destruction of traditional departmental autonomy over hiring, firing, tenure, and merit evaluations and decisions. The presumption is that a more collectively structured, impersonal, legalistic system, with absolutely clear-out standards, including a schedule of "handicapping points," would somehow serve women and minority scholars better than the older, more archaic, and "subjective" order.[6]

I think not. Briefly, here is why.

There are few matters more important for the modern academy than debates about evaluation of merit and tenure for women and minority persons in light of affirmative action. Those who only recently gained a toehold in higher education fear that program cutbacks, given budgetary crises, will not have neutral or evenhanded consequences but will, instead, disproportionately hit young, untenured faculty and newer programs, thus lopsidedly cutting women and, in fewer instances, minority persons. The question of how it has come to pass that women and minorities are underrepresented in the academy and whether this underrepresentation is ameliorating or worsening is one that requires empirical adjudication.[7] I shall not deal with that dimension of the problem here. Instead I shall take up attacks on merit and the meritocracy, which often go hand in hand with the insistence that the old, elitist standards must be waived or altered in order that the contributions of women and minorities to their departments, their universities, and their disciplines might be fairly assessed. Specifically, the question is: Should women and minority persons be compensated for the past sins of the society in ways that may require overriding older notions of quality and merit. This discussion leads, in turn, to a general consideration of the pursuit of excellence and the problem of equality. I aim, finally, to tie matters up through the theme of authority.

In her essay for this volume, Hu-DeHart discusses (in the higher case) merit, affirmative action, tenure, and tokens and tokenism in turn. Certainly no one with any sense of the reality of our current situation would claim that the academic meritocracy works in a perfectly just or fully defensible fashion. Women with feminist concerns, for example, may run into problems from colleagues who are either unaware of the new feminist scholarship or who believe that such scholarship, by definition, constitutes a form of special pleading and cannot possibly meet scholarly canons. In turn, women who are evaluated by their colleagues as having met such standards are sometimes subjected to derisive labeling from their sisters—called superwomen or tokens.[8] To undercut evaluations of scholarly distinction seen as part and parcel of a meritocracy implacably set against the attainment of equity by women and minorities, some members of those groups, together with radicals, have proposed eliminating qualitative distinctions and evaluations altogether. Others call, as does Hu-DeHart, for a purified "real" meritocracy, one which is genuinely race- and sex-blind and unbound to archaic tradition. Yet there is an inner tension in her argument. Her proposals for how to move toward an evenhanded, "real" meritocracy turn out to be far from sex- or color-blind.

For example, one of Hu-DeHart's chief complaints is that "women's problems" are not given proper consideration within the meritocratic system as it is set up under idiosyncratic departmental standards. One such problem, she continues, is the fact that few women professors enjoy the social and research-secretarial assistance of a husband in their professional work, a role wives frequently (or at least it used to be frequently) play for their husbands. The implication is that if departments were required by higher authorities, in the form of legal stipulations and in the interests of retributive justice, to be truly sex-blind they would somehow "see" *precisely* such sex-linked factors. This is a muddle. How are departments to "handicap" on the basis of sex in this way? Were one to try to take into account each individual's complete personal situation (married, not married; children, no children; help, no help) fairness would then dictate (as but one example) that the male professor who could get a signed affidavit that his wife does not and will not serve him in the older, more traditional ways must have his circumstance taken into account as a "handicap" as well. There are impossible problems inherent in any attempt to systematically plug such matters into evaluations of merit and scholarly distinction.[9]

One more efficacious way to move toward a "true meritocracy"—a way that keeps alive a commitment to quality—would involve reassessing how it is departments weigh diverse qualitative contributions by faculty in the areas of scholarship, teaching, and service. If a more systematic account were taken of quality teaching or heavy, robust involvement in such vital matters as important service, including student counseling—given the heavy demands placed on women and minorities in these areas—the merit system would work more evenhandedly. And one would preserve intact a commitment to assess the individual in his or her public role and according to public standards. However, this seems like so much beating around the bush, for I have not gone to the real heart of the problem the left frequently has in matters of excellence, distinctiveness, merit, and quality.

Two deep matters are at stake. First, a conviction that equality and excellence are not only in tension but are incompatible with one another; that moves toward greater equality must erode elitist notions of excellence; and that we must simply bite the bullet. (Those for whom the whole idea of merit is a complete sham don't even worry about the matter to this extent.) Second, the urge to "deauthorize" all personal "authority" and "authorities," whether of the scholar or of departments as evaluative bodies is an insistent underlying theme. As a way of stalking shibboleth four and of rounding out my argument on authority, I shall take up each of these deep matters in turn.

Problems emerge when a commitment to equality requires direct manipulation of the education process in a way that goes beyond expanding opportunities. "Strong compensation establishes an actual preference for disadvantaged groups [with dubious criteria for what is to count as 'disadvantaged,' ignoring poverty and class and concentrating only on sex and race] in college admissions or in the level of effort or resources expended on their education. This latter step involves attempting to compensate for differences in ability and motivation between more and less advantaged groups that are due to differences in home environment, early school and so on," writes economic and education theorist Michael McPherson.[10] It is programs of this sort—militant affirmative action one might call them—that have helped to bring about a reaction based on the conviction that schools are being used as tools to meet other goals often at the expense of the deeper purposes of higher education, including achievement based on merit and a commitment to that distinction between individuals that emerges as they confront a curriculum, pick and choose, and either re-create themselves through education or do not. This reaction in itself would not justify being skeptical. But the way the left has pegged a plethora of claims and aims, explicit and implicit, on affirmative action does raise questions. Affirmative action simply cannot bear the egalitarian weight placed upon it, particularly when that weight is borne by an instrument that itself is based on the perpetuation of gross inequalities given its silence on class-based injustices. Beyond this, affirmative action has come under fire from articulate members of "targeted groups" themselves. I shall look at the arguments of two such critics.

In his recently published autobiography, *Hunger of Memory. The Education of Richard Rodriquez*, Rodriquez, with great poignancy, explores his own reactions, as an officially categorized 'minority' to affirmative action. He is highly critical. He finds affirmative action part of a mistaken strategy. For those in the best position to benefit "from such reforms were those . . . least victimized by racism or any other social oppression—those culturally, if not always economically, of the middle class." Rodriquez here refers to people like himself: a well-educated Mexican-American, in his case, whose family was not desperately poor and whose children received excellent parochial, public, and higher educations.

What affirmative action ignores, what most strategies that aim explicitly to turn the schools into social reform institutions ignore, is the importance of class. It is, says Rodriquez

> easy to forget that those whose lives are shaped by poverty and poor education . . . are least able to defend themselves against social oppression, whatever its form. . . . All Mexican-Americans certainly are not equally Mexican-Americans. The policy of affirmative action, however, was never able to distinguish someone like me (a graduate student of English, ambitious for a college teaching career) from a slightly educated Mexican-American who lived in a barrio and worked as a menial laborer, never expecting a future improved. Worse, affirmative action passed as a program of the Left. In fact, its supporters ignored the most fundamental assumptions of the classical left by disregarding the importance of class and by assuming that the disadvantages of the lower class would necessarily be ameliorated by the creation of an elite society.[11]

The result, says Rodriquez, is bad faith on the part of educators, radicals, and society overall. Society "gets off the hook," ignoring the need for more fundamental reforms at other levels and putting the whole burden on educational institutions. Educators get off the hook by passing their provisional students even if they are confronted with evidence of a student's inadequate comprehension. Radicals can claim to be promoting sex and race equality when, in too many instances, their attitude toward women and minorities is deeply paternalistic. Women and minorities get used as a wedge to deepen the fissure in the merit system. In Rodriquez's angry words,

> The conspiracy of kindness became a conspiracy of uncaring. Cruelly, callously, admissions committees agreed to overlook serious academic deficiency. I knew students in college then barely able to read, students unable to grasp the function of a sentence. I knew nonwhite graduate students who were bewildered by the requirement to compose a term paper and who each day were humiliated when they couldn't compete with other students in seminars. . . . Not surprisingly, among those students with very poor academic preparation, few completed their courses of study. Many dropped out, blaming themselves for their failure. One fall, six nonwhite students I knew suffered severe mental collapse. None of the professors who had welcomed them to graduate school were around when it came time to take them to the infirmary or the airport. And the university officials who so diligently took note of those students in their self-serving totals of entering minority students finally took no note of them when they left.[12]

This is a harsh indictment. But it is not the usual reactionary lament. It comes from a man determined that equality in education not be bought at the price of sacrificing standards of excellence, for this is no equality at all and it only serves to erode further the authority of the scholar.

My second critic is a black writer who positions himself on the left. In his discussion of black conservatism, Jerry G. Watts argues that the impact of 1960s militancy for black students, scholars, and teachers has been mightily ambiguous. "One obvious benefit," he writes, "can be seen in the increased presence of black students and faculty on white campuses. . . . Yet the 'instant' quantitative inclusion of blacks in white academia may well have undermined long-run qualitative performance."[13] Watts goes on to indict the romantic antiintellectualism preached by many black "revolutionaries" who argued that concern about "established educational criteria" branded a black straight off as an "Uncle Tom." (This is a black version of women being labeled "tokens" or "male identified.") But his most bitter critique is reserved for white liberal intellectuals and scholars, themselves entrenched in the academy, who supported "radical chic," downgraded canons for scholarly endeavor for blacks as being unnecessary, racist, or elitist, even as they went about their own scholarly work. Why, Watts asks, is a defense of intellectual standards by definition conservative or reactionary?

My hunch is that the underlying presumption on which arguments such as those Watts criticizes emerge from the left and share a philosophical ground with the right, although each evaluates what flows from that ground in different ways. Let me explain by looking, briefly, at the concept of "equality" itself. Equality is a rich, difficult concept. The choice among apparently reasonable meanings of the term has implications for the kind of social policies one urges and for the kind of society one has. Indeed, we can account for the bitterness of the historic battles that have been fought over application of the idea of equality because, although we share and understand some rough, ready-to-hand notions about equality, we also fundamentally disagree about their application. The idea of equality involves moral claims and notions. It is tied to our ideas of fairness and justice.

Our society is, perhaps, unique among nations in building in, from its inception, a strong presumption for equality as one of the touchstones of our national identity and our political culture. All men (and I know, of course, the problem with the "men" formulation in matters of women and slaves) were declared equally created by the Founding Fathers. But this notion of equality, and its extension, have been variously interpreted and argued. Some say, in effect, a noble idea but balderdash because it is obvious that people are very different from one another, that is, *unequal by nature*. Such persons, then equate equality with sameness, inequality with differences. Since it is clear, they insist, that human beings differ, this means society will reflect those differences and invariably wind up with widespread social inequalities. There is something of a muddle in this formulation. Let me sort it out. The story goes like this. For conservatives, inequality (remember that differences are being construed as inequalities) is lodged in nature; social institutions must reflect this fact and are erected upon it. It follows that attempts to alter institutions to eliminate or reduce inequality will require nasty social surgery that will eliminate all human differences. It seems best, therefore, to allow natural differences—seen as inequalities—to work themselves out even if the result is a highly stratified, inegalitarian society.

But it strains credulity for us to believe that all those who are well placed have fully earned it and that their power and privilege simply flow from their being different—unequal—from the rest of us. Alas, the radical response has often been equally tendentious. Rather than challenging a view of equality that equates it with "sameness," many radical critics of American society implicitly accept this idea. Hence their vision of equality winds up with the fuzzy notion of a social world in which people are as indistinguishable from one another as possible—in the interests of equality. It is on this ground that arguments against individual distinction and merit are often erected. This is a vision satirized by Kurt Vonnegut in his short story "Harrison Bergeron," which appears in *Welcome to the Monkey House*. Vonnegut writes:

> The year was 2081, and everybody was finally equal.
> They weren't only equal before God and the law.
> They were equal every which way. Nobody was
> smarter than anybody else. Nobody was better
> looking than anybody else. Nobody was stronger
> or quicker than anybody else. All this
> equality was due to the 211th, 212th, and 213th
> Amendments to the Constitution, and to the
> unceasing vigilance of agents of the United
> States Handicapper General.[14]

In this delightfully ironic yet worrisome tale, Vonnegut portrays a future society in which all differences, all particular and unique human talents and gifts, have been compensated for downward in order to achieve the "equal society" in the belief that differences in themselves constitute inequalities. Thus ballet dancers, naturally gifted and trained to be lithe and limber, must dance with huge weights and irons on their legs. And so on.

But we are not stuck at this stalemate between defenders of reaction and proponents of a total egalitarian revolution who, as I have argued, ironically share certain presumptions. For we have other images of equality we can turn to *if* we recognize that equality is a goal of social and political policies and institutions and is not reducible to a statement about how people are, or are not, different from one another. It is a vision of greater economic equality, of a more secure social surround than that which many of our fellow citizens presently confront, that, in turn, provide for individual distinctiveness to emerge, that I have in mind.

Returning to the academy, it is the muddle-headed collapse of *difference* into *inequality* that leads many on the left to fight those distinctions between and among persons that necessarily emerge when colleagues make evaluations of one another's contributions. Not trusting in the capacities of individuals to make such judgments in a disinterested (in the best sense) manner, they would rather trust to a homogeneity imposed from above, or collectively lodged, and governed by a set of impersonal, legalistic standards of the sort I mentioned earlier. Such standards might include providing a handicapping schedule for specifiable conditions or states of being (race, sex.) Should this end be attained, we will, in our understandable and justifiable urge to improve the lot of the many, have forgotten the distinctiveness of the one. We will, as well, have furthered the process of "deauthorization" by undercutting genuine personal authority in one of the few areas in our social world where it still, however shakily, survives: in intellectual and scholarly endeavors and in the very personalism of academic decision making on department levels which allows one to attach decisions in real and particular persons rather than for judgments to flow from rule by "Nobody" (Hannah Arendt's characterization of modern bureaucratic governance).

At this point I come full circle, back to the elusive question of authority and to my (thus far) elusive comments on it. Baldly put, the problem is this: The left has generally failed to distinguish *authority* from *domination,* hence precluding "the possibility of specifying a non-coercive form of legitimation."[15] This collapse has dire consequences for the academy and our evaluations of sound scholarship, of genuine efforts to get at "the truth" of something, and ultimately on whatever substance inheres in the notion of academic freedom itself. A major source of our contemporary malaise is that individuals, in all spheres of life, have been increasingly deauthorized as political, social, and economic power is lodged more and more in impersonal and powerful bureaucratic structures and forms, public and private. The academy is one area where more personalized authority still exists, though here, too, the move is toward burgeoning and unaccountable bureaucracies. To seek the completion of this delegitimizing process is a terrible mistake. The difference between domination, or rule by force, and genuine authoritativeness, or the uncoerced recognition of a legitimate basis for the exercise of authority, is the difference between rule by bureaucratic managers (whether capitalist or socialist hardly matters) and rule to which real human beings and points of view are attached.[16]

Why is this important or even relevant to a consideration of academic freedom? To answer that question I will take up the problem of authoritative canons to guide faculty in their search for knowledge and in their presentations and evaluations of the results of that search—canons linked to the authority of individual scholars and of the academy overall. The left is often sarcastic or derisive in its treatment of the idea that such standards can or even should exist.[17] There is much in the story that invites sarcasm. We know all too well how ideological commitments can lurk behind the veil of value neutrality. But having said this, where do we go next? I want to share some apprehensions I have conjured with. It seems best to put the question squarely rather than to make unnecessary gestures. Does the left really want to undercut altogether the notion that there is some truth to the matter, whatever that matter might be? Do we, upon reflection, want to deepen the process of delegitimating the authority of scholars? Is a concern with standards fated to be a weapon in behalf of the status quo?

My answer to these questions is no. The truth is that not all opinions are created equal. The truth is that we can adjudicate between shoddy and serious scholarship, although there will and must be debates over what is to count as serious or shoddy. Given that conflict, it is a mistake to throw in the towel and claim that the quest for standards is itself fraudulent and self-serving. Let me make my case by taking up a recent scandal involving academic freedom and the question of scholarly canons.

The story involves one Robert Faurisson, an associate professor at the University of Lyon at the time the scandal erupted. Faurisson claimed that more than 30 years of painstaking research had convinced him that the Nazi gas chambers never existed and that the insistence that the Nazis practiced genocide was simply a lie endorsed by the official history of the victors.[18] Citing what he claimed to be mountains of documents, he declared the alleged gas chambers a lie of Zionist origin. Faurisson admitted that many Jews, though nowhere near six million, in fact only some thousands, died in camps. But he attributes these deaths to the fact that internment camps, where Jews were put for their own "protection," were a bit less than optimal—it was wartime, after all, so people who sickened could not get medical care, etc., though all that reasonably could be done was done to tend to them. But there was no extermination program of any sort.[19]

Now these claims fly in the face of historic evidence of every sort—first-person eyewitness testimony by victims and by camp authorities, documentation from allied liberators of the camps, on and on. It is important to be able to say that Faurisson is wrong, that his "demystification" is a lie based on a warped interpretation of highly selective material. But we can say this only if we accept that there is, in fact, some truth to be found and that to fly in the face of it is to put oneself beyond the pale of what is to count as scholarly work as opposed to the flimsiest political rhetoric.[20]

It is only because the opponents of Faurisson can speak from a vantage point of scholarly authority that they can effectively counter one such as he. If the project of deauthorization of scholars and scholarly merit in the interests of academic equality were complete, that is, if arguments that there is no such thing as merit and that qualitative evaluations are just a way to perpetuate rancid oligarchies had been altogether successful, there would no longer be scholarly legitimation. Instead, one would face a homogenized clash of self-interested opinion with Faurisson and his opponents facing one another on the same delegitimized plane. None in the dispute could claim more attention, more truth, than any other, and how the claims of each played politically would become the ultimately and only test of truth. (A crass utilitarian ethic is at work here.) This would be stunningly stupid. Better by far that Faurisson can claim the mantle of authority for himself and that other authorities can then show that he unjustifiably wraps himself and his work in that mantle; that, in fact, he has not made his case, hence he speaks with no genuine authority. Were there no longer an authoritative ground on which to stand and from which to speak, there would be no basis from which to indict the Faurissons of the world as frauds.

I hope that I have not set up some sort of mythic left or radical "strawperson" in order to make my case. The views I here attribute to left or radical critics of the academy permeate the air we breathe if we are, in some sense, radical or left critics ourselves, and they are, as well, views that can be quite explicitly attached to particular left-wing thinkers. I have done this at points in this chapter. My hope is that this challenge will prompt reflective individuals of radical views to recognize their own, perhaps unstated, commitments to "deauthorization" and against merit in the name of equality in order that they might question, in turn, whether they wish to deepen the present crisis of legitimation in the interest of an abstract goal. That goal—if it is equality—is better served through a steadfast commitment to human distinctiveness and difference even as one struggles for those structural changes in the American political economy that would allow distinctiveness to flourish.

NOTES

1. See the discussion by Ellen Schrecker, "Academic Freedom: The Historical View," in this volume. My arguments about academic freedom began as a discursive commentary on essays by Schrecker and Evelyn Hu-DeHart for the conference "Academic Freedom in the 1980s" sponsored by the National Emergency Civil Liberties Committee Foundation in New York City, May 21–22, 1982. Although my essay should not be read, save in those instances noted in the text, as a refutation of those by Schrecker and Hu-DeHart it would be instructive for the reader to play them off one another.

2. I here take partial issue with the case made by Hu-DeHart in her essay "Women, Minorities, and Academic Freedom," which appears in this volume.

3. Schrecker cites the academy for its historic cowardice. She seeks to undercut one of the primary claims made by those who argued that official Communist party members were not qualified for academic positions on the grounds that they were not free to pursue truth wherever it might take them, being bound by party orthodoxy. However politically motivated and dishonest these grounds it does seem disingenuous, at this late date, to claim, as Schrecker does, that the Communist party did not dictate in matters of scholarship or pedagogy to its academic members. It certainly did try to dictate to many of its writers, as powerfully described by Richard Wright in his posthumously published memoir *American Hunger* (New York: Harper & Row, 1977). Says Wright: "But the Communist party did not recognize the values that it had sworn to save when it saw them; the slightest sign of any independence of thought or feeling, even if it aided the party in its work, was enough to make one suspect, to brand one as a dangerous traitor" (p. 120). To admit the suppressive function of the Communist party is not, in any way, to justify its repression by the forces of order or to undercut the fact that left-wing scholars were often treated shamefully.

4. On this, see the discussion in Schrecker on academic freedom as a collective right. Much of my criticism was posed initially as a series of questions to her essay.

5. Schrecker, p. 40.

6. This is the specific thrust of the paper by Evelyn Hu-DeHart.

7. Hu-DeHart, in this volume, claims that "during this century," as higher education has expanded, opportunities have increased, and more women have received higher education, women have, at the same time, suffered a status decline in the academy overall. I do not think this is historically the case. For "during this century" there has been no generalized advance or retreat of women into or from higher education. Rather there have been periods when female professionalism and the number of women Ph.D.s rose (as in the 1930s) and periods when these declined (as in the 1950s), though there were no new barriers restricting female academic achievement or employment. To explain such cycles one would have to look to structural features of the American political economy as well as to the waxing and waning of cultural symbols and image of American womanhood.

8. Frankly, I think it is time to give these terms a decent, or better yet, an indecent burial. What purpose do they serve other than stigmatizing and pejorative ones? Tokenism is not a powerful analytic category—like repression or rights or class—we require because we cannot analyze certain phenomena without them. We can readily evaluate questions of women and minority status in the academy without resorting to

terms that bear no critical or theoretical purchase. For a woman to call another a token is for her to demean that woman and to undercut her achievement. The same holds for minorities and labels of Uncle Tomism. Whatever it is departments may do with women and minorities in their ranks in terms of pointing out what good guys they are given the presence of such individuals, this does not and should not require that women or minorities see themselves or others among them through the tokenist lens.

9. Some discussion of these problems in light of theories of distributive justice, forms of equality, and so on, may be found in Marshall Cohen, Thomas Nagel, and Tim Scanlon, eds. *Equality and Preferential Treatment* (Princeton, N.J.: Princeton University Press, 1979). See also my review in *Women and Politics* 1 (Fall 1980): 70–72.

10. Michael McPherson, "Values Conflicts in American Higher Education," typescript.

11. Richard Rodriquez, *Hunger of Memory. The Education of Richard Rodriquez* (Boston; David R. Godine, 1981), pp 149–51.

12. Ibid., pp. 154–55. There have been rather concerted attempts to discredit Rodriquez as a minority stalking horse for right-wing reaction; minimally, he is suspect as lacking proper progressive credentials. In this way his arguments are ignored and a general inability on the left to tolerate diversity in the ranks of minority groups—presumbly they should all think alike—is made evident.

13. Jerry G. Watts, "The Case of a Black Conservative," *Dissent* (Summer 1982): 301–03, 304.

14. Kurt Vonnegut, Jr., *Welcome to the Monkey House* (New York: Delacorte Press, 1968), p. 7.

15. Zelda Bronstein, "Psychoanalysis Without the Father," *Humanities in Society* 3 (Spring 1980): 201.

16. Ibid.

17. The overall thrust of Schrecker's eassay pushes this direction, as does Philip Green, *The Pursuit of Inequality* (New York: Pantheon, 1981).

18. Nadine Fresco, "The Denial of the Dead," *Dissent* (Fall 1981): 467–68.

19. Ibid., pp. 468–69.

20. See my essay on the epistemological dimensions of this debate in an essay called "Methodological Sophistication and Conceptual Confusion: A Critique of Mainstream Political Science on Women, Politics and Values," in *The Prism of Sex: Toward an Equitable Pursuit of Knowledge*, eds. Julian Sherman and Evelyn Beck (Madison: University of Wisconsin Press, 1980).

IV
Legal Perspectives: Editors' Note

The problematic nature of the notion of academic freedom is nowhere more obvious than when examined in its legal mode. One reason for this may be that in this context its instrumental qualities, rather than its normative presence, are focused upon. As Leonard B. Boudin shows, in his selective reviews of the Supreme Court's treatment of academic freedom, there is no clear dispositive legal grant of academic freedom—constitutional or otherwise. Although the Court over the years has dallied with the idea, it has consistently shied away from deciding any issue upon academic freedom grounds. However, as Elizabeth Schneider and Sanford Levinson develop in two very different contexts, the "law of academic freedom," such as it is, may be invoked for varied and often contradictory purposes.

Throughout this collection, the dual nature of academic freedom has been examined. This exploration continues in this section. Sanford Levinson's treatment of Princeton's arguments in the Schmid litigation graphically illustrates just how dangerous in its implications for academic freedom, in its broadest sense, is an assertion of a narrow, property-based claim of institutional academic freedom. This essay further shows how the courts avoid confronting the academic freedom conundrum directly, just as the Boudin article suggests will be the case.

In a sense, Princeton's assertion of its academic freedom differs little from that which Schneider would have universities and colleges invoke in defense of law school clinical programs. Of course, the contexts and contents of the assertion of institutional rights in the face of outside interference are not the same. Princeton wants to close its campus to leafleteers it doesn't like and to protect this practice from state and even judicial review. Schneider calls on colleges and universities to defend law school clinics as necessary and protected educational endeavors and to rebuff outside attacks on them. In both situations, the university argues that its academic freedom, the freedom of the university to govern itself, insulates it from some forms of social control.

As is made clear throughout this book, this strand of academic freedom—be it labeled institutional, corporate, or collective—is far more effective than individual claims of academic freedom protections. As Ellen Schrecker and others in this volume warn, faculty members can expect little protection from institutional assertions of academic freedom prerogatives against them and, in fact, are all too often sacrificed so that the institution can maintain hegemony over what it deems its proper area of control. The role of legal form here, as Schrecker and Schneider recognize, is often to provide "due process" protections to individual claimants and, in effect, to legitimate substantive infringements upon academic freedom in the name of academic freedom. Nonetheless, Schneider and Boudin, as well as other contributors to this collection, still look to the law as one tool available to protect academic freedom—at least until more effective political and social forms better able to protect unfettered inquiry are created.

•12•

Academic Freedom: Shall We Look to the Court?

Leonard B. Boudin

Arthur O. Lovejoy defined academic freedom very well many years ago as the

> ... freedom of the teacher or research worker in higher institutions of learning to investigate and discuss the problems of his science and to express his conclusions, whether through publication or in the instruction of students, without interference from political or ecclesiastical authorities, or from the administrative officials of the institution in which he is employed, unless his methods are found by qualified bodies of his profession to be clearly incompetent or contrary to professional ethics.[1]

This is a very broad definition, although limited to people "in *higher* institutions of learning" and to the "*teacher* or research worker." Today we would recognize at least two significant additions: first, that students and teachers in high and elementary schools are also entitled to academic freedom;[2] and second, that academic freedom goes beyond verbal expression and protects the students' freedom from corporal punishment, right to dress, religious freedom, and access to their records.[3]

As for teachers, academic freedom might include such subjects as the right to collective bargaining and to unrestricted personal behavior on and off the campus, as well as freedom from loyalty oaths.[4]

The arguments in favor of academic freedom are quite persuasive both conceptually and practically. The scholar, almost by definition, is an expert adviser or source of information for the community on issues of which he has special knowledge. Further, his opinions are not only competent, but disinterested. In addition, at a related, but different level, the educational institution itself must be recognized as an essential vehicle for transmitting to successive generations the knowledge already gained and for developing new ideas.

This was very well put by one of the world's greatest scientists and humanists, Albert Einstein. In 1954 he wrote the following to the Emergency Civil Liberties Committee at its conference in observance of his seventy-fifth birthday:

> By academic freedom I understand the right to search for the truth and to publish and teach what one holds to be true. This right also implies a duty: one must not conceal any part of what one has recognized to be true. It is evident that any restriction of academic freedom serves to restrain the dissemination of knowledge, thereby impeding rational judgment and action.[5]

The concept of academic freedom as a constitutional right is more difficult. This observation was anticipated by Lovejoy:

> The freedom of opinion, speech, and publication claimed for the university teacher is not in any extent significantly different from that usually accorded to other citizens in modern liberal states, and the reasons for maintaining it are in part the same.[6]

Academic freedom in the United States did not originate in federal or state constitutions, statutes, or judicial decisions. It was the product of the American Association of University Professors, which in the first two decades of this century developed a code of academic freedom.[7] Over the years the code gathered general acceptance among colleges and universities and had a clear impact upon the courts. Though I know of no constitutional or statutory provision that expressly establishes the legal right to academic freedom, many state statutes emphasize the importance of education and of educational institutions. Early in U.S. history the Ordinance of 1787 provided: "Religion, morality and knowledge being necessary to good government and the happiness of mankind, schools and the means of education shall forever be encouraged."[8]

The absence of a constitutional provision directly establishing academic freedom does not, however, negate its existence as a constitutional right. In a number of areas of law, the courts have found constitutional protection to exist without specific constitutional language.

An early example of this approach may be found in the famous passport cases of *Kent* and *Briehl v. Dulles*,[9] one of the great accomplishments of the National Emergency Civil Liberties Committee, in which the Supreme Court found a constitutionally protected right to travel, even though the right to travel or the right to movement is not explicitly stated in the Constitution. Also, although the Constitution does not explicitly make reference to the rights of association or of privacy, the first of these was found to exist by the Supreme Court in *NAACP v. Alabama*[10] and the latter in *Griswold v. Connecticut*.[11]

Strangely, the two cases that first touch upon academic freedom were based upon now questionable conceptions of property protection. In *Meyer v. Nebraska*,[12] an instructor in the Zion Parochial School of that state was convicted for teaching the German language, in violation of a state criminal statute requiring the English language to be used exclusively in elementary schools.

Justice McReynolds, writing for the Court, first paid respect to the legislature's desire "to foster a homogeneous people with American ideals prepared readily to understand current discussions of civic matters."[13] However, he held that "the means adopted . . . exceed the limitations upon the power of the state"[14] under the due process clause to deprive teachers of their Fourteenth Amendment right to teach "some language other than English. His right thus to teach and the right of parents to engage him so to instruct their children, we think, are within the liberty of the [Fourteenth] Amendment."[15]

Justice Holmes dissented in a companion case:

> I am not prepared to say that it is unreasonable to provide that in his [the child's] early years he shall hear and speak only English at school. But if it is reasonable it is not an undue restriction of the liberty either of the teacher or scholar.[16]

He said that "it appears to me to present a question upon which men reasonably might differ and therefore I am unable to say that the Constitution of the United States prevents the experiment being tried."[17]

Meyer v. Nebraska only deals inferentially with academic freedom as an important matter which should be diligently promoted and which was described as "useful and honorable, essential indeed to the public welfare."[18] But the Fourteenth Amendment right to which it referred was "the right of the individual to contract, to engage in any of the common occupations of life, to acquire useful knowledge . . . and generally to enjoy those privileges long recognized at common law as essential to the orderly pursuit of happiness by free men."[19]

In the second group of cases, headed by *Pierce* v. *Society of Sisters*,[20] the Court struck down the Oregon Compulsory Education Act of 1922 which required children between the ages of 8 and 12 to attend public school. The Court held that the statute deprived parents and children of their constitutional right to select schools and adversely affected the profitable business of private schools, diminishing the value of their property.

Referring to *Meyer* v. *Nebraska*, the Court stated that the Oregon statute had "unreasonably interfere[d] with the liberty of parents and guardians to direct the upbringing and education of children under their control."[21] There is not much here, then, on the subject of academic freedom as the notion has been developed.

The McCarthy period ushered in a new drive against "dissidents" in the field of education and elsewhere. This was nothing new in American history: There had been similar "red hunts" in World War I and its Palmer Raids aftermath and in the early 1940s the Rapp-Coudert legislative hearings in New York.[22] Loyalty oaths and legislative investigations were the weapons used in the 1950s. Indeed, at one time, three major congressional committees simultaneously pursued teachers: the Senate Judiciary Committee's Internal Security Subcommittee, the House Un-American Activities Committee, and Senator Joseph McCarthy's Subcommittee on Government Investigations. In addition, many of the states had so-called legislative investigating committees, of which the most virulent was that one established in New Hampshire, where the legislature authorized Attorney General Louis Wyman to investigate violations of the state's 1951 Subversive Activities Act. This led to several Supreme Court cases, two of which significantly relate to the issue of academic freedom.

In *Sweezy* v. *New Hampshire*,[23] the Court held that Paul Sweezy could not be compelled by the attorney general to answer questions about the Progressive party and about a lecture he had delivered at the University of New Hampshire. Chief Justice Warren stated: "We do not now conceive of any circumstances wherein a state interest would justify infringement of rights in these fields."[24] Justice Frankfurter, in his concurring opinion, referred to "the grave harm resulting from governmental intrusion into the intellectual life of a university" arising from "compelling a witness to discuss the content of his lecture."[25] He discussed at great length "the dependence of a free society on free universities. This means the exclusion of governmental intervention in the intellectual life of a university."[26]

Unfortunately for those concerned about free and open discourse, these brave words about academic freedom turned out, in the case of *Uphaus* v. *Wyman*,[27] to be an example of narrow elitism. Willard

Uphaus was the executive director of World Fellowship, Inc., a charitable organization that operated a summer camp in New Hampshire. It accurately described itself as "a religiously motivated movement . . . which seeks to bring together for fellowship and discussion the representatives of all faiths to the end that there may be peace and brotherhood and plenty for all men, women, and children."[28] It made guest lecturers available to the public on topics of contemporary interest.

Uphaus was subpoenaed because he and some of the speakers had been connected with organizations described as "subversive" by the attorney general and the House Un-American Activities Committee. He answered all questions concerning his own associations, denying that he had ever been a Communist or knew anyone to be a Communist, but declined to produce the names of his guests and his private correspondence concerning the guest lecturers.

The Supreme Court held that the attorney general was entitled to learn whether "subversive persons were in the state," the investigation therefore being undertaken in "the interest of self-preservation, the ultimate value of any society." It held that "this governmental interest outweighs individual rights in an associational privacy."[29]

The lectures given at World Fellowship were certainly as educational as those given at the University of New Hampshire or any other formal educational institution. Unfortunately, Uphaus was not a college professor and his camp was not a university. Although I must have some bias, since I represented Uphaus in the Supreme Court, it seems clear that the Court, and particularly Justice Frankfurter, had a respect for university teaching, scholarship, and scholars, which limited their vision of academic freedom. Needless to say, there were very strong dissenting opinions in the Uphaus cases.[30] In any case, a reading of Uphaus and Sweezy together does reveal a judicial awareness and support for academic freedom, albeit not explicitly articulated and very narrowly defined.

Thomas Emerson, the most thoughtful student of academic freedom, and author of The System of Freedom of Expression, summarizes the situation by pointing out that the Supreme Court has touched upon a small fraction of the total area of academic freedom and that it has used the principles of academic freedom to support the application of traditional legal doctrine.[31] Emerson then inquires as to whether we should recognize the establishment of "academic freedom as an independent constitutional right."[32] Pointing out that the Court established a new constitutional right, that of association, in NAACP v. Alabama, and another, the right to privacy, in Griswold v. Connecticut,[33] he discusses the advantages and disadvantages of establishing a constitutional right of academic freedom. One such constitutional provision would state that "academic freedom, being essential to the welfare and progress of the nation, shall be respected."[34]

Emerson suggests several reasons for elevating academic freedom into a constitutionally protected right: There exists a coherent body of principles built around the functioning of a major institution in our society, the system of education; there is some case law; and the fundamental principles are readily reducible to judicial rules. Emerson goes on to argue that a constitutional right may be found within the confines of the Constitution—either in the "liberty" part of the due process clause or in one of the unspecified rights reserved by the Ninth Amendment, or, like the right of privacy, from the emanations of a series of constitutional provisions. In his view, the concepts of freedom of expression in the First Amendment would protect the faculty member in his academic rights to expression and in his rights as a citizen.[35] They would also proscribe improper legislative limitation of the curriculum and would protect students' rights to form campus organizations, hear outside speakers, and demonstrate on the campus.

One practical impediment to the establishment of academic freedom as a constitutional right is that the Supreme Court seems hesitant in applying the principles of academic freedom, even when clearly appropriate. For example, in the Epperson case,[36] where an attack was leveled against an Arkansas law that made it unlawful to teach evolution the public schools, the Court decided the case on the ground that "[t]he First Amendment mandates governmental neutrality between religion and religion and between religion and non-religion."

A second problem raised by Emerson is that governmental presence in the academic world might prove to be repressive rather than liberating. This argument reminds me of the objections raised in the early 1930s by trade union opponents of the proposed Wagner Act.[37] That statute, it will be recalled, gave the National Labor Relations Board jurisdiction to protect trade union associations in two ways: by conducting collective bargaining elections and by eliminating employer unfair labor practices.

The statute as originally written was an important factor in the development of a growing, strong trade union movement. However, the fears just noted were realized when Congress amended the statute by passing the Taft-Hartley Act of 1947.[38] That statute not only created a series of employee unfair labor practices but established the so-called "noncommunist oath" as a condition to the use of the facilities of the NLRB. The result is history.

The lesson suggested by this example, which admittedly is hardly dispositive, is that academic freedom might be best protected by professional organizations such as the AAUP, by a moral atmosphere recognizing the importance of academic freedom, or by economic power based upon teachers' trade unions. This is obviously a practical rather than a philosophical problem. For the present, until the academic community shows itself willing and able to impose effective sanctions, adherents of a free society inside the educational system would do well to continue to assert in the courts their constitutional claims to academic freedom.

NOTES

1. Arthur O. Lovejoy, "Academic Freedom," *Encyclopedia of Social Sciences*, Vol. I (New York: Macmillan, 1930), p. 384.
2. Thomas I. Emerson, David Haber, and Norman Dorsen, *Political and Civil Rights in the United States*, 4th ed., Vol. I (Boston: Little, Brown, 1976), pp. 805–90.
3. Ibid.
4. Ibid., pp. 870, 887, 823.
5. Otto Nathan and Heinz Norden, eds., *Einstein and Peace* (New York: Schocken Books, 1968), p. 551.
6. Lovejoy, "Academic Freedom."
7. *See* "Developments in the Law—Academic Freedom," *Harvard Law Review* 81 (1968): 1045; "Academic Freedom and Tenure: 1940 Statement of Principles and Interpretive Comments," *AAUP Bulletin* 60 (June 1974): 270; Emerson et al., *Political and Civil Rights*, passim.
8. Ordinance of 1787, Art. III.
9. 357 U.S. 116.
10. 57 U.S. 449.
11. 381 U.S. 479.
12. 262 U.S. 390.
13. Ibid., p. 402.
14. Ibid.
15. Ibid., "Mere knowledge of the German language" said the Court, "cannot reasonably be regarded as harmful" (p. 400).
16. *Bartels v. Iowa*, 262 U.S. 404, 412.
17. Ibid.
18. *Meyer, supra*, 400.
19. Ibid, 399.
20. 268 U.S. 510.
21. Ibid., pp. 534–35.
22. Zechariah Chafee, *Free Speech in the United States* (Cambridge, Mass.: Harvard University Press, 1941); William Preston, *Aliens and Dissenters: Federal Suppression of Radicals, 1903–1933* (Cambridge. Mass.: Harvard University Press, 1963).
23. 354 U.S. 234.
24. Ibid., p. 251.
25. Ibid., p 261.
26. Ibid., p. 262.
27. 360 U.S. 72.
28. Affidavit of Willard Uphaus, quoted in *Wyman v. Uphaus*, 100 N.H. 436, 130 Atl. 2d 278.

29. 360 U.S. 72, 80.

30. 364 U.S. 388.

31. Thomas I. Emerson, *The System of Freedom of Expression* (New York: Random House, 1970), p. 610.

32. Ibid., p. 611.

33. Ibid.

34. Ibid., p. 612.

35. *Keyishian* v. *Board of Regents of the University of the State of New York*, 385 U.S. 589, 603. In this loyalty oath case, the Court, in dicta, spoke very directly about the academic freedom interests that inhere in the First Amendment. However, the Court typically relied upon more traditional grounds for its decision and failed in subsequent cases to follow through on the *Keyishian* reasoning.

36. *Epperson* v. *Arkansas*, 393 U.S. 97.

37. 29 U.S.C.A. §151 et seq.

38. U.S.C.A. §141 et seq.

•13•

Princeton Versus
Free Speech:
A Post Mortem

Sanford Levinson

Two years ago, Princeton University sought the aid of the U.S. Supreme Court in behalf of a radical redefinition of traditional notions of academic freedom. Princeton argued that academic freedom did not so much apply to faculty and students as it did to institutions, that the university is best conceived as property whose owners (trustees) hire employees (administration and faculty) to inculcate specific views into the minds of the consumers (students). From being a safeguard of the rights of scholars and students to teach and learn without fear of repression, Princeton tried to transform academic freedom into a guardian of the right of university adminstrators and boards of trustees to be absolute masters of the ideas that entered university grounds. A doctrine that has classically stood in behalf of the Socratic injunction to know oneself and to examine one's life, regardless of the pain that might be caused by the discoveries, would instead have justified, as a command of the First Amendment no less, protection of a university adminstration's desire to operate its campus as what Justice Fortas once described, referring to a repressive high school, as an "enclave of totalitarianism."[1]

Academic freedom has never commanded universal support, even within the academy itself; attempts to subvert its traditional

I am greatly indebted to my colleagues and friends Scot Powe and Betty Sue Flowers for the scrutiny each gave to drafts of this essay.

understanding, however, are rarely sponsored by an institution with the stature of Princeton. The very credibility that Princeton's name brings with it assures that its argument will be taken seriously. It therefore is important to understand the context within which its extraordinary arguments were made and why, in the word of the American Association of University Professors, they are "pernicious."[2]

On April 5, 1978, two members of what was then called the U.S. Labor party were arrested for having entered the grounds of Princeton University in order to distribute leaflets and other political material to students.[3] The members, Steven Komm and Chris Schmid, had not been invited onto the campus by any students or by any other Princeton authorities. Indeed, on at least one earlier occasion Schmid had specifically been denied permission to enter the campus on the basis of a university policy whereby members of the general public who wished to distribute material on campus had to receive permission from university officials. No standards were listed structuring the granting or denial of such permission, and no explanation had been given Schmid as to Princeton's refusal to allow him access to the campus. He had not thereafter sought permission.

Although some of the material concerned candidates who were running for office in the New Jersey primary scheduled to take place the following month, some of it elaborated as well general party positions. Whatever its title, the U.S. Labor party, headed by Lyndon LaRouche, is not a left-wing party. Its central political thesis seems to focus on the worldwide impact of a British-controlled conspiracy and its attempts to control the world economy. One aspect of this conspiracy involved attempts to weaken the South African economy by supporting efforts to "disinvest" in its business.

In April 1978, many Princeton students were actively encouraging precisely such "disinvestment" of funds managed by the Princeton Board of Trustees as part of the university's endowment. In what may strike some readers as a rueful irony, it was a "progressive," left-wing student, angered by the conservative posture of the U.S. Labor party's foreign policy, who brought to a university proctor's attention the fact that Schmid was on campus passing out offensive leaflets, apparently without permission. After questioning Komm and Schmid, who corroborated their status as uninvited strangers, the proctor arrested them and charged them with trespass. Whatever blame can be placed on Princeton for its overall policy or for going forward with the prosecution, none can fairly be placed on Princeton's administration for the initiation of this case.

I entered the case at this point at the behest of the New Jersey chapter of the American Civil Liberties Union and agreed to serve as co-counsel for Schmid and Komm. The case offered a relatively straightforward opportunity to test the limits of the rights of private property owners to restrict political expression on their property. The mid-1970s had seen a rout in the Supreme Court of claims of a right to access by political leafletters to commercial shopping centers. A 5–4 decision in 1968, the so-called *Logan Valley* case, had upheld such claims, but this decision was ultimately overruled by a new majority consisting, among others, of all of the judges appointed by Richard Nixon.[4] Still in place, though, was a 1946 decision, *Marsh v. Alabama*, which applied the First Amendment to a company town outside Mobile, Alabama, owned by the Gulf Oil Corporation.[5]

The Princeton litigation offered the opportunity to differentiate a private residential university from a shopping center. No one lives at a shopping center, regardless of the importance centers might otherwise play in modern American life. Princeton, on the other hand, is a typical residential university, inhabited by approximately 3,725 undergraduates who live and work within the enclosed space of the private campus. There are other major universities that are even more truly "company towns," such as Duke or Stanford, while others, like Harvard and New York University, are significantly less so. In any case the dispute was a perfect chance to test the continued vitality of *Marsh*, even given the demise of the shopping center cases.

There was a second reason to pursue the case with maximum vigor: New Jersey has one of the most progressive supreme courts in the country. A whole string of important and imaginative decisions came out of the court during the 1970s. Within several months of the U.S. Supreme Court's rejection of a federal constitutional right to equality in school financing, for example, the New Jersey Supreme Court found precisely such a right in the New Jersey constitution itself.[6] There was no appellate court in the country more likely than the New Jersey Supreme Court to take seriously an argument defending Schmid's rights. Moreover, it was easy to interpret the New Jersey constitution as covering the case, so the *Marsh* problem could ultimately be avoided if need be. From the outset, then, we intended to appeal at least as high as the New Jersey Supreme Court if we lost below, and I confess that I maintained a blithe confidence of ultimately prevailing before that court, whatever happened below.

The initial trial took place in the local municipal court, where Princeton[7] argued that its property rights prevailed over Schmid's First Amendment and state constitutional rights. The judge, after several months' deliberation, convicted Schmid of trespass and fined him $15 plus costs. (Komm had been dropped as a defendant by mutual agreement.)

Then, as the case was wending its way up on appeal, an extraordinary event occurred: The New Jersey Supreme Court on its own motion took the case even before argument in the intermediate appellate court. In addition, the court invited Princeton, which had lost official connection with the case once it entered the appellate process, to participate in the oral argument. Nicholas deB. Katzenbach, attorney general under Lyndon Johnson and now general counsel of IBM—as well as a member of the Princeton Board of Trustees—appeared for the university administration.

With Katzenbach's oral presentation to the New Jersey Supreme Court in February 1980 appeared for the first time the argument that Schmid's asserted claim of a right of access to Princeton's campus threatened the university's academic freedom. Prior to his argument, Princeton's (and the state's) claim had been couched forthrightly in terms of its rights as a property owner. Perhaps Princeton was embarrassed by so publicly presenting itself as similar to a shopping center owner; perhaps Katzenbach recognized that pure property rights were in a precarious situation in New Jersey and needed the bolstering of other arguments. In any case, "academic freedom" moved into stage center.

The New Jersey Supreme Court held unanimously that Schmid's conviction was invalid. It sidestepped the *Marsh* company-town argument and instead based its decision squarely on the New Jersey constitution, which "imposes upon the State government an affirmative obligation to protect fundamental individual rights. . . ."[8] Among the most important of these rights is political speech. "Where political speech is involved, our tradition insists that government 'allow the widest room for discussion, the narrowest range for its restriction.' "[9] To allow Princeton to invoke New Jersey's trespass law in order to prevent the peaceful distribution of political material would violate New Jersey's commitment to free speech.

The court was undoubtedly encouraged in its decision by a June 1980 opinion handed down by the U.S. Supreme Court. Justice Rehnquist, writing for the Court, held that the earlier shopping center decisions protected owners only against claims asserted under the First Amendment.[10] The California Supreme Court, however, had interpreted the California constitution to require access to a shopping center by political petitioners. The court agreed unanimously that California was fully empowered to limit the owners' property rights even if the U.S. Constitution did not on its own require such limitations. The case, *Robins v. PruneYard*, thus presented an increasingly common joinder of traditional civil libertarian and states' rights concerns, and the New Jersey court accepted the implicit invitation to be more protective of speech than even the U.S. Constitution.

Princeton refused to accept the New Jersey decision as final and appealed to the U.S. Supreme Court. As a result of *PruneYard*, Princeton's assertions of rights derived from owning the property slipped into the background. Its brief and argument were devoted entirely to asserting its own protected status under the First Amendment, purportedly as "academic freedom." The university tried to distinguish itself from a shopping center by pointing to its more noble commitment to the life of the mind; the university seemed unconcerned by the paradox of its argument that this commitment itself justified far more repression at a university than was to be tolerated at a shopping center.

The Court ultimately dismissed the case as moot.[11] Princeton had, since the initiation of the case, changed its rules to allow far more access to the campus, and Schmid did not challenge the propriety of the new standards. The effect of its dismissal was to leave in place the New Jersey decision. The Pennsylvania Supreme Court has interpreted that state's constitution similarly in a case involving Muhlenberg College,[12] and like cases will almost undoubtedly arise in other states. The arguments made by Princeton will, equally undoubtedly, continue to be heard from aggrieved university administrators, perhaps addressed yet once again to the Supreme Court. Analysis of Princeton's argument may help to defeat it in its future reincarnations.

I have been referring to "Princeton" and "Princeton's" arguments. It should be noted, though, that the terminology itself contains the seed of the fundamental issue posed by the case. At no time, for example, did the administration of Princeton University, which made the decision to go through with the prosecution of Schmid and then to appeal the adverse decision of the New Jersey court, formally consult with the faculty or students of the university. No one suggested that Schmid's presence presented a threat to his or her own rights of free inquiry. It was entirely appropriate that Katzenbach, a member of the Board of Trustees, argue the case, for in fact the genuine adversary of Schmid was the board—and the administration hired by the board—rather than the faculty or students of the university (save perhaps the one student whose complaint led to Schmid's arrest).

Who counts as "the academy" is an obviously crucial question in any discussion of "academic freedom." Two polar views were presented by the case. The first, which was presented by Schmid and by the American Association of University Professors as *amicus curiae*, emphasized that "academic freedom" is a liberty interest enjoyed by teachers and scholars themselves. The second, presented in behalf of Princeton University, shifted the focus from the individual faculty and students to the rulers of the university as a corporate whole. "Princeton University" under this second view is not a collection of noted scholars and their students, equally devoted to fearless dissection of ideas; instead, it is a nonprofit corporation organized for educational purposes and under the legal control of its Board of Trustees, who hire a broad range of employees, inlcuding professors, to carry out their wishes.

I do not know why IBM allowed its general counsel and at least two members of his staff to devote significant time and energy to asserting the claims of Princeton's Board of Trustees, but it should be clear that nothing in this latter version of "academic freedom" poses a threat to the owners of corporate America. Corporate contributors eager to control the tunes played by faculty pipers might well be eager to have "academic freedom" defined in terms of *their* interests, as members of university boards, rather than as the interests of the faculty and students of a university. Indeed, perhaps the principal motivating factor behind the decison of the AAUP to participate in the case by filing an extremely strong *amicus* brief was its perception that a decision upholding "Princeton's" authority could have had significant ramifications for the general distribution of power between university administrations and their faculties. If Princeton were successful, "academic freedom" would consist only of those freedoms university administrators chose to respect or to guarantee by contract.

In asserting its right to stand as a synecdoche for the whole of Princeton University, then, the university administration was making a very controversial claim. It is perhaps an undue burden on the reader to write "Princeton's administration" instead of "Princeton" throughout this essay, but it is misleading to accept the latter as an innocent condensation. We must be self-conscious about the way we imagine the "legal fictions" we call corporations and how we define the relationship between the inchoate whole and the living individuals who constitute its parts. Political struggles are often contests over who gets to speak in the name of a sacred symbol, whether it is the Constitution, the U.S. government, the Marxist tradition, or Princeton University.

For ease of writing, I shall use "Princeton" or "Princeton's" in the following pages, but the reference is really to the specific members of the board and administration who controlled the conduct of the case. Princeton University as I conceive it did not lose in the *Schmid* case;

Princeton University as conceived by the board did indeed lose, and that loss represents a real victory for the genuine tradition of "academic freedom" so shamelessly misused by Katzenbach and his cohorts.

Princeton's central argument was presented as follows:

> Universities, public or private, are so involved with the values which the First Amendment secures from governmental interference as to make "[t]he freedom of a university to make its own judgments as to education . . . a special concern of the First Amendment." *University of California v. Bakke,* 438 U.S. 265, 312 (1978). A community of scholars engaged in research and education -the search for knowledge and its dissemination—is central to the purposes of a university and to "the pursuit of truth which the First Amendment was designed to protect." *Adler v. Board of Education,* 342 U.S. 485, 511 (1952) (Douglas, J., dissenting). Unfettered educational choices are as crucial to the function of a university as the editorial choices of a newspaper. Like a newspaper, and unlike a company town or a shopping center, the property of a University is devoted to expressive purposes and is constitutionally protected from governmentally mandated access.[13]

Princeton's key move is the identification of the freedom of the "community of scholars engaged in research and education" with the freedom of the administration of a university to set the intellectual agenda for that community. These are two sharply different notions of "academic freedom." Although the initial theory of academic freedom developed in nineteenth-century Germany emphasized the threat of governmental interference in the affairs of the university, the American elaboration of that theory quickly recognized that threats to the freedom of unfettered inquiry could come from many sources, many of them nongovernmental. The stress on governmental interference was understandable in a European context, where members of the academy traditionally controlled the institutions within which they taught; indeed, on occassion they controlled the municipality within which the institution was located as well. But this pattern of academic control of academic institutions has not been a feature of the American experience, which instead has placed our great private universities, with no significant exceptions, under the control of nonacademics, usually organized as boards of trustees or overseers. To be sure, academics may sometimes be members of such boards, although almost never of the institution at which they teach, but the laity is in firm legal control of the academic institution within which the teaching takes place.

A recurrent problem in this country, therefore, has been the tension between student and faculty, on the one hand, and these lay boards, on the other, over what ideas are suitable for examination. Indeed, Fritz Machlup has noted "the fact that, in the brief history of academic freedom in the United States, it has been chiefly from the boards of trustees that pressures have been exerted upon professors." It was those boards that challenged both the *Lehrfreiheit* of the professor—the freedom to teach, inquire, and publish one's ideas—and the *Lehrfreiheit* of the student.[14]

It should also be noted, moreover, that the American notion of academic freedom expanded its German predecessor in one crucial respect: "Academic freedom" was interpreted to encompass the right of teachers to participate in ordinary politics and public debate without having to answer to university authorities for the propriety of their views. For example, one of the most important conflicts over academic freedom in the history of American universities took place at Stanford University in 1903. Jane Stanford, the powerful widow of railroad mogul Leland Stanford, the university's founder, was outraged by Professor Edward Ross's public suggestions that railroads be regulated in the public interest. (He had earlier offended conventional sensibility by opposing the election of William McKinley to the presidency.) Even though the source of interference was entirely private, and the conduct complained of tangential to Ross's central teaching duties, the American Economics Association had no trouble issuing a report accusing Stanford of violating the academic freedom of Ross and other members of the faculty.[15]

It is this understanding of "academic freedom" that is powerfully captured in the remarks of Justice Frankfurter, concurring in a 1957 case, *Sweezy v. New Hampshire*, which invalidated the punishment directed at the noted Marxist economist Paul Sweezy for his failure to answer legislative inquiries about lectures he had delivered at the state university:

> In a university knowledge is its own end, not merely a means to an end. A university ceases to be true to its own nature if it becomes the tool of Church or State or any sectional interest. A university is characterized by the spirit of free inquiry, its idea being the ideal of Socrates—"to follow the argument where it leads." . . . [16]

That specific case, of course, did indeed involve governmental interference. But Frankfurter's own reference to a university's becoming subordinated to the view of a particular church demonstrates the breadth of his concept. To be sure, churches might be protected in their educational enterprises by the free exercise clause of the First Amendment, but that is a value wholly different from academic freedom.

Princeton, however, wished to redefine academic freedom in a way that leaves far behind any necessary commitment to free inquiry. Instead, Princeton emphasizes the purported First Amendment right of private universities to exercise "unconstrained philosophical and curricular choices," even if such choices in fact limit the free inquiry of faculty or students. "Thus," wrote Katzenbach, "*a private university* may choose an educational philosophy which seeks to expose students to widely differing viewpoints, as does Princeton, or it *may choose to indoctrinate students in a particular ideology or set of beliefs.*"[17] Under this interpretation, the state must not only be formally indifferent to the choice, but it must also be prevented by the First Amendment from attempting to safeguard the values of free inquiry spelled out by Frankfurter.

In the useful distinction drawn by Amy Gutmann, Princeton's argument is a fine example of "corporate pluralist" theory. Under this view, academic freedom is a safeguard, not of individual rights of unfettered inquiry, but rather a protection of the rights of groups or corporate entities to carve out protected space in order to promote their preferred views of the world. Both traditional liberalism and corporate pluralism join in a fear of an overweening state that has the power to set limits on the intellectual marketplace. The liberal marketplace, though, is one of individuals; the corporate pluralist's market, on the other hand, is one of contending groups. The concern of the corporate pluralist is not the defense of individual autonomy but rather the protection of corporate autonomy. Such autonomy "supports pluralism by permitting diversity among institutions of higher education. There will be Catholic, Jewish and Fundamentalist, libertarian, socialist as well as liberal universities as long as some groups of trustees decide to dedicate their universities to these purposes."[18]

As Gutmann shrewdly points out, corporate pluralism, while guaranteeing a pluralistic society, does not at all guarantee that any given individual within the society will be committed to traditional values of free inquiry. "If every private university shields its students from the burden of being exposed to ideas it deems unworthy of consideration, then the marketplace of ideas will have no privately educated and informed consumers. The idea that 'society as a whole is enriched' by every university promoting its own theory of the good life ignores the fact that the idea of intellectual enrichment presumes a thinking subject."[19]

There is no doubt, of course, that Princeton University in fact is committed to the idea of liberal education and the concomitant encouragement of actively thinking subjects. But the theory of academic freedom adopted by the university in its presentation to the U.S. Supreme Court treats liberal education as only one among many possibilities offered in the educational supermarket.

In thus confusing the concepts of traditional academic freedom and the unrestrained power of university overseers or administrators, Princeton makes it impossible to comprehend the extent to which they may be in radical opposition. Acceptance of its argument would make the sentence "Stanford University violated Ross's academic freedom" meaningless in precisely the same sense that a sentence referring to a "married bachelor" makes no sense in our ordinary language. But the suggested sentence *is* meaningful, instantly understood by any competent speaker of the language, and it is vitally important to maintain the ability to differentiate between the two concepts.

I am not arguing that the state necessarily should have the right to impose its own notions of education, including liberal ones, upon schools organized around different principles. Pluralism is an important political value, not lightly to be disregarded. In the language of constitutional law, moreover, both the free exercise clause and more general notions of freedom of association ought to be read to protect all sorts of schools in their idiosyncratic visions of life, even if they include the suppression of inquiry along certain paths. The point, though, is that this has nothing to do with academic freedom and must therefore be defended in terms of other theoretical notions.

Indeed, at no time in the litigation did we, as Schmid's attorneys, challenge Princeton's discretion to choose its faculty or decide what subjects should be taught with what pedagogical method. Both we and the AAUP pointed out, however, that even these discretionary rights, which surely lie at the center of institutional autonomy, are scarcely absolute. Title VII of the Civil Rights Act of 1964, for example, has properly been read to constrain the right of a university to engage in racial or gender discrimination in hiring its faculty. Nonetheless, all but the most confirmed statist would presumably concede that private universities can at least under some circumstances confine their teaching faculties to believers in a particular religious or political ideology.

What made Princeton's claim extraordinary, even beyond its attempted redefinition of academic freedom, was the scope of control of student life that was asserted to be constitutionally protected. One must repeat: The case did not concern what was taught in Princeton's classrooms or what books were available in its libraries. It did concern the right of a political leafletter to pass out his wares on the Princeton campus. It was this incursion of an alien idea on campus that brought forth the onslaught of New Jersey's trespass law by the university.

The decision of the New Jersey Supreme Court invalidating the conviction was actually quite moderate. For better or worse, the court did not construe the New Jersey constitution to require access by a leafletter to any and all residential colleges. Indeed, the court specifically analyzed the educational purposes of Princeton University itself—including its commitment, as articulated by Princeton's President William G. Bowen, to create "a milieu in which every individual, whether the steadiest proponent of the majority viewpoint or the loneliest dissenter, is encouraged to think independently."[20] The court held that Schmid's presence presented no threat to Princeton, given its purposes, although it left open the possibility that a different decision would be reached for a university with different purposes.

Princeton objected to the very assessment of its purposes by the court: "Where private property is primarily used to promote private educational, ideological or religious objectives," wrote Katzenbach, "the right to decide what is or is not compatible with those objectives is as much a First Amendment right as is formulating the objectives in the first place."[21] This claim of plenary authority is remarkable; it claims for university administrators a freedom denied even the president. In *United States v. Nixon*, the Court at one and the same time recognized a limited right of "executive privilege" but held as well that the president was bound by judicial determination as to whether the claim was justifiable in any particular case. Under Princeton's formulation, though, the very claim of institutional autonomy would foreclose all further judicial review. It is not surprising that the courts were not receptive to the argument.

The question remains, though, as to how courts should analyze the issues presented in cases before them. Rejection of Princeton's extreme claim of autonomy does not supply a standard of review, and there are good reasons for being wary of the New Jersey Supreme Court's test, which emphasizes the relationship between institutional purposes and the challenged behavior.

Consider a Catholic university, for example, which uses state trespass law to sanction a stranger who come onto campus in order to pass out leaflets in support of a proabortion political candidate or bill before a legislature. Under the New Jersey test, it is unclear that *that* use of state power would be unconstitutional, for the university's purpose has never included commitment to the same liberal ideals as those endorsed by Princeton. Thus, Princeton argued in its initial brief, seeking review by the U.S. Supreme Court, "[A] primary purpose of a Catholic university and a primary use of its physical facilities may be to instruct in the Catholic religion. Presumably it may extend an invitation to the general public to visit its campus so long as no speech or activity offensive to its religious beliefs takes place, and it may exclude those who do not abide by the rule."[22] It is possible that this is a correct statement of New Jersey law even after *Schmid*.

There is, to be sure, a surface plausibility to Princeton's argument. Indeed, I am willing to agree that Notre Dame need not grant the freedom of access to its campus to a Jehovah's Witness who wishes to pass out leaflets denouncing the Catholic religion. There is no good reason to interpret the First Amendment, or any state constitutional analogues, to require such access, since the general social order has no particular interest in maximizing the confrontation by its citizens with the full range of ideas about religion.

The state certainly cannot censor the expression of religious ideas on its property, including state universities. The Supreme Court was quite right in holding last year that a public university could not prohibit a student religious group from using public buildings for its meetings.[23] That, the court held, was precisely the content censorship that the First Amendment is designed to limit, for the university was more than happy to allow the presentation of all other ideas in its building, so long as none of them encouraged belief in God.

A private university organized around a religious creed, however, need feel under no state-imposed duty to engage in self-criticism by welcoming those who would attack its central premises on campus. The question, though, is whether my concession necessarily applies to the example given above, where the interloper was concerned not to attack Catholicism, per se, but rather to articulate the merits of a political position or candidate. I believe that it does not apply.

There is an exceedingly simple reason why the rights of university administrators, whether at Princeton, Notre Dame, or Brigham Young, cannot extend so far as Princeton's argument would have them: These universities' students are *more* than students. As Justice Douglas noted, "Students—who by reason of the Twenty-sixth Amendment, become eligible to vote when 18 years of age—are adults, who are members of the college or university community."[24] The specific facts of the *Princeton* case certainly demonstrate the cogency of Justice Douglas's observation. Not only were more than 85 percent of the student body citizens of the United States and, being over 18, eligible to vote; approximately 1,500 students were registered to vote in the Borough or Township of Princeton themselves. It is not simply that the students are registered voters and thus potentially active members of the political community; it is also relevant that they genuinely reside on the university campus and can therefore be personally reached only by those with access to the campus.

It is no part of my argument that Princeton University could be prevented from limiting its teaching faculty, if it so wished, to registered Republicans. Indeed, I agree with the university's argument that a private university could limit admission overall to adherents of a particular political ideology. But it requires a strained reading of the Constitution, as well as fallacious arguments in political theory, to argue that a residential university could prevent the introduction on campus of all non-Republican ideas by prohibiting entrance into the campus by any person with disapproved ideas. That would deny voting citizens of the United States freedom to interact with their fellow citizens—whether students or outsiders—in conversation about the great issues of the polity, including, of course, the merits of candidates running for office.

Lawyers' discourse tends to discuss such issues under the rubric of the First Amendment, since that is the basis of most judicial opinions. I prefer to emphasize a different clause of the Constitution—the guarantee in Article IV that the "republican form of government" shall be preserved in the states. Practicing lawyers are usually ignorant of that clause because the Supreme Court, in 1847, indicated that it was "nonjusticiable," that is, courts would not enforce the clause. Given our culture's emphasis on the judiciary, that was enough to consign the clause to oblivion. Yet, as Yale professor Charles Black has reminded us, we do not in fact need the First Amendment as a sign of the importance of freedom of speech and press, for these values are incarnated in the very notion of a republican form of government, which presupposes an active and alert citizenry standing eternally vigilant against governmental attempts to limit their liberty.[25]

Princeton's students, like those of the other universities named, "are free citizens of their State and country. Just as all other citizens they must make decisions which affect the welfare of the community and nation. To act as good citizens they must be informed. In order to enable them to be properly informed their information must be uncensored."[26] Those words were written by Justice Hugo Black in the landmark *Marsh* decision extending the protections of the First Amendment to a so-called "company town." Oddly enough, the plaintiff, Grace Marsh, was a Jehovah's Witness, and Black never made clear what the relationship was between the quoted sentences and her particular interests, which were at the farthest remove from those of decision-making citizens. Black does, however, eloquently spell out the vision of a republican political order, and his arguments indicate as well why neither Princeton, Notre Dame, nor Brigham Young can be permitted to treat its entire campus as an enclave closed to alien ideas.

As the Court put it so well on another occasion, "[S]elf government suffers when those in power suppress competing views on public issues 'from diverse and antagonistic sources.' "[27] It is, of course, not only governmental officials who exercise power; the New Jersey Supreme Court emphasized that protections of the state constitution "are also available against unreasonably restrictive or oppressive conduct on the part of private entities...,"[28] at least when these entities have generally opened their property to some degree of public use. The courts found that Princeton, indeed like almost all universities, did generally invite the public onto its property, whether to attend public lectures, visit the museum, or hear concerts. Chris Schmid was fully welcome on Princeton's campus so long as he did not try to indicate his political views; this made all the difference to the court. Princeton's actual interest in keeping Schmid off its property were almost nonexistent, as demonstrated by the fact that the university in fact changed its policy subsequent to the initiation of the case and set up procedures by which uninvited strangers like Schmid could indeed get access to the campus. The potential costs to the ability freely to engage one another in political discourse—what the New Jersey constitution refers to as the "right to consult for the common good"—were severe, and a state truly devoted to republican government could not exact such costs from its citizenry.

The Republican-form-of-government rationale for access to the grounds of private universities has, it should be emphasized, a limited scope, especially if we are focusing on the circumstances under which the state should intervene in the operation of a private university. One might well prefer a university that opened itself, and its students, to the broadest range of ideas and experiences imaginable, but there is no good argument that the Constitution requires every university to incarnate this ideal. What Schmid won in the Princeton case is best defended not in the name of general liberal ideals of free inquiry but in behalf of the much more limited ideal of political self-governance. That ideal, important as it is, captures only some of the First Amendment doctrines enunciated by the U.S. Supreme Court and it is important to understand their limited application to private universities.

The past two decades has seen the extension of First Amendment protection to such activities as commercial speech,[29] at least soft-core sexual explicitness,[30] and the right to use "vulgar" or "offensive" language at least in speech directed at adults.[31] It is not clear to me that any of these protections need necessarily be extended to Schmid, even if he is protected in passing out his leaflets, since none speaks to the central value of republican governance.

Commercial speech is the easiest example to distinguish from the political speech that a university cannot exclude. That the state cannot prohibit a lawyer or druggist from advertising does not entail that she or he has a right to come onto a university campus and pass out leaflets indicating the current price for goods and services. One can even concede that student-consumers have an interest in learning such information, but the role of consumer does not rise to the same level as that of citizen, and a university administration can decide that an academic atmosphere is best maintained by limiting the incursion of commerce.

Cultural expression, including alleged pornography, is a harder issue. The argument made above implies the right of a pamphleteer to enter Notre Dame's campus to pass out leaflets endorsing a law that would decriminalize homosexuality or other behaviors condemned by the Catholic Church. Once an issue enters the political process, I believe, a university cannot prevent communication about it to its students, so long as the methods of communication do not otherwise disrupt university operations. Does this mean, however, that a person has a right to enter the campus and pass out leaflets endorsing homosexuality itself or containing vivid narrative descriptions of the pleasures attached to uninhibited sexual expression?

I am inclined to think not. Although sexual identity and expression are incredibly important, they are analytically separable from protection of the overall process of democratic self-governance. The religious and associational rights of Notre Dame, Brigham Young, or similar institutions are entitled to prevail. Thus I think that a private university could ban the sale on its campus of *Playboy* (let alone *Hustler*), although my argument suggests that it could not prevent the distribution of *Human Events* or the *Monthly Review* (let alone *The Public Interest* or *The Nation*).

More difficult issues are presented by the regulation of "vulgar" speech. The Supreme Court upheld the right of Paul Cohen to wear a jacket saying "Fuck the Draft." Must Princeton or Notre Dame allow Schmid to wear a jacket saying "Fuck British imperialism" as he passes out his protected leaflets?

There is one strain of republican-governance theory, especially that associated with philosopher Alexander Meiklejohn, which emphasizes the rationalism and decorum of political debate.[32] Under this model, political discussions are conducted with emphasis on the reasoned elaboration of one's viewpoint, with "emotion" and epithet kept to a minimum. This strain sees little worth protecting in the public use of "Fuck the Draft." Indeed, to the extent that universities stand for the general values of structured discourse, they necessarily oppose the reduction of complex issues to single-phrase labels. Insofar as one generally permits even the state to engage in time, place, or manner regulation of public speech, perhaps one wants to recognize a university's right to insist that political argument be conducted in a manner befitting the overall commitment of the university to reason.

I suspect that we will be more or less sympathetic to such limitations on the style of discourse depending on our general acceptance of the rationalist model that lies behind them. In my own case I have become progressively disillusioned with rationalist models of behavior and thus more accepting of the importance of displays of emotion, including the use of angry epithets that put their hearers on notice about the intensity of the speaker's feelings. I thus fully support the *Cohen* case and the "liberation" of public discourse. As an academic myself, though, I retain enough respect for structured discourse to be aware of the costs of argument by epithet. My present inclination is to allow private universities to prohibit certain modes of expression, though the case is obviously a close one.

The final example is perhaps the most volatile: Does a private university have to allow a march on its campus objecting to its central values, including political ones? For example, does Yeshiva have a constitutional duty to allow the Nazis to march on campus in order to call for the elimination of political rights of Jews? Again, I note that my earlier argument indeed requires that a Nazi leafletter be granted access to Yeshiva to pass out material supporting Nazi political views. Similarly, and more realistically in terms of contemporary politics, a supporter of the PLO has a right to enter Yeshiva in order to distribute material opposing American support in Israel. Does this entail that Yeshiva, like Skokie, has no right to prevent a march?

As a preliminary matter, one might ask if a university generally prohibits marches, in order, for example, to maintain a suitable decorum. If that was the case, then we would in fact simply be considering another version of the "manner-of-expression" problem treated above. There would be no reason to believe that the university was trying to censor the expression of *particular* views, even as it was admittedly trying to censor some of the language by which they were presented. But what if a university allowed marches in behalf of its football team or world peace, but then attempted to prevent a particular march, organized by outsiders to express obnoxious or hateful views?

Although the question is a close one, here, too, I am inclined to let the university prevail. Part of the reason has to do with the place of marches along the spectrum from reasoned argumentation to sheer emotional display. Another, perhaps more important, has to do with the actual financial costs of a march, whether defined in terms of picking up the litter or hiring additional police in order to prevent fistfights between marchers and the audience.

Princeton made such financial arguments, but they were correctly minimized by the court, in part because Schmid was not claiming a right of access by an unlimited number of U.S. Labor party members at any one time. The rules as modified by Princeton, and implicitly endorsed by the New Jersey Supreme Court, allow access to a limited number of outsiders, on a apparent first-come, first-served basis. Princeton will not have to go out and hire extra security personnel because of an inundation of outsiders.

One can easily imagine, however, a university's having to spend sizable sums of money should the Klan announce its desire to march through it. I see no good reason to impose such costs on private universities, especially as the economic crisis makes every dollar of increasing marginal import. Indeed, in this last instance, it is even possible to link the university's concern with a defensible notion of "academic freedom," since a university administration might well be able to show that diversion of its funds to protecting marchers would require cutbacks in its academic program.

This essay has been written within the perspective of classical liberalism and its commitment to an unfettered marketplace of political ideas. It is no secret, however, that that perspective has been subjected to significant criticism from a variety of sources, both right and left. Insofar as it rests on a conviction that the invisible hand will produce favorable results from an unconstrained intellectual marketplace, it is liable to the charges leveled against more orthodox laissez-faire theory. No contributor to this book believes enough in classical economics to support an unfettered economic marketplace. Why should the intellectual marketplace be treated any differently?

Alexander Meiklejohn, one of the architects of modern civil liberties theory, confessed that he was "[not] able to share the . . . faith that in a fair fight between truth and error truth is sure to win. And if one had that faith, it would be hard to reconcile it with the sheer stupidity of the policies of this nation—and of other nations—now driving humanity to the very edge of final destruction."[33] One can only imagine what Meikeljohn, who wrote those words in 1960, would think today, as Congress agrees to fund the MX missile because the "Great

Communicator" who is president says it is necessary to do so to provide a bargaining chip.

The level of public debate, including that on university campuses, might corroborate as well the 1965 insight of Herbert Marcuse that "[u]nder the rule of monopolistic media—a mentality is created from which right and wrong, true and false are predefined whenever they affect the vital interests of society."[34] For Marcuse this perception supported his ultimate argument in behalf of "liberating tolerance"—"intolerance against movements from the Right and tolerance of movements from the Left."[35] It is thus not at all clear that he would have supported the state's limiting the power of a university to bar the entrance to its campus of supporters of the "wrong" ideas—of political "untruth," as it were.

Princeton, of course, did not defend itself on such grounds; its policy was formally, and actually, neutral, but one can well imagine other universities doing so. Moreover, the gestation of the *Princeton* case in the anger of a left-wing student over the views of the U.S. Labor party reminds us that the right can, in fact as well as in theory, be the victim of left-wing intolerance, even if most examples of academic unfreedom in this book involve suppression of the left.

I do not wish to dismiss the views of Meiklejohn and Marcuse; serious intellectuals, given the ravages of the twentieth century, can no longer quote John Stuart Mill or Oliver Wendell Holmes as if they had the last words. Yet I am basically content, in this essay, to remain within the classical liberal framework, if for no other reason than my conviction that no alternative theory likely to be adopted in contemporary America will offer more protection to that speech and political activity I endorse. Moreover, I do believe that the "best" society would in fact be maximally protective of political discourse.

Whatever one's ultimate theory of civil liberties, though, I think that Princeton's particular conduct and arguments are objectionable. Repression was not justified in the name of truth or commitment to a particular substantive vision of human liberation. Instead, it was predicated on a mixture of pure property ownership and the alleged right to indoctrinate the young into the owners' favorite political views, however pernicious. No theory of civil liberties—left, right, or liberal—should find that rationale plausible. Harder problems can thus be saved for another case and another essay.

NOTES

1. *Tinker v. Des Moines Independent Community School District*, 393 U.S. 503, 511 (1969). That case involved an attempt by the local schools to prohibit the wearing of black arm bands to protest the Vietnam War.

2. Brief *amicus curiae* of the American Association of University Professors submitted to the U.S. Supreme Court in the case of *Princeton University* v. *Chris Schmid*, No. 80-1576, p. 30.

3. Most of the facts detailed in this and the following pages are taken from the brief submitted by appellee Chris Schmid to the U.S. Supreme Court in *Princeton University v. Schmid*, No. 80-1576. Additional facts are based on my personal knowledge of the circumstances of the case, in that I both was teaching at Princeton at the time and also served as co-counsel to Schmid following his arrest. In my capacity as co-counsel, I was the principal author of the briefs submitted to the New Jersey and U.S. Supreme Courts in Schmid's behalf.

4. *Amalgamated Food Employees Union v. Logan Valley Plaza*, 391 U.S. 308 (1968), was first modified in *Lloyd Corp.* v. *Tanner*, 407 U.S. 551 (1972), and then flatly overruled in *Hudgens v. National Labor Relations Board*, 424 U.S. 507 (1976).

5. *Marsh v. Alabama*, 326 U.S. 501. (1946).

6. *Robinson v. Cahill*, 62 N.J. 473, 303 A.2d 373 (1973).

7. Under New Jersey law, the complainant in a trespass case can present the case in behalf of the state before the municipal court that hears the case, and Princeton exercised this right. All appeals beyond the municipal court, however, were handled by first the Mercer County prosecutor's office and then the New Jersey attorney general.

8. *State v. Schmid*, 84 N.J. 535, 423 A.2d 615 (1980), at 423 A2d 627.

9. Ibid.

10. *Pruneyard Shopping Center v. Robins*, 447 U.S. 74 (1980).

11. *Princeton University and New Jersey v. Chris Schmid*, 455 U.S. 100 (1982).

12. *Pennsylvania v. Tate*, 432 A.2d 1382 (1981).

13. Brief submitted by Princeton University to the U.S. Supreme Court, p. 7 (citations omitted).

14. Fritz Machlup, "On Some Misconceptions Concerning Academic Freedom," *AAUP Bulletin* 41 (1955): 753, reprinted in *Academic Freedom and Tenure: A Handbook of the American Association of University Professors*, ed. Louis Joughin, (Madison: University of Wisconsin Press, 1967), p. 182. Excellent general histories of academic freedom in the United States include Richard Hofstadter and Walter Metzger, *The Development of Academic Freedom in the United States* (New York: Columbia University Press, 1955) and Laurence Veysey, *The Emergence of the American University* (Chicago: University of Chicago Press, 1965), pp. 384–418.

15. See Veysey, pp. 397–407.

16. 354 U.S. 234, 255 (1957).

17. Princeton brief, p. 8 (emphasis added).

18. Amy Gutmann, "Is Freedom Academic? The Relative Autonomy of Universities in a Liberal Democracy," in *Liberal Democracy*, ed. J. Roland Pennock and John W. Chapman. See also the student note on the *Schmid* case, *Testing the Limits of Academic Freedom*, 130 U. PA. L. REV. 712 (1982).

19. Ibid, p. 270.

20. William G. Bowen, "The Role of the University as an Institution in Confronting External Issues," quoted in *State v. Schmid*, 423 A.2d at 631 n. 11,

21. Jurisdictional statement submitted to the U.S. Supreme Court in behalf of Princeton University, p. 9.

22. Ibid.

23. *Widmar v. Vincent*, 4154 U.S. 263 (1981).

24. *Healy v. James*, 408 U.S. 169, 197 (1972) (Douglas , J., concurring).

25. See Charles L. Black, Jr., *Structure and Relationship in Constitutional Law* (Baton Rouge: Louisiana State University Press, 1969).

26. *Marsh v. Alabama*, 326 U.S. 501, 508 (1946).

27. *First National Bank of Boston v. Bellotti*, 435 U.S. 765, p. 777, note 12 (1978).

28. 423 A.2d, p. 628.

29. *Virginia State Board of Pharmacy v. Virginia Citizens Consumer Council, Inc.*, 425 U.S. 748 (1976).

30. To put it mildly, judicial doctrine relating to explicit presentation of sexually related speech is extraordinarily tangled, but no one aware of contemporary American culture can doubt the overall shift in what is now tolerated as opposed to as recently as 10 or 15 years ago. For representative Supreme Court cases, see, *Jacobellis v. Ohio*, 378 U.S. 184 (1964); *Jenkins v. Georgia*, 418 U.S. 153 (1974); *Miller v. California*, 413 U.S. 15 (1973); and *Paris Adult Theatre I v. Slaton*, 413 U.S. 49 (1973).

31. *Cohen v. California*, 403 U.S. 15 (1971).

32. Alexander Meiklejohn, *Free Speech and Its Relation to Self-Government* (New York: Harper, 1948). See also Frederick Schauer's extremely illuminating recent book, *Free Speech: A Philosophical Enquiry* (New York: Cambridge University Press, 1982).

33. Alexander Meiklejohn, "The First Amendment Is an Absolute," *Supreme Court Review* 245 (1961): 263.

34. Herbert Marcuse, "Repressive Tolerance," in *A Critique of Pure Tolerance*, Robert Wolff et al. (Boston: Beacon Press, 1965), p. 95.

35. Ibid, p. 109.

•14•

Academic Freedom and Law School Clinical Programs

Elizabeth M. Schneider

Over the last 20 years, the academic curriculum of American law schools has been substantially changed through the development of law school clinical programs in which students work on actual legal cases and/or simulated problems for academic credit.[1] The move toward clinical education, particularly "live-case" clinics, resulted from a growing interest in delivery of legal services to the poor, and law as a tool for social change in the 1960s, and a recognition that the traditional law school curriculum was not sufficiently focused on the development of problem solving and other lawyering skills.[2] It has also been fueled recently by increased attention to competency and professional responsibility of lawyers by the legal community and public generally.[3] Clinical legal education is now part of the academic curriculum of most law schools.[4] Many law schools have "live-case" clinical programs that function as part of the law school, in which students get academic

I want to acknowledge the important contributions of Professors James Stark of the University of Connecticut Law School, Elliot Milstein of the American University Law School, and Dean Rivkin of the University of Tennessee Law School in the work of the Committee on Political Interference and to thank them for their helpful comments on an earlier draft of this essay. The first two sections of this article are adapted from *Political Interference in Law School Clinical Programs*, Tentative Final Draft, Report of the AALS Section on Clinical Legal Education, Committee on Political Interference (November 1982), which Professor Stark and I co-authored.

credit for work on actual cases, under the supervision of attorney/teachers paid by the law school. The majority of these live-case clinics still handle public interest cases involving civil rights, civil liberties, poverty law, or environmental law.[5]

Since the early years of clinical education, state legislators and private groups have all too often attempted to interfere with the curriculum of law school clinical programs, particularly those of state law schools. The goal has been clearly articulated: to stop law school live-case clinics from involvement in public interest litigation. Recently there has been a resurgence of attacks on clinical programs through legislation, litigation, and public pressure, as part of a broader war on legal services and public interest legal groups, spearheaded by the Reagan administration and supported by legislators, private right-wing groups, and corporations.[6] Forces outside the law school are thus attempting to restrict the content of clinic litigation and interfere with basic litigation decisions that are at the heart of the educational function of clinical programs. Since clinical programs operate as intrinsic parts of the overall educational program of law schools, these attacks infringe on academic freedom. This interference violates what has been termed "individual" academic freedom,[7] the ability of individual clinic teachers to teach what they want and carry on the litigation they need to teach with, as well as "institutional" academic freedom,[8] the law school's abililty to regulate its curriculum and fulfill its education task.

In response to these attacks, efforts have been made to mobilize a national constituency of legal educators and lawyers groups. The Clinical Legal Education Section of the Association of American Law Schools, the membership organization of law schools, convened a Committee on Political Interference in 1982, to investigate the problem.[9] This committee's work has primarily involved the preparation of a report, which James Stark of the University of Connecticut Law School and I, as chair of this committee, co-authored. This report proposed that the American Bar Association (ABA), which accredits law schools, enact an accreditation standard that would link law schools' affirmative protection of clinic independence from outside interference to law school accreditation. The report, and the problem of political interference in law school clinical programs, have received national attention.[10]

The assertion by clinical law teachers of equal entitlement to the protections of academic freedom afforded regular law teachers is not entirely new, but the report represents a significant effort to expand the reach of the concept to include a less traditional segment of legal academia. While clinical education is now a mainstay of American legal education, it has still not overcome its second-class status. Within many law schools, clinical programs are not perceived by deans and regular faculty as important as traditional classroom courses, clinical work or methodology is not integrated into the regular classroom,[11] and clinical teachers are not accorded equal status, salary, or treatment with the regular faculty.[12] Most clinical teachers are not on a tenure track, but have short-term contracts or limited appointments.[13] Thus frequently there are tensions among clinical teachers, deans, and regular faculty members, many of whom have mixed feelings about clinical education and the public interest content of much clinical work. In addition live-case clinical programs are expensive and severely tax the resources of many law schools.[14] As a result of these financial burdens, as well as other factors, many law schools are now developing simulation programs, in which students deal with hypothetical, as opposed to actual, cases or placement programs in which students are placed for supervision with lawyers outside the law school, as opposed to "in-house" clinical programs, which are part of the law school program.

Precisely because clinical education has a second-class status within legal education, it needs the protection afforded by academic freedom. While this "protection" may be somewhat limited, since academic freedom has not historically protected all segments of the academy,[15] but only the more established segments, it can have an important practical impact on the maintenance and expansion of live-case clinical programs. In addition, because the ideology of academic freedom plays an important legitimating role, the claim that clinical education is equally entitled to the protection of academic freedom makes a crucial link between the educational function of clinical and traditional classroom teaching, a link that could have profound implications for the form and content of legal education.

THE PROBLEM OF POLITICAL INTERFERENCE IN LAW SCHOOL CLINICAL PROGRAMS

Efforts by groups outside the law school to restrict the public interest content of law school clinical programs began in the 1960s as soon as clinical education first took hold. In 1969, a joint committee of the American Association of University Professors (AAUP) and Association of American Law Schools (AALS) investigated claims of political interference with a law school-legal services program at the University of Mississippi Law School. Its report concluded that political pressure by members of the state bar, state legislators, and the governor's office caused the law school to sever its clinical affiliation with the legal services program on the ground that it had been involved in "civil rights activities" and to terminate illegally the contracts of two professors who wished to remain connected with the clinic.[16] In the early 1970s there were threats made by state legislators in New Jersey and Connecticut to clinical programs at Rutgers Law School, Newark, and the University of Connecticut Law School. The governor of Connecticut labeled the University of Connecticut legal clinic as "nothing more than an agency designed to destroy our government and its institutions" and threatened to cut off state funding.[17]

Over the last several years, political interference appears to be on the rise, particularly in state law schools. The focus has been on clinics engaged in public interest representation in such areas as civil rights, civil liberties, environmental law, and prisoners' rights.[18] These attacks have been directed at clinic litigation efforts perceived as threatening the financial or political interests of the state or private groups.

Legislators have attempted to restrict the types of cases that law school litigation programs at the universities of Iowa, Colorado, and Idaho handle. Iowa's "in-house" Prisoner Assistance Clinic, Complex Civil Litigation Clinic, and Legal Services externship program were threatened with termination by a bill introduced in the 1981 legislative session by six members of the Iowa House of Representatives in retaliation for the clinic's successful prosecution of several large-scale prison conditions suits against the state penitentiary.[19] The bill would have prohibited the expenditure of any state funds for the representation of clients in litigation against any governmental body, and specifically the representation of inmates, by persons associated with the law school's clinical program.[20] Though the bill passed in a House committee, it was defeated by the full body.[21]

A similar bill, introduced twice in the Colorado state legislature, was directed against a seminar on constitutional litigation at the University of Colorado Law School taught by Jonathan Chase, in which students worked on civil rights cases. This bill, apparently a response to a lawsuit handled by Chase that challenged a Nativity scene, focused on him, not the seminar program, since it prohibited "law professors at the University of Colorado from assisting in litigation against a governmental unit or political subdivision."[22] In 1981, this so-called "Skip Chase" bill passed both houses of the legislature but was vetoed by the governor. In 1982, it passed the House of Representatives but did not get out of committee in the Senate. The Idaho House of Representatives voted 55–11 in 1982 to prohibit any public institution from offering "a class, legal clinic or other educational opportunity in which students participated in any lawsuit against the State or its political subdivisions."[23] Fortunately, this measure was also defeated in Senate committee.[24] A bill to curb clinical representation at the University of Arkansas has also been reported,[25] and in Connecticut, a high-ranking state official recently threatened to introduce legislation to curtail the activities of the law school's criminal law clinic, which successfully challenged a provision of Connecticut's death penalty statute.[26]

Outside interference has also resulted from litigation. The University of Tennessee's Law School clinical program was recently investigated by the university as a result of motions made by the state attorney general to dismiss the clinic's application for attorneys' fees in a clinic civil rights case on the ground that clinic attorneys were state employees and that the fee request circumvented the budget process.[27] This led the university's board of trustees to convene a special committee to study the clinic. This inquiry has led to an unwritten agreement that the clinic would not initiate any "significant" suits against the state and the severance of the clinic from the legal services program with which it was previously joined.[28]

Attacks on a University of Oregon Law School clinic, the Pacific Northwest Resources Center, have been repeatedly mounted by private groups through the courts and through pressure on the State Board of Higher Education.[29] In one incident, in 1981, the clinic, funded at that time by the National Wildlife Federation, angered powerful members of the timber industry by bringing a lawsuit to halt timber-cutting practices in Idaho. Lawyers for the timber industry were able to question two clinical instructors, the dean of the law school, two former clinic students, and several university officials under oath concerning the clinic's relationship with the university.[30] In addition, the timber groups have pressured university officials and the State Board of Higher Education to restrict the clinic's legal work and withhold funds from the university pending administrative review.[31] A recent attempt by one of the same private timber companies to harass the Oregon clinic in another environmental lawsuit spurred the Political Interference Committee to enlist the AALS to file an amicus curiae brief on behalf of the plaintiffs. This brief argued that "it will harm American legal education if the fact that a party is represented by a law school clinic can be used to divert the time and attention of the court from the merits of the litigation and to burden that party and the law school with annoying discovery and other wasteful pretrial proceedings."[32]

These documented attacks against law school clinical teachers, university administrators, and clinical programs are not isolated instances. They are determined efforts to restrict the content of the litigation that clinics handle. Individually and collectively, they constitute a significant chill on the educational independence of American law schools. As one clinical teacher has stated, "There is no question that we worry constantly that our willingness to represent unpopular clients and our success in suing governmental bodies will cost us our chances to provide high quality clinical training to our students."[33]

THE REPORT ON POLITICAL INTERFERENCE

The Report on Political Interference in Law School Clinical Programs identified four different grounds on which outside interference with the operations of law school clinical programs is unwarranted and perhaps unlawful. First, outside attacks on law school educational programs threaten the institutional independence of law schools, their institutional academic freedom. Second, these attacks undermine the academic freedom of individual clinicians in their capacity as teachers. Third, externally imposed restrictions on law school clinics conflict with the ethical obligation of clinicians, as attorneys, to exercise independent judgment on behalf of their clients and to take controversial cases. Fourth, interference with clinical curricula impinges upon protected First Amendment rights of associational and academic freedom and raises serious constitutional problems.

Institutional Academic Freedom

The report argued that external attacks on law school clinics constitute a serious challenge to the independence and institutional integrity of American law schools. The choice of subject matter or emphasis, choice of types of cases the clinic will handle, and litigation decisions are important educational decisions. Law school faculties commonly review proposed subject matter guidelines for clinics, just as they review course coverage and catalog descriptions for substantive courses in their curricula. To the extent that outside individuals or groups interfere with this process, they are challenging perhaps the most critical academic function of law school faculties.

In 1966, the AAUP published a Statement on Government of Colleges and Universities. This policy states that "when an educational goal has been established, it becomes the responsibility primarily of the faculty to determine appropriate curriculum and procedures of student instructions."[34] It states further that when "external requirements influence course content and manner of instruction or research they impair the educational effectiveness of the institution."[35] Section V contains the following language:

> The faculty has primary responsibility for such fundamental areas as curriculum, subject matter and methods of instruction, faculty status, and those aspects of student life which relate to the educational process. On these matters the power of review and final decision lodged in the governing board or delegated by it to the president should be exercised adversely only in exceptional circumstances and for reasons communicated to the faculty.[36]

Outside political interference with law school clinical programs violates this policy statement and threatens the autonomy of law school faculties in designing high-quality skills training programs for their students.

However, the institutional academic freedom issues posed by outside efforts to regulate legal educational curriculum are particularly complex because of the "outside" regulation that the ABA and other groups already exercise directly or indirectly. In recent years, for example, the Indiana Supreme Court and the South Carolina Supreme Court adopted rules mandating extensive curricular requirements for students who wish to take bar examinations in those states, a development assailed by many law teachers.[37] In addition, several high-level committees of legal educators and the ABA Section of Legal Education and Admissions to the Bar have incurred criticism for their efforts to suggest or mandate skills training in American law schools.[38]

The report argues that these outside efforts to regulate law school curriculum are different because their impetus is presumptively educational—to enhance the professional preparation of law students in the practice of law. By contrast, the impetus for the outside attacks on clinical education is manifestly political and ideological. These efforts can result in restrictions of clinics that threaten the ability of law schools to provide first-rate skills training. In addition they can impair, however subtly, the ability of law schools to inculcate in students traditional values of zealous advocacy and professional independence. Outside political attacks on clinical programs thus pose dangers to the institutional independence of law schools different in kind from forms of professional regulation—and very disturbing in their potential effects.

Individual Academic Freedom

In addition to undermining the institutional autonomy of law schools, political interference with clinical programs threatens the academic freedom of individual clinical teachers. At the present time, AALS bylaws and ABA standards both incorporate AAUP principles of academic freedom and tenure.[39] Under AAUP guidelines, a teacher is entitled to "full freedom in research and in the publication of the results" and "to freedom in the classroom in discussing his [sic] subject," as long as he is "careful not to introduce into his teaching controversial matter which has no relation to his subject."

Neither the AALS nor the ABA presently has specific guidelines regarding academic freedom for clinical faculty. But the report argues that clinical teachers are, first and foremost, teachers, and should be recognized as such. The selection of individual cases to handle and the methods of handling those cases, like the selection of casebooks and teaching approaches, are at the very heart of the educational function of clinical programs. So long as these decisions reasonably serve that educational function—a judgment that only the law school faculty is capable of making—they should be protected by academic freedom, particularly since, to a greater extent than the decisions of classroom teachers, they are made in a public forum.

Professional Responsibility

Outside interference with clinical programs poses especially sensitive problems because clinical faculty act in a dual capacity, as teachers and as attorneys. Thus, in addition to raising academic freedom issues, by interfering with the clinicians' exercise of independent judgment, and, particularly, the decision to undertake controversial cases, political attacks on clinicians may violate fundamental ethical principles, including those contained in the ABA Code of Professional Responsibility, which sets forth binding standards of conduct for lawyers.

The Code of Professional Responsibility provides that there can be no interference with a clinical teacher's legal decisions concerning the handling of clinic cases—decisions such as choice of parties, forum, and legal remedies. In addition, Canon 5 of the code states the fundamental principle that "[a] lawyer should exercise independent professional judgment on behalf of a client." The Ethical Considerations that explain these rules provide that a lawyer must "disregard the desires of others that might impair his free judgment."[40] Since "[n]either his personal interest, the interests of other clients, nor the desires of third persons should be permitted to dilute his loyalty to his client,"[41] a lawyer must resist employer pressures against independent judgment.[42] He "shall not permit a person who recommends, employs, or pays him to render legal services for another to direct or regulate his professional judgment in rendering such legal services."[43]

Another section of the code stresses that every lawyer should aid in making legal services fully available, and the accompanying Ethical Considerations require each lawyer to accept a share of the burden of rendering legal services in those matters unattractive to the bar in general. Thus, a lawyer cannot justify refusal to handle cases on the ground of "personal preference to avoid adversary alignment against judges, other lawyers, public officials or influential members of the community"[44] and cannot decline to handle legal matters that are "repugnant" because of the "the subject matter of the proceeding [or] the identity or position of a person involved in the case."[45] Similarly, an ABA ethical opinion on this issue states that

[J]ust as an individual attorney should not decline representation of an unpopular client or cause, an attorney member of a legal aid society's board of directors is under a similar obligation not to reject certain types of clients or particular kinds of cases merely because of their controversial nature, anticipated adverse community reaction or because of a desire to avoid alignment against public officials, governmental agencies or influential members of the community.[46]

These principles have been held to apply equally to law school clinical programs.[47] In Informal Opinion No. 1208, the ABA Ethics Committee considered the ethical implications of law school guidelines that would bar clinics from suits against the state, as well as guidelines that would require prior approval for such suits from a clinic governing board on a case-by-case basis.[48] This opinion resulted from threats made by the Connecticut governor to the University of Connecticut Law School clinical program in the 1970s. It concluded that neither set of restrictions was ethically permissible on the ground that "[l]awyer-members of a governing body of a legal aid clinic should seek to establish guidelines that encourage, not restrict, acceptance of controversial clients and cases."[49] Opinion No. 1208 clearly establishes that law schools should resist efforts at interference with the attorney-client relationship when they arise.

Constitutional Considerations

The report argues that law school clinical programs must be accorded a high measure of constitutional protection from state interference because of the dual sources of First Amendment activity involved in clinical education. Outside interference with clinical curricula restricts law teachers' and law schools' right of academic freedom as well as clients', teachers', and students' rights of association for the purpose of litigation. While any form of interference burdens the exercise of these rights, state legislation that conditions funding of state law school clinics on the nonexercise of these rights raises particular constitutional problems. Bills like those proposed in Iowa, Colorado, and Idaho impermissibly dictate the subject matter and content of law school curriculum by effectively prohibiting state law school clinics from engaging in the very type of public interest litigation that has been the educational mainstay of most clinical programs.

The Report on Political Interference argues that the crucial educational function served by law school clinical programs protects clinic decisions concerning case selection and choice of defendants from state interference as an academic freedom interest. The Supreme Court has recognized an academic freedom interest deriving from the rights of expression and association guaranteed by the First and Fourteenth Amendments for individual teachers.[50] An institutional right to protection against "governmental intervention in the intellectual life of a university" has also been recognized by some justices.[51] The Court reaffirmed in 1982 that "the First Amendment . . . does not tolerate laws which cast a pall of orthodoxy over the classroom"[52] and has stated that "[to] impose any strait jacket upon the intellectual leaders in our colleges and universities would imperil the future of our Nation."[53] The report argues that restricting clinic litigation to cases that do not challenge state action unconstitutionally "impose [s] [a] strait jacket" on law school curricular choices and casts a prohibited "pall of orthodoxy" over the law school.

Law school clinical programs generally involve representation of individuals or groups exercising rights to association through litigation. Clinic teachers and student interns are also exercising these rights through participation in litigation. An unbroken line of Supreme Court decisions establishes that activities related to association for the purpose of litigation are protected against state action by the First and Fourteenth Amendments and that state restrictions on the exercise of associational rights must be justified by proof of actual harm to a compelling state interest.[54] Indeed, the Supreme Court has recognized that "[a]ssociation [for the purpose] of litigation may be the most effective form of political expression,"[55] and thus has affirmatively sought to protect public interest litigation. The right to sue the state is implicit in this protection of First Amendment associational rights expressed through litigation. Just as the freedom to criticize the government is essential to meaningful exercise of free speech rights, freedom to sue the state is essential to a meaningful exercise of associational rights.[56]

Because of the importance of these First Amendment rights at stake, the report concludes that laws that restrict suits against the state brought by clinical programs, particularly at state law schools, have serious constitutional defects. Efforts to restrict First Amendment activity through the threat of withdrawal of state funds rather than outright prohibition appear to violate the constitutional requirement that the state cannot condition receipt of state funds on the waiver of constitutional rights.[57] Second, differential treatment of state law school clinic programs based on the subject matter of their curricula raises serious problems of unequal treatment for clinical programs that may violate the constitutional guarantee of equal protection.[58]

Need for an ABA Standard

Finally, the report argues that there is a need for an ABA standard as a means of affirmatively encouraging law schools to protect and ensure clinic independence from outside interference. It proposes that the law school's responsibility to do so should be explicitly tied to the ABA's professional accreditation process in order to have a potential sanction for noncompliance. The primary argument made in support of the standard is economic. Outside interference in clinic programs is increasing at the same time that budgetary pressures, particularly on state law schools, have intensified. The present economic situation underscores the need for a vigorous defense of live-case clinical education because law school administrators are now even more likely to feel substantial pressure from legislators and private groups who control the university's financial purse strings. Implementation of a standard would be an important means of supporting resistance to those pressures.

The proposed standard requires "law schools . . . [to] ensure that clinical or other litigation-related programs are free from political interference." It defines litigation enterprises within law schools as educational programs and specifies that decisions concerning subject matter emphasis and case selection and handling are both educational and legal decisions. It affirmatively states that "basic tenets of academic freedom and principles of institutional self-governance require that these decisions be made by clinic teachers and law schools" free from outside interference. It explicitly argues that "choice of individual cases and methods for handling those cases" must be "left to the discretion" of teachers in charge of the clinic program, "provided such choices serve the educational objectives of the enterprise." Finally, it urges law schools to "avoid establishing guidelines that prohibit acceptance of controversial clients or cases or cases aligning the clinical program against public officials, government agencies or influential members of the community."

While the standard is still under consideration by the ABA, the Council of the Section of Legal Education and Admissions to the Bar of the ABA has, as a result of the report, adopted a policy statement on the problem, which it has sent to all deans of ABA-approved law schools. The policy statement incorporates the arguments made in the report and reads as follows:

> The Council has received several reports of inappropriate interference in law school clinical activities. Improper attempts by persons or institutions outside law schools to interfere in the ongoing activities of law school clinical programs and courses have an adverse impact on the quality of the educational mission of affected law schools and jeopardize principles of law school self-governance, academic freedom, and ethical independence under the ABA Code of Professional Responsibility. In appropriate ways, the Council shall assist law schools in preserving the independence of law school clinical programs and courses.[59]

In considering the effectiveness of the committee's approach, it is worth noting that since the committee was convened, the deans of both the University of Oregon Law School and Cleveland-Marshall Law School have vigorously responded to threats of outside interference with clinical programs at their schools by wholeheartedly supporting the programs.[60]

OUTSIDE INTERFERENCE, LEGAL EDUCATION, AND ACADEMIC FREEDOM

The problem of outside interference in the American university has a long history. Outside interference has come from both private and government sources. The earliest examples of such interference—the cases of Richard Ely, Edward Bemis, Scott Nearing, and Edward Ross—arose from private efforts, trustees, and other influential individuals pressing for the removal of teachers who had publicly advocated controversial ideas. For example, Richard Ely was accused by a former member of the Board of Regents of the University of Wisconsin for believing in "strikes and boycotts, justifying and encouraging the one while practicing the other" in 1894.[61] However, during the First World War and in the latter half of the twentieth century, outside interference came more from an alliance of government and private sources. In World War I, "[a]ll over the nation, partriotic zealots on boards of trustees, in the community, and on the faculties themselves, harassed those college teachers whose passion for fighting the war was somewhat less flaming than their own."[62] The McCarthy period saw the rise of outside interference in the form of loyalty oaths, legislation, and government investigations, as exemplified by the cases of Sweezy, Adler, and Keyishian.

In very few of these instances of private or governmental interference did the universities come to the aid of the threatened individual teacher and consider the threat to individual academic freedom to be a threat to institutional academic freedom. The case of Richard Ely was an exception. Ely was ultimately exonerated by the Wisconsin Board of Regents, which issued a report defending the threat to academic freedom on institutional grounds.[63] Walter Metzger concludes that the different resolution of Ely's case rested on the key role of the president of the university—his relationship with Ely and his evaluation of the potential loss to Wisconsin because of Ely's stature.[64] Others have concluded that it was due to Ely's concession that the charges, if proven, would constitute unfitness.[65] In any event, the Ely case highlights the critical role that a supportive university administration can play in responding to threats to individual academic freedom.

In analyzing the problem of outside interference and its implications for academic freedom, it is important to identify the different sources of outside interference, the different interest groups affected and their different perceptions of the threat to academic freedom. There are five levels of interest groups within the university whose interests may be affected: trustees, administrators, faculty as a whole, individual teachers, and students. Where the threat to academic decision making takes the form of outright government intervention into such traditionally autonomous areas as faculty hiring or promotion and student selection or student funding, the interests of several of these groups may coincide. The case against government intervention usually commands the greatest support, and threats to institutional autonomy are quickly perceived.

Where outside interference, whether governmental or private, is directed at the elimination of individual teachers and/or programs who are controversial, the interests of these groups may well diverge. Outside pressures in the affairs of the academy in this context have traditionally resulted in an internal self-policing mechanism where the university acts as a transmission belt for political pressures from the outside.[66] University trustees, administrators, and faculty have frequently sacrificed outspoken or controversial professors in the name of "defend[ing] their collective freedom" to keep outsiders from interfering with issues such as curriculum development, hiring, or promotion.[67] The ideological means for this process has been the espousal of objectivity as a fixed principle of scholarship and the elimination of open advocacy of controversial ideas or social change from acceptable academic discourse. Thus, university presidents, boards of trustees, and faculty who, subject to outside pressure, do not want to support outspoken teachers or advocacy programs that are attacked from the outside may also pose a danger to academic freedom. They may either define the teacher or the program's work as failing to meet an objectivity standard or may simply not consider their interest in institutional autonomy to be threatened by these attacks.

The problem of political interference in the law school clinical context highlights some of these issues with some additional wrinkles. First, law schools have a mixed identity: part traditional academic institution, where scholarly objectivity is the rule, and part trade school. This results in a number of dichotomies, reflected in differing views concerning the form and content of curriculum: theoretical and scholarly work versus advocacy activities, classroom teaching versus clinical activities, simulation versus live-case clinics, appellate case analysis based on the notion that there are objective legal principles versus analysis of social and political values and the manipulability of legal doctrine.[68] The trade school aspect, and the close link between law schools and the legal profession, have meant that law schools have submitted to a greater degree of outside regulation and control over accreditation and curriculum content than other academic institutions or professional schools.[69]

Second, the subject of the interference in the clinical context is activity that constitutes open advocacy of one side—litigation. While there are many law teachers who have been involved in litigation on the side, the activity challenged here is litigation, necessarily partisan activity, conducted on behalf of an educational program of the law school itself. It engages the law school in a form of advocacy and violates some fundamental norms concerning the ideological neutrality of the academy. Thus it is not surprising that most of the attacks have been directed at state law schools, since there are greater pressures in favor of ideological neutrality at state law schools. Indeed, the discourse of academic freedom, which has maintained the distinction between public and private, legitimizes the state's argument that state-funded clinical programs should not be able to sue the state.

Third, the controversial nature and second-class status of clinical education as perceived by many law school administrators and faculty mean that these groups do not necessarily perceive that their interests in institutional autonomy are threatened by outside attacks on law school clinics. Because of the way in which clinical education is viewed, and the expense of live-case clinical programs, outside pressure might well be successful in pushing law schools simply to sacrifice these programs. It thus becomes crucial to persuade law school administrators and faculty that live-case clinical education is an essential part of the law school curriculum so that they will perceive that their institutional autonomy over curriculum is threatened and support, rather than sacrifice, the clinics.

The strategy of the Report on Political Interference attempted to respond to these particular problems. Its approach, to use the pressure of the "outside" national legal organization, the ABA, which accredits law schools, as the means of encouraging law school administrators and faculty to stand behind clinical education was an effort to use the outside regulatory mechanism of accreditation that already exists in an affirmative way. The committee believed that, without outside pressure, many law school deans and faculties would not come to the defense of law school clinics and perceive that their institutional autonomy was threatened. This was somewhat of a risk, because law school faculties have occasionally reacted negatively to the role of the ABA and outside groups in regulating curriculum. The report recognizes this problem and attempts to distinguish between the type of outside interference that regulates educational matters and that which attacks clinical education. Criticism of this approach has not been voiced.

In addition, the committee recognized that it had to persuade law school administrators and faculty that their institutional autonomy was threatened by these attacks and that they had to resist them. The committee understood that institutional autonomy arguments had strong appeal and sought to utilize them. It also recognized that, particularly in light of the uncertain status of clinical education, institutional support was necessary to protect the academic freedom of individual clinical teachers. The report therefore emphasized the institutional prong of the academic freedom argument and gave it priority.

Finally, the report recognized the necessity of persuading law school deans and faculties that the contents of the threats to both individual and institutional academic freedom were the same in the clinical context as they were in the traditional academic setting. The report expands the definition of what is appropriately "academic" by arguing that clinic litigation decisions fall within the traditional rubric of protections of academic freedom. This argument links the educational nature of decisions made about which cases to litigate and how to handle them with decisions respecting choice of substantive law and pedagogic approach in the regular classroom. The report argues that outside interference with clinical caseloads impinges on the individual academic freedom of clinic teachers by limiting the clinic teachers' ability to teach what they believe in the same way that classroom teaching choices are protected, affecting institutional autonomy in the same way as interference with the traditional classroom.

This link, and the crucial similarity of clinical and nonclinical educational functions, have not been widely accepted within the legal educational community. Law school deans and faculty do not always see these academic enterprises as equal. Lack of perception of this similarity has traditionally been an obstacle to both full recognition of the importance of clinical education within the law school curriculum and efforts to integrate clinical and classroom approaches.

The claim of academic freedom in this context performs both important ideological and pragmatic functions. It empowers clinical education by putting it on a par with more traditional academic enterprises. It contains a "transformative" seed—the notion of the similarity of the pedagogic function and analytic task of both clinical and classroom teaching[70]—and attempts to transcend the theory/practice, scholar/litigator, objective/subjective dichotomies that hamper the development of innovative legal educational curriculum.[71] As a practical matter, assertion of academic freedom may also provide a basis, albeit limited, to unify the regular faculty, law school administration, and clinic teachers in response to outside threats to clinical education.

However, because of the practical status of clinical education within the law school, there are serious limitations in the assertion of the institutional as well as the individual claim of academic freedom. The individual claim is inherently limited because many clinical teachers are not equal members of the regular faculty, are not on tenure tracks, and have short-term contracts. The institutional claim is limited because many law school faculties do not see clinical education on a par with traditional courses and because live-case clinics often impose special financial burdens. Indeed there is a real risk that one way law schools may respond to increased outside pressure, financial or otherwise, without appearing to modify curriculum or sacrifice institutional control is simply to substitute simulation or placement clinics for the more expensive live-case clinics, a result that many clinic teachers believe is educationally unsound.[72]

The emphasis in the report on the arguments concerning institutional autonomy, rather than individual academic freedom, reflects this reality. For most live-case clinics, there is still a basic question of survival within law school academic programs. Because of the need to unify law school faculties in support of still marginal clinical programs and teachers, the argument on institutional autonomy in the report is primary. Without institutional support, there can be no protection of academic freedom for individual clinic teachers. Success of the individual academic freedom argument rests on the institution's view that interference with live-case clinics threatens an essential aspect of the curriculum and is not dispensable. Thus, recognition of a threat to institutional autonomy as well as a threat to individual academic freedom is essential to any unified response to outside interference. The uncertain status of clinical education underscores the strategic priority given to the institutional autonomy argument.

However, the institutional autonomy argument is also problematic. The assertion of institutional autonomy raises serious questions as to who speaks for and defines both the institution and its definition of "autonomy" and highlights important issues of self-governance and control of educational decisions. In the Report on Political Interference this comes down to the question of who controls or should control clinic litigation decisions—deans, law faculties, or clinic teachers—a question which the proposed standard does not clearly answer. Moreover, institutional autonomy is increasingly being asserted as the basis of a new claim of academic freedom made by the university to protect its definition of its corporate interests and protect it from outside regulation. This claim goes beyond the scope of the institutional autonomy argument presented in the report—that is, that which is necessary to support individual academic freedom. The implications of this newly articulated claim of institutional autonomy must be explored.

The classic view of academic freedom in the United States has been that it protects the individual scholar's ability to teach; the individual strain is thus the "genuine tradition of academic freedom."[73] However, the vague rhetoric of academic freedom, expressed in legal doctrine, masks the difference between protection of the individual's right to teach and publish and protection of the corporate interests of the university and conceals the potential conflicts between them. Outside interference directed against a controversial teacher or program necessarily highlights these conflicts because there is "a fundamental tension between the academic freedom of the teacher to be free from the university administration and the academic freedom of the university to be free of interference."[74]

Although case law over the last several years "indicates a greater growth of individual academic freedom as a 'penumbra' right under the First Amendment than much judicial recognition of institutional autonomy,"[75] there has been substantial dicta on the importance of institutional freedom.[76] During the McCarthy era, Justice Frankfurter wrote that "the dependence of a free society on free universities means the exclusion of governmental intervention in the intellectual life of a university."[77] Justice Powell emphasized the importance of university autonomy in *University of California Regents v. Bakke,* where he wrote that "[the] freedom of a university to probe its own judgment as to education includes the selection of its student body."[78] Justice Powell also recently noted, in his dissent in *Cannon v. University of Chicago,* that "Title IX trenches on the authority of the academic community to govern itself."[79] But the concept of institutional autonomy has been "more an ideological expression of academic custom and usage than a specifically enunciated legal doctrine even though academic abstention is implicitly based on judicial recognition of [it]."[80]

However, "institutional autonomy" has recently been argued as a basis for private university exclusion of leafleteers on campus,[81] against federal regulation of universities, programs, and policies, under Title IX,[82] and as the basis for a privilege protecting the university from disclosure of information concerning faculty hiring, promotion, and tenure in Title VII actions.[83] In each of these contexts, institutional autonomy is asserted to protect the university administration's view of "the university's" self-interest. The unstated assumption implicit in these formulations is that the interests of the university administration, the interests of the faculty as a whole, and the interests of individual teachers are the same.

This assumption is made explicit in the recent decision of the U.S. Supreme Court in *NLRB v. Yeshiva.*[84] In *Yeshiva,* the Court refused to enforce an order of the NLRB requiring collective bargaining between the faculty and administration at a private university on the ground that the faculty played a managerial role in the governance of the university. The Court rejected the board's argument that the professional interests of the faculty and interests of the institution were "distinct separable entities with which a faculty member could not simultaneously be aligned."[85] Instead, the Court ruled that the faculty's professional interests could not be separated from those of the institution.[86]

Justice Brennan dissented on the ground that the majority failed to understand the nature of the faculty's role in university governance.[87] He argued that the majority wrongly decided the case precisely because it confused the individual interests of the faculty with the institutional interests of the university and saw them as "one and the same."[88] Brennan emphasized that although these interests may coincide, they may also diverge since "[t]he university administrator has certain economic and fiduciary responsibilities that are not shared by the faculty, whose primary concerns are academic and relate solely to its own professional reputation."[89] Significantly, he noted that "the notion that a faculty member's professional competence could depend on his undivided loyalty to management is antithetical to the whole concept of academic freedom."[90] He concludes that the majority's "rose-colored" view of governance as "collegial decision making" fails to take account of the degree to which education has become "big business," the work of operating the university transferred from the faculty to an autonomous administration, which "faces the same pressures to cut costs and increase efficiencies which confront any large industrial organization."[91]

This blurring of distinctions between the interests of the administration, the interests of the faculty as a whole, and the interests of individual faculty members reflected in Yeshiva is also manifested in recent legal writing endorsing the institutional claim of academic freedom. One commentator has proposed a theory of "academic collective interests" as a way of resolving individual Title VII employment challenges in academic institutions based on a view of a coincidence of interests between the faculty and administration; under this approach, the administration can assert these "collective" interests.[92] Other writers have argued that the university's choice (read administration's) choice of educational philosophy should be protected under the First Amendment,[93] that the university should have an independent claim of freedom of association and a right of free speech in hiring and promotion practices,[94] and that institutional academic freedom should be viewed as a right "derived" from the individual faculty member's academic freedom.[95]

These approaches overstate the convergence of interests and minimize the divergence of interests and potential conflicts between faculty and administration. Although the interests of university administration, faculty generally, and individual faculty members may sometimes converge (on issues of governmental regulation, for example), they more frequently diverge and may even be in conflict. Without confusing these separate interests as identical, the maximum possibility of alliances in resisting outside threats to individual academic freedom should be preserved. Spelling out the permissible governance roles in practice, however, may be difficult.

The inherent tension between these divergent interests emerged in the drafting of the proposed Standard on Political Interference. Most clinic teachers believe that once a general subject area like civil or criminal law or women's rights is approved by the faculty, clinic teachers should have primary control over caseload decisions. Questions of case selection and handling must ultimately be left to clinic teachers, both because of academic freedom and the additional ethical obligations of the attorney/client relationship. The ABA ethical opinion on clinic interference clearly rejects case-by-case approval by members of a governing board and approves only broad guidelines. Case-handling decisions are a necessary aspect of an ongoing attorney/client relationship. However, the faculty as a whole clearly has residual power over the educational objectives of the program.

The proposed standard acknowledges both institutional and individual responsibility. It states that both clinical teachers and law schools have authority over "decisions concerning subject matter emphasis, case selection and handling" and then specifies that "choice of individual cases and methods of handling these cases (including such issues as choice of parties, forum and remedies) must be left to the discretion of teachers in charge of the clinic or litigation related program, provided such choices serve the educational objectives of the enterprise." The report attempts to leave authority over content and litigation decisions to the individual clinic teachers, while acknowledging ultimate authority in the "law school" to determine whether educational objectives are met. However, the standard fails to define explicitly who the "law school" is—the administration or the faculty.

The language of the proposed standard reflects the difficulty in resolving these tensions. The committee did not want to spell out the respective roles of clinic teachers, faculty, and administration because it did not know what governance structure would best protect clinic independence. What was clear was the importance of giving primary authority over pedagogical content, subject matter, and approach to clinic teachers. However, it was not clear how to define the respective roles of faculty and law school administration. In some schools, neither faculty nor administration support live-case clinical programs; in others, both do. However, since the parameters of institutional authority and control over clinical programs are not well defined in many schools, there was a fear that by delineating the roles too specifically, the committee might ultimately hurt clinic independence.

But even if we recognize that the institutional claim of academic freedom may be dangerous because it tends to blur the distinct and sometimes conflicting interests of the administration, faculty, and individual faculty members, the question still remains as to the proper scope of the claim. By arguing institutional autonomy, are we necessarily endorsing a corporate view of academic freedom that asserts the primacy of the administration's interest in all circumstances? In the report, the institutional autonomy argument has been made to ensure the traditional protection of academic freedom to individual clinic teachers and programs. The law school's perception that its institutional autonomy is threatened by this interference is necessary to establish institutional support and develop a united response precisely because clinical teachers and clinical education have an uncertain status in legal education. Institutional autonomy is the means to protect the individual clinician's freedom to teach.

In this sense, the institutional autonomy argument is developed as a kind of collective means to protect the individual teacher's academic freedom. The individual strand alone cannot adequately protect individual academic freedom, so institutional academic freedom is also necessary.[96] Thus, the institutional claim should be seen as a corollary or prerequisite to the exercise of individual academic freedom: essential to protect the institutional "robust exchange of ideas," which is at the heart of the vision, if not the reality, of academic freedom; an affirmative support against interference with critical and controversial teaching and scholarship. Amy Gutmann agrees with this limitation in her perceptive analysis of the corporate pluralist implications of the argument for institutional autonomy. She argues that an institutional claim of academic freedom, applicable to both private and public universities, should "only be invoked by universities dedicated to defending the traditional academic freedom of their faculty."[97] However, she wisely cautions that it "should not be so broad as to permit any university to defend itself against those governmental regulations that are compatible with or instrumental to achieving a university's self-proclaimed educational purposes."[98]

A final question remains as to whether the report's affirmative use of the rhetoric of academic freedom is purely instrumental, perhaps even dangerous because it reinforces a sense that the rhetoric is meaningful, that the vision of academic freedom is borne out by practice, or that there is such a thing as "academic freedom."[99] Academic freedom is, as others have noted in this book, a concept that does not take account of inequality of power, resources, or basic issues of governance and control and that plays a mystifying and legitimating role. Most significantly, it does not start us on the process of defining the vision of the academy that we want. However, separating out the individual and institutional strands of the doctrine is an important first step in demystifying the notion of academic freedom, exposing the conflicts in the ideology, and identifying what we might want to maintain. Assertion of academic freedom from a self-conscious perspective that understands its uses and limitations may allow for the possibility of gaining space and building alliances for genuinely critical and controversial teaching and scholarship, as well as providing a context for the articulation of "transformative" educational projects.

APPENDIX

Standard proposed by the Report on Political Interference in Law School Clinical Programs of the Committee on Political Interference of the Clinical Legal Education Section of the Association of American Law Schools (1982)

Interference in Law School Clinic or Litigation-Related Programs

Law schools should ensure that clinical or other ligitation-related programs are free from political interference. Litigation enterprises within law schools are educational programs; emphasis, case selection and handling are both educational and legal decisions. Ethical precepts governing legal practice, [and] basic tenents of academic freedom and principles of institutional self governance require that these decisions be made by clinic teachers and law schools free from unwarranted interference by outside agencies.

In the interest of principles of academic freedom and to safeguard the independence of the lawyer-client relationship, choice of individual cases and methods of handling those cases (including such issues as choice of parties, forum and remedies) must be left to the discretion of teachers in charge of the clinic or litigation related program, provided such choices serve the educational objectives of the enterprise. Law schools must affirmatively protect the independence of both the case selection and the case handling process.

Law schools should seek to avoid establishing guidelines that prohibit acceptance of controversial clients or cases that prohibit acceptance of cases aligning the clinical program against public officials, government agencies or influential members of the community. Acceptance of such cases is in line with the highest aspirations of the bar to make legal services available to all.

NOTES

1. The terms "clinical programs" and "clinical education" in this article refer to live-case in-house clinical programs.

2. See, generally, *Clinical Legal Education*, Report of the Association of American Law Schools-American Bar Association Committee on Guidelines for Clinical Legal Education (1980); Warren F. Burger, "The Special Skills of Advocacy: Are Specialized Training and Certification Essential to Our System of Justice?" 42 *Fordham Law Review* 227 (1973); Michael Meltsner, and Peter Schrag, "Report from a CLEPR Colony," 76 *Columbia Law Review* 581, 584–87 (1976); American Bar Association, Section of Legal Education and Admissions to the Bar, Report and Recommendations of the Task Force on Lawyer Competency: The Role of the Law Schools (1979); Robert Keeton, "Teaching and Testing," 40 *Maryland Law Review* 20 (1981); American Bar Association, Task Force on Professional Competence, Interim Report (1982).

3. *Clinical Legal Education*, p. 7.

4. Ibid.

5. Appendices, Selected Summaries of Law School Clinical Legal Education and the Legal Profession, 29 *Cleveland State Law Review* 735-815 (1980).

6. See for example, "Insult to the Poor and the Constitution," *New York Times* editorial, December 13, 1982, p. A.20.

7. Ellen Schrecker, "Academic Freedom: The Historical View," this volume; Sanford Levinson, "Princeton versus Free Speech: A Postmortem," this volume. See generally Harry T. Edwards and Virginia Davis Nordin, *Higher Education and the Law* (Cambridge, Mass.: Institute for Educational Management, Harvard University, 1979) p. 4.

8. Edwards and Nordin, *Higher Education and the Law*. A recent spate of law review articles discusses the institutional autonomy aspect of academic freedom. See, "Academic Freedom and Federal Regulation of University Hiring," 92 *Harvard Law Review* 879 (1979); "Preventing Unnecessary Intrusion on University Autonomy: A Proposed Academic Freedom Privilege," 69 *California Law Reivew* 1538 (1981); Richard Yurko, "Judicial Recognition of Academic Collective Interests, A New Approach to Faculty Title VII Litigation," 60 *Boston University Law Review* 473 (1981); "Testing the Limits of Academic Freedom," 130 *University of Pennsylvania Law Review* 712 (1982).

9. Although the committee and the report have used the term "political interference," this essay uses the terms "outside interference" and "political interference" interchangeably.

10. See "Limits Urged on the Litigation That Law Schools May Undertake in Clinics," *Chronicle of Higher Education*, January 26, 1983, p. 8; "Report Scores Political Interference in Clinics," *New York Law Journal*, February 28, 1983, p. 8; "Council States Policy on Clinic Interference," *Syllabus* (American Bar Association Section on Legal Education and Admissions to the Bar), June 1983, p. 4.

11. See Michelman Committee Report on curriculum of Harvard Law School (1982); Frank W. Munger, "Clinical Legal Education: The Case Against Separatism, 29 *Cleveland State Law Review* 715 (1980); Melkel-Meadow, "The Legacy of Clinical Education: Theories About Lawyering," 29 *Cleveland State Law Review* 555 (1980).

12. "Teachers of Clinical Law Seek Recognition, Better Treatment," *Chronicle of Higher Education*, January 19, 1983, p. 5; Elwood Gordon Gee, "Survey of Clinical Legal Education in Survey and Directory of Clinical Legal Education 1978–79," (New York: Council on Legal Education for Professional Responsibility, 1979), p. xvii; Ralph S. Tyler and Robert S. Catz, "The Contradictions of Clinical Legal Education," 29 *Cleveland State Law Review* 693 (1980).

13. Idem. See also Memorandum to the Personnel Committee from the Clinical Faculty Group re: Status of Clinical Faculty at New York University Law School, March 23, 1983.

14. See Peter Swords and Frank K. Walwer, "Cost Aspects of Clinical Education," *Clinical Legal Education*, p. 133.

15. See generally, Richard Hofstadter and Walter Metzger, *The Development of Academic Freedom in the United States* (New York: Columbia University Press, 1955); Schrecker, "Academic Freedom."

16. "The University of Mississippi," *AAUP Bulletin* (Spring 1970): 74–86.

17. Conversation with Professor Elliot Milstein, American University Law School, July 6, 1982.

18. However, there has also been a recent effort by members of a civil rights group to prevent a clinic attorney's private *pro bono* representation of the Ku Klux Klan in a demonstration case at the University of Connecticut Law School. They sued the attorney on the ground that the use of state funds violated state antidiscrimination statutes. Conversation with James Stark, University of Connecticut Law School, June 16, 1983.

19. Memorandum from Barbara Schwartz, re: University of Iowa Law School Legislative Interference with Clinical Programs at the University of Iowa, June 25, 1982, to author. (On file with author.)

20. Ibid.

21. Ibid.

22. Conversation with Jonathan Chase, now dean of Vermont Law School, July 7, 1982.

23. Conversation with John Bonine, June 15, 1982.

24. Ibid.

25. Conversation with Dean Rivkin, University of Tennessee Law School, June 20, 1982.

26. Conversation with James Stark, University of Connecticut Law School, June 16, 1983.

27. Conversation with Dean Rivkin, University of Tennessee Law School, June 16, 1983.

28. Conversation with Jerry Black, University of Tennessee Law School, June 20, 1982.

29. See generally, "Seeing the Forest for the Trees," *Willamette Week*, December 29, 1980–January 5, 1981, p. 3.

30. Letter from John Bonine, University of Oregon Law School, to Elliot Milstein, dated November 12, 1982. (On file with author.)

31. Ibid.

32. *Harold Thomas, et al.* v. *Peterson*, Civ. No. 82-2056 (U.S.D.C. D. Ida.). Memorandum of Association of American Law Schools as *amici curiae* with respect to plaintiffs' motion to strike, p. 2.

33. Memorandum from Barbara Schwartz.

34. AAUP Statement on Government of Colleges and Universities, 1966, 44.

35. Ibid.

36. Ibid, p. 43.

37. See, for example, Richard W. Nahstoll, "Current Dilemmas in Law School Accreditation," 32 *Journal of Legal Education* 236, 241 (1982).

38. Ibid, 241–42.

39. AALS bylaws, 6-8(d) states: "A faculty member shall have academic freedom and tenure in accordance with the principles of the American Association of University Professors." The ABA Standards and Rules of Procedures or Approval of Law Schools

contain verbatim the text of the 1940 AAUP statement of principles on academic freedom and tenure in Annex 1 to its rules.

40. Ethical Consideration (EC) 5-21.
41. EC5-1.
42. EC5-23.
43. Disciplinary Rule S-107(B).
44. EC2 28.
45. EC2-29.
46. ABA Formal Opinion No. 324 (August 9, 1970).
47. ABA Informal Opinion No. 1208 (February 9, 1972).
48. Ibid., p. 1. The opinion assumed that "the governing body of the Law School Clinic is a hierarchy consisting of the Law School faculty and its committees and its Dean, the university administration and the university board of trustees. Some of the individuals in this hierarchy are lawyers and some are not." The Guidelines for Clinical Legal Education note that "[t]he functioning of a [clinic] advisory group raises problems, however, particularly in the area of interfering with the attorney-client relationship. ABA Formal Opinions No. 324 and No. 334 indicate that an advisory board is significantly limited in its role once a case has been accepted." Clinical Legal Education, p. 20.
49. Clinical Legal Education, p. 3. However, the opinion suggests that lawyer-members of the board would only be subject to a disciplinary sanction for establishment of and participation in a prior approval, case-by-case clinic case selection process, although across-the-board restrictions on suing the state are "counter to the ethical precepts urged upon lawyers in the Code of Professional Responsibility." Informal Opinion No. 1208, 3.
50. Sweezy v. New Hampshire, 354 U.S. 234 (1957); Keyishian v. Board of Regents, 385 U.S. 589 (1967).
51. Sweezy, 262 (Frankfurter, J., concurring); Regents of the University of California v. Bakke, 438 U.S. 265, 311-316 (1978) (Powell, J., concurring); Cannon v. University of Chicago, 441 U.S. 677, 730, 747 (1979) (Powell, J., dissenting).
52. Board of Education, Island Trees v. Pico, U.S. , 102 S. Ct. 2799 (1982), citing Keyishian, 385 U.S., p. 603.
53. Sweezy, p. 250.
54. See NAACP v. Button, 371 U.S. 415 (1963); In re Primus, 436 U.S. 412 (1978).
55. NAACP v. Button, p. 431.
56. In an analogous context, the Third Circuit rejected an effort to enforce a Pennsylvania contract provision between the state and legal services that barred the award of attorney's fees in civil rights actions to state-funded legal services offices. Shadis v. Beal, 685 F.2d 824 (3d Cir. 1982), cert denied, sub nom. O'Bannon v. Shadis, 51 U.S.L.W. 3331 (November 8, 1982). It held that this provision violated public policy in favor of enforcement in civil rights actions as expressed in 42 U.S.C. § 1988. Indeed, in Shadis the Third Circuit emphasized the illegitimacy of Pennsylvania's even less direct effort at stifling the prosecution of public interest suits:

> What the Commonwealth has attempted to do here is to buy immunity from CLS lawyers. In return for a steady, partial subsidy, the Commonwealth has demanded that CLS not seek attorney's fees in cases brought against the commonwealth. . . . The obvious effect of this, if the agreement is enforced, is to cause CLS not to bring actions against the Commonwealth. In end result, an important member of the plaintiffs civil rights bar would be removed from the scene and the vigorous enforcement of the laws would be materially quelled. Shadis v. Beal, 685 F 2d at 831 citing Shadis v. Beal, 520 F. Supp. 858, 864 (ED Pa. 1981) [emphasis added]

57. The Supreme Court has repeatedly held that the state cannot condition receipt of funds on a waiver of First Amendment rights. *Sherbert v. Verner*, 374 U.S. 398 (1963) (state may not condition receipt of unemployment benefits on persons's willingness to accept Saturday employment that violates her beliefs); *Pickering v. Board of Education*, 391 U.S. 563 (1968) (Board of education may not dismiss teacher on the grounds that teacher wrote letter critical of board); *Shelton v. Tucker*, 364 U.S. 479 (1960) (school may not condition teacher's reemployment on teacher's signing of affidavit that lists all organizations to which teacher belongs or contributes). The Supreme Court has explained why this is impermissible:

> [The government] may not deny a benefit to a person on a basis that infringes his constitutionally protected interests. . . . For if the government could deny a benefit to a person because of his constitutionally protected speech or associations, his exercise of those freedoms would in effect be penalized and inhibited. This would allow the government to "produce a result which [it] could not demand directly." *Speiser v. Randall*, 357 U.S. 513, 526. Such interference with constitutional rights is impermissible. *Perry v. Sindermann*, 408 U.S. 593, 597 (1972)

Since the state cannot directly dictate the subject matter of law school curriculum or prohibit public interest litigation challenging state action, the report argues that it cannot "produc[e] that result" through the threat of denial of funds to state law schools. But see *Maher v. Roe*, 432 U.S. 464 (1976), where the Supreme Court held that the constitutional protection afforded a woman's reproductive choice did not prevent Connecticut from making "a value judgment favoring childbirth over abortion and implement[ing] that judgment by the allocation of public funds." 432 U.S., p. 474.

58. The report argues that differential treatment of state law school clinics on the basis of whether they sue the state raises serious issues of equal protection as "informed by" the First Amendment. See *Carey v. Brown*, 447 U.S. 455, 460-61, 466-71 (1980) (state statute allowing the picketing of a workplace but not of a residence is invalid); see also Thomas I. Emerson, "The Affirmative Side of the First Amendment," 15 *Georgia Law Review* 802–03 (1981); Kenneth L. Karst, "Equality as a Central Principle in the First Amendment," 43 *University of Chicago Law Review* 20 (1975). But see *Regan v. Taxation with Representation of Washington*, 51 L.W. 4583, U.S. Sup. Ct. (May 24, 1983) (lobbying restrictions on nonveterans' tax-exempt organizations, not applied to veterans' organizations do not violate equal protection). The report contends that since fundamental rights are involved, the state must show more than a "rational basis" for its differential subsidization. Discriminatory governmental subsidization of first amendment activities is only constitutionally valid where the discrimination "serves a substantial governmental interest and [where] the statute is narrowly tailored to serve that end." *Buckley v. Valeo*, 424 U.S. 1, 95–96 (1976).

The report argues that under this standard such legislative restrictions on law school clinics cannot pass constitutional muster. State refusal to fund law school clinics' public interest litigation serves no legitimate governmental interest but is instead "aimed at the suppression of [the] dangerous ideas" advanced by clinical teaching and practice of public interest litigation. *Speiser*, 357 U.S., p. 519.

The report contends that laws that seek to restrict clinic litigation, such as those proposed in Iowa, Idaho, and Colorado, would not meet the "substantial governmental interest" test. In *Island Trees v. Pico*, 102 S. Ct. 2799 (1982), the Supreme Court held that a school board's exercise of discretion concerning a library's contents is unconstitutional if it is "intended . . . to deny . . . access to ideas with which [they] disagree. . . . " 102 S. Ct. at 2810. In each of these states it is clear that the legislation is designed to stifle the exercise of First Amendment activity and to deny students "access to [First Amendment protected litigation and educational experiences] with which [the state] disagrees."

However, several months after the report was written, the Supreme Court issued its decision in *Regan v. Taxation with Representation of Washington.* Although this opinion recognizes that differential state subsidization "aimed at the suppression of dangerous ideas" may pose equal protection problems, 51 U.S.L.W. at 4586, that opinion raises questions as to the viability of this argument in the report.

59. Memorandum D8383-25 to deans of ABA-approved law schools from James P. White, Consultant on Legal Education to the American Bar Association, re: Statement of Council Policy Regarding Interference in Law School Clinical Activities, Feburary 21, 1983, reprinted in *Syllabus* (American Bar Association, Section of Legal Education and Admissions to the Bar), June 1983, p. 4.

60. Letter from Dean Derrick Bell of the University of Oregon Law School to Provost Richard J. Huie, University of Oregon January 28, 1983. Letter from Dean Robert J. Bogomolny, Cleveland-Marshall College of Law, to Dr. Walter V. Waetjen, president, Cleveland State University, October 7, 1982. (On file with author.)

61. Hofstadter and Metzger, *The Development of Academic Freedom in the United States,* pp. 426 ff. In 1894, Edward Bemis was dismissed from the University of Chicago for a speech against the railroad companies while the Pullman Strike was going on. Reported in the press, the speech caused the president of the university "a great deal of annoyance" (p. 427). In 1903, Edward Ross was threatened because Jane Stanford, the influential widow of Leland Stanford, was outraged because of his public support of Eugene V. Debs and his advocacy of municipal ownership of railroads (p. 428). Scott Nearing was fired from the University of Pennsylvania for publicly opposing the use of child labor in coal mines in 1915 because an influential mine owner member of the Board of Trustees pressured the president of the university. See Bertell Ollman, "Academic Freedom in America Today: A Marxist View," this volume.

62. Hofstadter and Metzger, *The Development of Academic Freedom in the United States,* pp. 495-96.

63. The regents report stated: "As Regents of a University with over a hundred instructors supported by nearly two millions of people who hold a vast diversity of views regarding the great questions which at present agitate the human mind, we could not for a moment think of recommending the dismissal or even the criticism of a teacher even if some of his opinions should, in some quarters, be regarded as visionary. Such a course would be equivalent to saying that no professor should teach anything which is not accepted by everybody as true.. *This would cut our curriculum down to very small proportions."* [emphasis added]. Ibid, p. 427.

64. Ibid, p. 431.

65. Schrecker, "Academic Freedom: The Historical View."

66. Ibid.

67. Ibid.

68. See generally, Michelman Report; Munger, "Clinical Legal Education"; Jerome Frank, "Why Not a Clinical Lawyer-School?" 81 *University of Pennsylvania Law Review* 907 (1933); *Gary Bellow and Bea Moulton, The Lawyering Process: Clinical Instruction in Advocacy* (Mineola, N.Y.: Foundation Press, 1978); Bellow, "On Teaching the Teachers: Some Preliminary Reflections on Clinical Education as Methodology," *Clinical Education for the Law Student* (New York: CLEPR, 1973); Duncan Kennedy, "Legal Education and the Reproduction of Hierarchy: A Polemic Against the System," *Journal of Legal Education* 32(1982): 591-615; David Kairys, ed., *The Politics of Law* (New York: Pantheon, 1982).

69. See Stevens, *Law School* (1983), particularly Chap. 13; Scott Slonim, "New Accreditation Proposals Critiqued," 65 *American Bar Association Journal* 1505 (1980):

Slonim, "State Court Tells Law Schools What to Teach," 67 *American Bar Association Journal* 26 (1981).

70. "Clinical legal education is not a separate substantive subject or set of substantive subjects, but a mode of teaching. Its objectives are very much the same as those of more traditional modes of law school teaching: to provide our students with the opportunity to develop—and to guide them in developing—a breadth of perspectives, a depth of insight, and a vigorously systematic set of analytic and behavioral techniques which they can train on the varied problems that confront lawyers and the law." Report of the Clinical Faculty Group to the Personnel Committee on the Status of Clinical Faculty, New York University Law School, March 23, 1983, p. 1. See also sources in notes 11 and 68.

71. See sources in note 68.

72. The following is a useful description of the different formats of simulation and fieldwork in the clinical context from the Report of the Clinical Faculty Group to the Personnel Committee on the Status of Clinical Faculty. Significantly it concludes that "an effective clinical program should offer students the opportunities for both simulation and fieldwork." For a different view, namely, that simulation programs should replace live-case clinics, see Tyler and Catz, "The Contradiction of Clinical Legal Education."

Simulation involves role-playing techniques. Students do not deal with real clients or real cases; they perform as lawyers (or in other roles designed to be instructive regarding lawyers' roles) in artificial situations constructed to simulate reality. Thus, they may interview or counsel other students or actors playing the role of client; they may negotiate, advocate, mediate, or try cases in which other students, actors, and faculty play the roles of witnesses, opposing counsel, administrators, and judges.

Simulation has a number of virtues as a clinical teaching technique. Because the instructor completely controls the environment, the students' activities can be designed for maximum educational potential; they can be paced according to the students' developing capabilities; they can be tailored to individual students' special needs; and they can be guaranteed to occur—that is, for example, a trial *will* be held; it will not be aborted by a last-minute settlement or plea bargain. Students can be permitted to make educational mistakes and learn from disastrous consequences which it would be impossible to visit on real clients. Students can be shifted from role to role in order to develop multiple perspectives on a single situation. "Real time" can be expanded or collapsed, so as to relate activities in a way that enables the students to see processes as a c o h e r e n t whole.

Fieldwork exposes students to real clients, cases, legal institutions, and their operating personnel. In the most common form of fieldwork at New York University, the students serve as co-counsel to clinical faculty members, representing clients or handling cases in actual practice. In a minority of clinics, they serve as co-counsel or assistants to staff attorneys in public law offices, under the general supervision of a clinical faculty member.

Fieldwork, too, has unique virtues as a teaching tool. It provides students with experiences that cannot be realistically simulated and requires them to deal professionally with a broad array of types of people whom they do not encounter in law school and who cannot be realistically portrayed by those they do. Precisely because the environment is not artificially structured, it confronts the students with the constant surprises that abound in practice, deprives them of the comfortable assurance that everything is under control, demands that they cope with a world in which everything is not under control, and gives them a chance to examine how they function in such a world. It arouses tensions and anxieties that no simulation can. It furnishes a proving ground for both students and faculty, to ensure that the insights, perspectives, and conceptualizations developed by simulation techniques continue to bear pertinently and accurately upon reality.

An effective clinical program should offer students the opportunities for both simulation and fieldwork. At New York University, most of the fieldwork clinics now include simulation components.

73. Levinson, "Princeton Versus Free Speech."

74. *Cooper* v. *Ross*, 472 F. Supp. 803, 813 (E.D. Ark. 1979). Grant Cooper was an assistant professor at the University of Arkansas at Little Rock who sued the university and its administrators because he was not reappointed to the faculty because of both internal and external pressure. He claimed that his membership in the Progressive Labor party and his public acknowledgment of his Communist beliefs were protected under the First and Fourteenth Amendments. The Court ruled that he was entitled to reinstatement but not back pay.

75. Edwards and Nordin, *Higher Education and the Law*, p. 4. For general background on academic freedom and the law, see William P. Murphy, "Academic Freedom: An Emerging Constitutional Right," 28 *Law and Contemporary Problems* 447 (1963); "Academic Freedom—Its Constitutional Context," 4 *University of Colorado Law Review* 600 (1968); "Developments in the Law: Academic Freedom," 81 *Harvard Law Review* 1045 (1968).

76. Edwards and Nordin, *Higher Education and the Law*, p. 4.

77. *Sweezy* v. *New Hampshire*, 354 U.S. 234, 262 (1952) (Frankfurter, J., concurring).

78. *Regents of the University of California* v. *Bakke*, 438 U.S. 265, 311-316 (1978) (Powell, J., concurring).

79. *Cannon* v. *University of Chicago*, 441 U.S. 677, 730 (Powell, J., dissenting).

81. Edwards and Nordin, *Higher Education and the Law*, p. 17. For cases involving claims of institutional autonomy, although not necessarily explicitly characterized as such, see *Haverford College* v. *Recher*, 379 F. Supp. 1196 (E.D. Pa. 1971); *Regents of the University of Minnesota* v. *NCAA*, 560 F.2d 352 (8th Cir. 1977); *Wayne State University* v. *Cleland*, 590 F.2d 627 (6th Cir. 1978); *Kinda* v. *Muhlenberg College*, 621 F.2d 532 (3d Cir. 1980).

82. *Princeton University and New Jersey* v. *Chris Schmid*, 455 U.S. 100 (1982). See "Testing the Limits of Academic Freedom."

82. In *Cannon* v. *University of Chicago*, the University of Chicago argued that admissions decisions of private universities should not be subject to judicial scrutiny because it would have "an adverse effect on the independence of members of university committees." *Cannon*, 441 U.S., p. 709, cert. granted, No. 82-792 51 U.S.L.W. 3611 (February 22, 1983).

In *Grove City College* v. *Bell*, 687 F.2d 689 (3d Cir. 1982), Grove City College argued that the Department of Education could not force it to comply with Title IX because enforcement of the regulation would curtail the college's freedom of association and that of the students. The college asserted that enforcement would "impermissibly interfere with the College's autonomy and the values which it seeks to promote among its students." 687 F.2d at 689. The Third Circuit rejected this argument. The petition for *certiorari* presented this issue for review by the Supreme Court, 51 U.S.L.W. 3428 (November 30, 1982). See "Academic Freedom and Federal Regulation of University Hiring;" David Kroll, "Title IX Sex Discrimination Regulation: Private Colleges and Academic Freedom," 13 *Urban Law Annotated* 107 (1977).

83. See generally, "Preventing Unnecessary Intrusion on University Autonomy." In *Blaubergs* v. *Board of Regents*, No. 79-42 (M.D. Ga. May 24, 1979), Maija Blaubergs, an assistant professor at the University of Georgia sued the Board of Regents of the university and others because she had been denied promotion to the rank of associate

professor and her employment was terminated. During discovery, she sought to question one professor, James A. Dinnan, who had served on the College of Education Promotion Review Committee that had considered her application for promotion, under oath. During the deposition, he refused to answer how he voted, asserting an "academic freedom" privilege. The district court rejected his claim and ordered him to testify; he refused, and was held in contempt, ordered to pay a fine of $100 per day or 30 days, and if he continued to refuse, to serve 90 days in prison. The Fifth Circuit denied his motion for habeas corpus or mandamus, but granted his motion for expedited appeal. *Blaubergs v. Board of Regents, expedited appeal granted sub nom. In re Dinnan* 625 F.2d 1146 (5th Cir. 1980). On the merits of the appeal, the Fifth Circuit affirmed the district court's rejection of Dinnan's claim of privilege. *In re Dinnan,* 661 F.2d 426 (5th Cir. 1981) and the Supreme Court denied *certiorari, Dinnan v. Blaubergs,* 50 L.W. 3963 (June 7, 1982).

Both the Fifth Circuit opinion and the question presented to the Supreme Court in the petition for *certiorari* do not clearly distinguish whether Dinnan's claim of academic freedom was individual or institutional, although the Fifth Circuit opinion treats it effectively as an institutional claim. According to one commentator, Dinnan argued that his individual right of academic freedom was violated misapplying the individual strand of academic freedom, and he should have claimed an institutional right of academic freedom. "Academic Freedom Privilege," p. 1547. It is not clear from the opinions whether the Board of Regents or other administrators asserted an independent institutional academic freedom privilege, since the case was on appeal from Dinnan's contempt order. However, the American Association of University Professors issued a statement expressing its fear that access to university records in faculty renewal cases will jeopardize academic freedom. AAUP, "A Preliminary Statement on Judicially Compelled Disclosure in the Nonrenewal of Faculty Appointments," *Academe* (February–March 1981): 27. The case has received much national attention. See "Tenure Sexism and Jail," *Washington Star,* October 20, 1980, p. 51A; "Jailing of a Professor Heightens Fears for Campus Independence," *New York Times,* September 14, 1980, p. 1; "The Professor and the Judge," *Washington Post,* October 14, 1980, p. A14; "Professor's Jailing: Is Academic Freedom at Issue?" *Boston Globe,* August 3, 1980, p. 41.

84. 444 U.S. 672 (1980).

85. Ibid., p. 688.

86. Ibid.

87. Ibid., p. 691, 702.

88. Ibid., p. 700.

89. Ibid., p. 701.

90. Ibid., p. 700.

91. Ibid., pp. 702–03.

92. Yurko, "Judicial Recognition of Academic Collective Interests," p. 525.

93. "Testing the Limits of Academic Freedom," p. 715.

94. "Academic Freedom and Federal Regulation of University Hiring," pp. 886, 888.

95. "Testing the Limits of Academic Freedom," p. 715.

96. "Preventing Unnecessary Intrusions on University Autonomy: A Proposed Academic Freedom Priviledge," p. 1549.

97. Amy Gutmann, "Is Freedom Academic? The Relative Autonomy of Universities in a Liberal Democracy" in *Liberal Democracy,* ed. J. Roland Pennock and John W. Chapman (New York: New York University Press, 1983): 27b.

98. Ibid.

99. For differing views on this issue generally, see Edward Sparer, "Fundamental Human Rights, Legal Entitlements and the Social Struggle: A Friendly Critique of the Critical Legal Studies Movement," *Stanford Law Review,* forthcoming; Karl Klare, "Labor

Law as Ideology: Toward a New History of Collective Bargaining Law," 4 *Industrial Relations Law Journal* 450 (1980); Lynd, "Government Without Rights: The Labor Law Vision of Archibald Cox," 4 *Industrial Relations Law Journal* 483 (1981); Duncan Kennedy, "Critical Labor Law Theory: A Comment," 4 *Industrial Relations Law Journal* 503 (1981); and Kairys, *The Politics of Law.*

Postscript

Scott Nearing

At the beginning of the 1880s there was a profoundly religious Quaker named Joseph Wharton. He came from a well-to-do family, and he was president of Bethlehem Steel Corporation. Bethlehem Steel was very closely interwoven with the arms trust group in Pennsylvania. That whole area there, including Du Pont to the south, that whole area was an arms production, dynamite manufacturing area.

Joseph Wharton didn't wear a collar button or a cuff button or a watch chain. He was an austere Quaker. He was also rich enough to give three quarters of a million dollars to the University of Pennsylvania to found the Wharton School of Finance and Economy. He was the patron saint of that department of the university.

Mr. Wharton believed in protection, not free trade, which was one of the greatest controversies of the period. When he gave this gift to the university he also gave a statement upholding and supporting protection as against libertarian forces. He came to the university again and again. He made speeches to the students publicizing Bethlehem Steel and protection and these other elements for which he was one of the most vocal champions. And when I got to teach at the Wharton School in 1906, from 1906 to 1915, it was already an accepted thing that you were for protection, that you were for big business, and so on.

I was from a coal and lumber county in northeastern Pennsylvania. I had been born and brought up in a company town in which the Morris Run Coal Company owned the roads, the schools, the churches, the shops, the houses. My grandfather was the superintendent of the Morris Run Coal Company, and he ran the town and all of its activities. He was known as Czar Nearing. I did not follow along in this aspect of my grandfather's footsteps.

In the county where I grew up lay a number of important coal strips, coal veins. And in this county stood some of the finest timber that you ever saw. It was a land of rich natural resources. One of the first memories that I have was getting an opportunity to talk as a

This statement by Scott Nearing is the edited version of two interviews with Ruth and Bud Schultz on May 16, 1981, and later on July 24, 1982, at his home in Harborside, Maine. Scott Nearing's statement is one in a series of personal accounts of political repression the Schultzes are collecting in preparation for a book on this topic.

youngster in favor of the conservation of natural resources. I remember this very distinctly. I didn't know very much and I couldn't say very much, but I was already, what shall I say, ready to talk against the family interests.

I started to teach at the Wharton School when I was twenty-three. From that time forward, I found myself in a little group, a little complex of young men who held what you would then call the liberal progressive point of view of Bob LaFollette and Theodore Roosevelt. We were a rising generation of progressive thinkers, young people who had more or less the same background. We were beginning to recognize domination by big business over not only the pocketbook of the country, but the mind of the country.

I don't know why I was the one in our group who eventually got fired. I suppose it was because I was rather vocal. As a youth I was exceedingly shy. I had definite difficulty expressing myself in public. I couldn't teach and I couldn't speak. So I went to Temple University and took courses in public speaking, public presentation they called it. It was a four-year program, which I finished in three years at the same time I was finishing my work at the University of Pennsylvania. That's why I had a little advantage over the rest of those young fellows because I had bulwarked myself with this program in public address.

At this time the employment of children in industry for wages had become a controversial issue. There was a labor department of the state government but comparatively little regulatory legislation. And nobody paid any attention to the factory laws we had. They weren't intended to be enforced. There was no child labor law except a very loose and very limited one. The employers and manufacturers did about as they pleased.

There were inspectors who were stationed in the factories and were supposed to look at the children who were handling the spindles in the textile mills or doing the other routine work of the factories. These factory inspectors were supposed to say yes or no when the question was: "Should that boy or girl do that particular job? Is it too dangerous or too dirty for the boy or girl to do?" But they were paid by the employers to protect the employers from being sued later on. If the inspectors found that the employers had "conformed with the law," when a kid got hurt the employer was not responsible.

Pennsylvania child labor became notorious in the textile mills, in the glass factories, in the nut and bolt shops, and other shops producing small things children could easily handle. And it was notorious in the mines. Children would work both inside and outside the mines. Those children who worked inside the mine did various chores like tending door. All through the mine there were doors or wooden partitions that sealed up each section so it was more or less poison proof. When they shot off blasts in one section, the partition was closed so the other side of the partition continued to have fresh air. These children stayed by the doors to open and close them at the proper times.

The breaker boy worked on the outside of the mine. Coal was hauled out in mine cars by mule or by hand and later by electricity and then dumped over a rather steep place where it slid down an incline. As it went down, breaker boys picked out the stone and the slate and the other so-called impure matters and left the coal to slide on down the hill. It was picked up there and put into railroad cars.

Breaker boys were any age over four or five. Any smart boy or smart girl at four or five or six or ten who could separate stone and slate from coal might make a good breaker boy or breaker girl or could tend doors. They worked as long as the mine worked. And the mine worked as long as it had orders. Sometimes it would start up and work two hours. Sometimes it would start up and work eight or nine hours.

A friend of mine, Sally Cleghorn, said of that time: "The golf links lie so near the mill that almost any day the working children can look out and see the men at play." It was true. The golf course was here and the mill or mine tipple was just over yonder. They were both operating at the same time.

I became interested in the conditions surrounding the employment of children in factories, mines, and other workplaces in my native state. Child labor had become so notorious that the Pennsylvania Child Labor Committee was set up to oppose it. I joined that group and after two years I was made the secretary. I gave many speeches throughout the state condemning the exploitation of children. I went to women's clubs and other organizations where people had no idea there was such a thing as child labor. But the university authorities thought I should confine my activities to the classroom and should not speak in public.

I didn't get promoted, although promotion was rather general in our time. I taught at the Wharton School for nine years and until the last year I was only an instructor. Now, usually after the first three or five years if you didn't get promoted you were dropped from the teaching staff. Generally speaking, if you did your job, and unless there was some extreme reason like a divorce or a scandal or something of that kind, you were promoted. Either you did your job and got promoted or you didn't do your job and were dropped.

When promotion time came around and they passed me up, the *North American*, a Philadelphia businessman's paper with an editor who was more or less of our way of thinking, became concerned. It raised the question: Why is this particular teacher passed over? Nevertheless, year after year I was kept on as a teacher but not promoted academically.

In the meantime I began to get more speaking engagements outside the university. Macmillan had published six of my books. Two of them were textbooks which were selling very well. I didn't think I was going to be able to make a living teaching for more than a few years; I'd probably get kicked out. You see, a teacher has an ethical problem. The ethical problem is: Shall the teacher keep his job, period, and do whatever he must do to hold it, or should he risk the livelihood of his family by telling the truth, whatever it happens to be, and perhaps find himself out on the street. In that case you have a profession and you can't practice it anymore. I knew in advance what I was going to do.

I saw what was probably coming and I put into the bank every month, regularly, a sum of money from my lectures and books which was large enough to provide my family and me with a year's living, if I were unemployed. I carried a mininum of a year's living in the bank, untouched for other purposes, so that if I really got stuck, here was twelve months of food, clothing, and shelter for the family. I built a war chest, if you want to call it that, to fight this thing through.

I was dismissed on the sixteenth of June, 1915, in a curt letter from the provost of the university, Edgar F. Smith. He wrote, "Dear Mr. Nearing: Your services at the University will not be continued after this year." In other words, you're fired. They never talked to me. I never saw them. They didn't even bother to explain except to say, you'll not be hired another year. And they waited until the faculty left the university, until the whole place was just in vacation, then they pulled this thing off.

I taught as well as I could. My classes were well-attended. The boys and the girls in the classes were, what shall we say, well satisified. They thought they were learning something.

A *North American* reporter went to see J. Levering Jones, who was one of the most influential of the trustees. There were twenty-three trustees representing twenty-three points of view of business. The reporter said, "Why have you dismissed this man?"

Mr. Levering Jones said, "When I dismiss a stenographer, do I have to give a public reason?"

244

So that was our status. Like any stenographer, if you didn't "do your job," out you went. And that was the extent of academic freedom in 1910 and throughout that period. There was no tenure, no such thing.

A book, *The Nearing Case,* is about my dismissal. It was written by Professor Leightner Witmer, who was head of the Psychology Department of the University of Pennsylvania. Witmer and I were at swords points on the war which was on then. Professor P.H. Shelling, head of the English Department, was extremely pro-British and extremely pro-military in his outlook. However, these professors supported me. Witmer said, "If they can do that to you, they can do that to me. They don't have to give you a reason. They don't have to even give you a notice. You're fired!"

One hundred percent of our faculty at the Wharton School were for me and against this dismissal. But it was already done. I was already one of the army of unemployed.

Of course my activities contributed to my dismissal. The Pennsylvania State Manufacturers Association was opposed to child labor legislation or any other form of industrial legislation. They wanted freedom to do as they pleased and they didn't want the state to step in and interfere in any way. And they didn't just *try* to influence the state legislature, they *influenced* it.

The university went to the legislature every year with a list of appropriations they would like to have made. They had been getting about a million dollars a year from each legislature. The story is that when the university came to the legislature in 1915 to ask for money, legislators said, "How about that fellow Nearing on the Child Labor Committee? What is he doing? Does he have to stay?" That undoubtedly was related to my dismissal.

Then I was invited to go to the University of Toledo, which was a municipal university, owned and operated by the city through a board of nine trustees. I had a friend on the Board of Trustees of the university, Dr. John S. Pyle, a surgeon with liberal leanings. As a matter of fact, he was a socialist at the time. Altogether there were enough trustees representing the trade union movement and the LaFollette forces who were in favor of academic freedom and worked to secure my appointment.

By the time the war was two years gone, things were different from what they had been in 1915 when I was hired at the University of Toledo. You were now told: "Sit down. You're rocking the boat." The boat was on the way to war. Everyday, everyday, everyday, the rah-rah boys in various positions, preachers and teachers and newspapermen were saying, "Whatever you do, don't rock the boat."

The war hysteria mounted. The right to conduct meetings was cancelled. Cancelled? There weren't any meetings. When people like us tried to hold meetings against the war, we were called traitors.

People who opposed the war were fired now without it disturbing anybody. They lost their jobs widely and freely. I was fired from Toledo in 1917. But if I had "sat down and not rocked the boat," there would have been no further question about my job.

A meeting of the Board of Trustees was held to vote for my dismissal or retention at the university. One of the trustees who supported me was named Ben Johnson. He was a lawyer, a liberal lawyer. In some way or other he was persuaded not to go to the trustees' meeting when the vote on my retention came up. Nobody could find him. And that gave them a majority of one.

The most crucial people on the board were liberals and they could stand just so much pressure. I wasn't surprised that they did what they did. Why not? After all, it was their bread and butter. And the pressure of the times and the pressure of Toledo and big business were too great.

Another thing happened in Toledo. Federal agents took all my papers. I was teaching at Chautauqua Summer School at the time. My house was empty except that my secretary was staying there. They came with a search warrant and took all my opened and unopened letters, everything they could lay their hands on, including research notes for a book I was preparing.

Sometime later I wrote a pamphlet that was published before the end of the war. It was a simple little thirty-two–page pamphlet called *The Great Madness*. President Wilson said in one of his speeches at the time, "Madness has entered everything," describing the war situation, and I took that idea as the title for the pamphlet. It analyzed the causes of the war: the political causes, the economic causes, and so on, showing that it was not a war of patriotism or a war for democracy, but a definite businessmen's war.

The war was making the machine go. You've got to recollect that in 1913, before the war started, we were in a very bad depression, and in order for the machine to start again, you had to have orders. The war served that purpose.

An indictment against me under the Espionage Act was finally handed down in New York after the end of the war. That was in 1918, the fall of 1918. It was a major matter that carried up to a twenty-year sentence in the penitentiary.

I was charged with writing *The Great Madness* pamphlet, and this pamphlet, they felt, would interfere with recruitment and enlistment in the armed forces of the United States. The "evidence" was that any young man reading this pamphlet might or would refuse to go into the armed forces, or to enlist, or to be conscripted. Therefore it was treasonable and therefore I should be punished and therefore the indictment.

The Espionage Act that ostensibly was enacted to cope with the German spy system was used against people like me who opposed the war. Why not? What's the spy act really for except to prevent people of a certain point of view from influencing policy?

We had a meeting of interested people in New York about the indictment. We said: Now here's a chance to publicize our views about the war. What we wanted to do was to make the most of the publicity for peace, for socialism, for a better world.

Because the pamphlet was part of the indictment, we used it in presenting our case. When I was on the stand, my attorney, Seymour Stedman of Chicago, said, "Mr. Nearing, turn to page three of this pamphlet. Would you read paragraph two?"

And so I read that. Then he said to the jury, "My client will now defend this paragraph." We spent eight days going through the pamphlet, paragraph by paragraph, and I gave a detailed explanation each time we had another paragraph coming. The newspapers were full of it. Magazines were full of it. We said we didn't care if we were to be found guilty or not. We were interested in furthering the cause of peace and socialism in America. It was the obvious thing to do.

In the end, the jury acquitted me for writing the pamphlet and convicted the Rand School for publishing it.

Toledo was the last teaching job I held. After that, nobody would hire me. I had intended to make teaching my life job. I prepared myself to teach and I went on teaching until I was fired. Since then I've been homesteading in the hills of Vermont and then in the hills of Maine. I've been writing all the time, writing as much as I could or should, and speaking up on every possible occasion.

Index

Academic freedom: definition, 5–7, 15, 17, 20, 22, 25, 30, 31, 32, 36–37, 46, 47, 163, 172, 179, 181, 182, 186, 189, 193, 194–96, 198, 210, 219, 224, 225, 229; as civil liberty, 15, 18, 36, 193; as myth, 17, 20, 22; as ideal, 18, 19, 22, 25, 47, 53–55, 211; as ideology, 224; as constitutional right, 179, 182, 186, 193, 198, 226, 227; as repression, 15, 52–56, 151, 161, 164, 183; as value free, 6, 7, 8, 52; as privacy right, 8; as procedural right (due process), 6–7, 180; as self-regulation, 7, 26, 52, 164, 180, 222; as necessary to critical thought, 9, 10, 55; as not protecting radicals, 29, 40, 46, 102, 162, 164; and employment crisis, 121; as protection against outside interference, 6, 15, 26, 33, 55, 162, 164, 179, 194–97, 210, 220–30; in corporate mode, 26, 36, 46, 47, 179, 193, 197–98, 205, 225, 229; institutional, 101, 102, 114, 179, 189, 193, 210, 214–15, 224, 225; individual, 6, 8, 26, 36, 180, 193, 210, 216, 224, 225, 227, 229; threats to, 22, 46, 70, 73, 102, 103, 195

Acquinas, St. Thomas, 66

Adler v. *Board of Education*, 195, 220

administration (administrators), 51, 86, 91, 189, 221, 222, 226; as violators of academic freedom, 19, 27, 36, 40, 46, 54; access to positions as, 155; increase in, 49

admissions, 6, 101; open, 85

advertising, corporate political, 110–11

affirmative action, 7, 90, 94, 119, 141–48, 157, 165, 168; and merit, 146; and feminist movement, 81; and part-time teachers, 126; goals of, 148, 168; as mistaken strategy, 168–69

Alger, Horatio, 2, 129

Allen, Raymond J., 34

alumni, 8

Amalgamated Food Employees Union v. *Logan Valley Plaza*, 191

American Academy of Science, 148

American Anthropological Association, 129, 131

American Association of University Professors (AAUP), 28–29, 34, 36, 39, 40, 70, 90, 182, 186, 189, 193, 194, 198, 211, 215, 216

American Association of University Women, 142

American Bar Association, 210, 215, 219, 223; accreditation process, 219; section on legal education, 215, 220; code of professional responsibility, 216–17

American Civil Liberties Union (N.J.), 190

American Economics Association, 196

American Economics Review, 70

American Enterprise Institute, 27, 111

American Federation of Teachers, 90

American Philosophical Association, 131

American Sociological Association, 128, 131

Anderson, John, 72

anti-intellectualism, 101, 163, 169

Arendt, Hannah, 172

Collins, Randall, 78
Colorado, University of Law School, 212
Columbia University, 30, 49, 86; Law School, 80
Communist Party, 30–35, 36, 38, 40, 185
community college, 19, 65, 85, 86, 94, 124; Kingsborough, 86
Committee for Economic Development, 107
Commoner, Barry, 72
company town, 191, 192, 201
computer science, 65
Conant, James Bryant, 34
Connecticut, University of, Law School, 210, 211, 217
contract, right to, 183
Control of the Campus, 9
corporal punishment, 181
corporate: influence/interference with university, 1, 2, 5, 8–9, 22, 72–74, 102, 112–14, 194; influence on public history, 132–34; concentration, 103–05; profits, 3, 9, 48, 61, 104, 105, 107–09, 112–13; research contracts, 8, 18, 73, 91, 94; regulation of, 107–09; political advertising, 110, 111; Political Action Committees, 110, 111; interdependency, 104–06; networks, 103–07, 109
cost benefit analysis, 2, 3
Council on Foreign Relations, 107
credentialling, role of higher education, 70–00
critical education, 4, 9, 10, 63, 94, 164
critical thought (thinking), 49–51, 102
creationism, 26
curriculum: 4, 6–9, 26, 48, 72, 85, 94, 101, 168; determined by government, 9; and academic freedom, 73; and liberal arts, 85, 88; critical,

88, 94, 97; narrowing of, 101, 155; in law schools, 209–30

Dahl, Robert, 3, 11
Darwin, Charles, 66
Davis, Jerome, 29
demography, 8, 15, 119, 121, 134
Denton, Jeremiah, 70
Department of Agriculture, 8, 70
Department of Commerce, 107
Department of Defense (Pentagon), 7, 8, 9, 71, 72, 100
Department of Health and Human Services, 9, 100
Department of Labor, 100
Dewey, John, 28
discrimination, 11, 119; against radicals, 15; race and sex, 142, 146, 147, 156, 161, 198; in tenure, hiring, firing, promotion, 6; and economic structure, 28
Douglas, Justice William O., 200
draft, 30
dress, right to, 181
DuBois, W.E.B., 63
Duke University, 72, 85, 191
Dupont, 8
Durkheim, Emile, 21

economics/economy, 52, 71, 81, 89; new reality, 5, 119; under capitalism, 47–48; business, 103–06, 107–08; growth, 5; Marxist, 92; decline in, 51, 90; crisis, 61, 87, 90, 151; equality in, 144
Einstein, Albert, 1, 66, 182
Ely, Richard, 27, 28, 220, 221
Emergency Civil Liberties Committee, 182
Emerson, Steve, 107
Emerson, Thomas, I., 186
Emory University, 85
energy crisis, 2

252

Hoover, Herbert, 75
Horkheimer, 81
House UnAmerican Affairs Committee (HUAC), 40, 184, 185
humanities, 5, 61, 71, 113, 121, 122, 123, 156; renewed emphasis, 10; education necessary, 4; function, 87; for women, 89, 123, 152
Hunger of Memory: The Education of Richard Rodriguez, 168

IBM, 192
Idaho, University of, Law School, 212
immigration, 67
individualism, 80
inflation, 2, 71, 101
International Research Council, 10
Internal Securities Sub-Committee of Senate Judiciary Committee, 36
Iowa, University of, Law School, 212
Islamic studies, 107

Johnson, Ben, 246
Johnson, Lyndon, 192
Jones, J. Levering, 244

Katzenbach, Nicholas deB, 192, 193, 194, 197, 199
Kaysen, Carl, 4
Kent and Briehl v. *Dulles*, 182
Kerr, Clark, 5, 85, 86
Keyishian v. *Board of Regents*, 220
Komm, Steve, 190–91
Kopkind, Andrew, 10, 11
Korean War, 34
Kristol, Irving, 73, 113

Labor market, 5, 19, 49, 78–81, 83–85, 87, 95, 121–22, 123–27
Laffer, Arthur, 73
LaFollette, Robert, 241, 245
LaRouche, Lyndon, 190
Lasersfeld, Paul, 75

legitimation, 7, 15, 56, 63, 163, 172, 211, 229; of system, 3, 4, 50; by radicals, 51; and equal opportunity, 119; of repression, 161; of authority, 173
Lenin, V.I., 21
liberal arts, colleges, 85, 87, 94; value of, 65–66, 86, 88; decline in, 48, 65, 71, 85, 86, 88, 101; at Harvard, 86, 87; and critical thought, 88
Locke, John, 21
Logan Valley, see *Amalgamated Food*, etc.
Lovejoy, Arthur O., 30, 181, 182
loyalty oath, 181, 184; California, 26
Luxemberg, Rosa, 21
Lyon, University of, 173

Machlup, Fritz, 196
Mailer, Norman, 64
Manne, Henry, 9
Marcuse, Herbert, 81, 82, 205, 206
Marquit, Erwin, 57
Marshall, Alfred, 75
Marsh v. *Alabama*, 191–92, 201
Marx, Karl, 21, 66, 81
Marxist/Marxism, 47, 52, 127; in universities, 32, 56, 90, 92; lack of intellectual recognition, 46, 93; unscientific approach of, 46; errors of, 81; tradition of, 195
Maryland, University of, 46, 47, 56, 70, 92
Massachusetts Institute of Technology, 73
Massachusetts, University of, 164
maternity leave, 147, 148
mathematics, 65
May, Ernest R., 130
McCarthy, Joseph/McCarthyism, 35, 39, 70, 73, 184, 220, 226
McKinley, William, 243
McPherson, Michael, 167
McReynolds, Justice James C., 183

254

physics, 9
Pierce v. Society of Sisters, 183
Plato, 3, 21, 65, 86
pluralism, 93, 197–98
Political Action Committees, 111–12
political science, 45, 51, 56, 152
political speech, 192, 203, 204, 219
post-behavioralism, 7
potato famine, 66
Powell, Justice Lewis F., Jr., 226
press, freedom of, 1
Princeton University, 6, 145, 189–95, 197, 198–99, 200, 202, 205, 206
privacy, right of, 8, 183, 185, 186
privatization, 63
productivity, 1, 2, 87, 96; of women scholars, 144, 145
professional responsibility, 26, 244; of lawyers, 209, 214, 216–25
Progressive Party, 184
promotion, 6, 20, 26, 51, 151, 226, 243, 244; discrimination, 6; merit, 144
property rights, 179, 183, 189–93, 199, 202, 206
publications, 6, 181; non-traditional, 52, 154; criteria for judging, 21, 51, 102, 103
Public Historian, The, 131
public history, 131–34
Puerto Rico, 67
Pullman Strike, 45
Pyle, John S., 245

Queens College, 36

Radical(s), 28, 29, 45, 55, 56, 73, 161, 165, 168, 174; professors, 15, 50, 51, 162, 163; movements, 21; as danger to academy, 29, 50; as legitimators, 50; repression of, 54, 69, 93; scholarship, 56, 163; on increase, 51, 90
Rand School, 247

Rapp-Coudert Committee, 31, 36, 45, 184
Reagan, Ronald, administration of, 8, 22, 23, 63, 70, 75, 77, 100, 112, 113, 210; National Commission on Excellence in Education, 4; hostility to education, 67; economic policies, 71, 112
records, access to, 234
recruitment, 94; on campus, 7, 94; of faculty, 126
Reed College, 37
regulatory policy, 1, 73; regarding business, 107–09
Rehnquist, Justice William H., 192
Reich, Wilhelm, 81, 82
religious freedom, 181, 186
research, corporate grants, 1, 8; Defense Department, 7, 71, 72, 100; Department of Agriculture, 70; sponsored, 18, 72; contracts, 8, 9, 18; decline, 4, 102
residential university, 190, 200, 201
Robins v. PrunYard, 192
Rockefeller Foundation, 38
Rodriguez, Richard, 168
role model, female faculty as, 141, 150, 151, 155
Roosevelt, Theodore, 242
Ross, Edward, 196, 198, 220
ROTC, 7, 71
Rutgers University, 19, 37, 39, 71; Law School, 211

Saint Augustine, 21
Samoff, Joel, 45, 46
San Juan, 67
Schmid, Chris, 179, 190–94, 198, 199, 200, 202, 203, 205
Scholastic Aptitude Test (SAT), 9
Science & Society, 33
Securities and Exchange Committee, 108

Senate Judiciary Committee, 36, 70, 184

Servicemen's Readjustment Act of 1944, 4

Shakespeare, William, 65

Shelling, P.H., 245

shopping centers, 191, 192–93

Shor, Ira, 50

Smith, Edgar F., 244

Society for Applied Anthropology, 131

socialism, 54, 247; struggle for, 55

sociology, 9, 64, 90, 131, 152

social science, 5, 7, 61, 71, 113, 121, 122, 156; education necessary, 4; renewed emphasis, 9; value free, 49; and bourgeoise ideology, 50; for women, 89, 94, 152; decline in, 102

Southern California, University of, 73

Soviet Union, 31; perceived threat, 4, 23

Spinoza, 21

Stanford, Jane, 196

Stanford, Leland, 196

Stanford University, 154, 191, 196, 198; Center for Research in International Studies, 10

Stark, James, 210

Stedman, Seymour, 247

State University of New York (SUNY), Stony Brook, 69

stratification, 19, 64, 74, 79, 80, 85, 101, 102

students, 15, 26, 49, 51, 71, 79, 83, 95, 181, 189, 193, 194, 196, 198, 200, 201, 202, 221; access to education, 65–67; academic freedom of, 26, 70, 181, 186, 193, 221; as citizens, 200, 201, 203; careerism of, 99, 100; demands of, 61, 100 196; risk taking by, 4, 5; movement, 87, 90; aid to, 67, 70, 74, 99

Summers, Lawrence, 107

superwomen, 148–51, 166

Sutherland, Arthur, 37

Sweezy v. New Hampshire, 184, 196, 220

Sweezy, Paul, 184, 185, 196

System of Freedom of Expression, The, 186

systems analysis, 3, 82

Taft-Hartley Act of 1947, 186

technical education, expansion of, 85, 86; disadvantages, 95, 96

Temple University, 242

Tennessee, University of, Law School, 213

tenure, 15, 20, 30, 51, 74, 90–92, 95; system of, 90, 92, 151; criteria for, 93, 122, 153–55; for women, 143, 144, 146, 151, 153–55, 156, 158; for part-time faculty, 126; excludes dissenters, 92, 93; for radicals, 69, 102; and discrimination, 6, 122; and secrecy, 154, 155; for law teachers, 211, 216, 226

Texas, University of, 130

Thucydides, 21

token/tokenism, 148–51, 166, 169

Toledo, University of, 30, 57, 245, 247

trade unions, 84, 186

travel, right to, 182

trespass, 190, 191, 192, 199

trustees, 8, 27, 36, 40, 47, 196, 213, 221–22; University of Pennsylvania, 29, 45; Rutgers, 37; as owners, 189, 191, 194; Princeton, 189, 190, 192, 193

tuition, 18, 19; at CUNY, 66; rise in, 70, 101

United States Labor Party, 190, 205, 206

United States v. Nixon, 198

About the Editor
and Contributors

CRAIG KAPLAN practices law in New York City with Levinson, Mogulescu and Kaplan. During 1981–83 he was special counsel to the National Emergency Civil Liberties Committee. Kaplan teaches at New York University and is completing his doctorate in political science at the Graduate Faculty of the New School for Social Research.

ELLEN SCHRECKER teaches history at New York University and has also taught at Harvard, Princeton, and the New School. A member of the National Writers Union, Schrecker is the author of a forthcoming study, *Academic McCarthyism* (Oxford) and has written *The Hired Money: The French Debt to the U.S., 1917–1929*. Her articles and reviews have appeared in *Antioch Review, The Nation, Humanities and Society*, and elsewhere.

EMILY K. ABEL has taught history and women's studies at a number of colleges and universities. Her book, *Terminal Degrees: The Job Crisis in Higher Education*, will be published by Praeger in 1984.

STANLEY ARONOWITZ is a professor of sociology at the City University of New York Graduate Center. His most recent books are *Working Class Hero: A New Strategy for Labor* (1983), and *The Crisis in Historical Materialism* (1981).

LEONARD B. BOUDIN is a senior partner in the New York City law firm of Rabinowitz, Boudin, Standard, Krinsky and Lieberman. He has written extensively on constitutional and international law and has taught at the law schools of Harvard University, Yale University and the University of California.

JEAN BETHKE ELSHTAIN is a professor of political science at the University of Massachusetts. During 1981–82 she was at the Institute for Advanced Study in Princeton. Author of *Public Man, Private Woman: Women in Social and Political Thought* (Princeton) and the editor of *The Family in Political Thought* (University of Massachusetts Press), Elshtain has published articles and reviews in *Politics and Society, Political Theory, Telos*, and elsewhere.

EVELYN HU-DeHART is an associate professor of history at Washington University in St. Louis. She is the author of *Missionaries, Miners and Indians: A History of Spanish Contact with the Yaqui Indians*, as well as numerous articles on Latin American history. Hu-DeHart received her Ph.D. from Stanford University and was a Fulbright scholar in Brazil.

ROBERT LEKACHMAN is Distinguished Professor of Economics at the Lehman College and Graduate Center campuses of the City University of New York. His most recent books, both published by Pantheon, are *Capitalism for Beginners* and *Greed Is Not Enough: Reaganomics*.

SANFORD LEVINSON teaches at the School of Law at the University of Texas. He is the co-editor of *Processes of Constitutional Decisionmaking*, 2nd edition (Little, Brown), and writes frequently for *The Nation* on legal matters. Levinson received a Ph.D. from Harvard and a J.D. from Stanford University.

JOSEPH S. MURPHY is the Chancellor of the City University of New York. He assumed this position after having served as president of Bennington College and president of Queens College of CUNY. Murphy is the author of *Political Theory: A Conceptual Analysis* and has published articles on philosophy, political theory, and education.

BERTELL OLLMAN is a professor of politics at New York University. He is the author of *Alienation: Marx's Conception of Man in Capitalist Society* and *Social and Sexual Revolution: Essay on Marx and Reich*. He is also co-editor of *The Left Academy: Marxist Scholarship on American Campuses* and *Studies in Socialist Pedagogy*. Ollman is the creator of Class Struggle: A Marxist Board Game.

FRANCIS FOX PIVEN is a professor in the political science program, Graduate School and University Center, City University of New York. Along with Richard Cloward, she has written *Regulating the Poor: The Politics of Turmoil, Poor People's Movements*, and, most recently, the *New Class War: Reagan's Attack on the Welfare State and Its Consequences*.

ELIZABETH M. SCHNEIDER is an associate professor at Brooklyn Law School. From 1980 to 1983 she was a staff attorney and administrative director, Constitutional Litigation Clinic, Rutgers Law School, Newark. She has litigated and published extensively in the field of women's rights and recently chaired the Political Interference Committee of the AALS's Section on Clinical Legal Education.

MICHAEL USEEM is professor of sociology at Boston University. He is the author of *The Inner Circle: Large Corporations and Business Politics in the U.S. and U.K.* (Oxford), *Protest Movements in America*, and *Conscription, Protest and Social Conflict*. His articles have appeared in the *Chronicle of Higher Education, Social Policy*, and elsewhere.